Legal Conversation as Signifier

ELGAR STUDIES IN LEGAL THEORY

Series Editor: Wojciech Sadurski, *Sydney Law School, University of Sydney, Australia*

Elgar Studies in Legal Theory is a new series designed to cultivate and promote high quality works of scholarship on all aspects of legal theory. The focus of the series is on the development of original thinking in legal theory, with topics ranging from law and language, logic and legal reasoning, morality and the law, critical legal studies, and transnational law. Innovative work is encouraged from both established authors and the new generation of scholars.

Titles in this series include:

Understanding the Nature of Law
A Case for Constructive Conceptual Explanation
Michael Giudice

Comparative Law as Critique
Günter Frankenberg

Law's Political Foundations
Rivers, Rifles, Rice, and Religion
John O. Haley

Authority in Transnational Legal Theory
Theorising Across Disciplines
Edited by Roger Cotterrell and Maksymilian Del Mar

Legal Conversation as Signifier
Jan M. Broekman and Frank Fleerackers

Legal Conversation as Signifier

Jan M. Broekman

Frank Fleerackers

Faculty of Law, KU Leuven, Belgium

ELGAR STUDIES IN LEGAL THEORY

Edward Elgar
PUBLISHING

Cheltenham, UK • Northampton, MA, USA

Published by
Edward Elgar Publishing Limited
The Lypiatts
15 Lansdown Road
Cheltenham
Glos GL50 2JA
UK

Edward Elgar Publishing, Inc.
William Pratt House
9 Dewey Court
Northampton
Massachusetts 01060
USA

A catalogue record for this book
is available from the British Library

Library of Congress Control Number: 2017936585

This book is available electronically in the **Elgar**online
Law subject collection
DOI 10.4337/9781788110204

MIX
Paper from
responsible sources
FSC® C013056
FSC
www.fsc.org

ISBN 978 1 78811 019 8 (cased)
ISBN 978 1 78811 020 4 (eBook)

Typeset by Columns Design XML Ltd, Reading
Printed and bound in Great Britain by TJ International Ltd, Padstow

Contents

Preface

This book's title could be read in everyday language as: 'Talking about law produces meanings'. Indeed, a legal conversation does not take place in a courtroom, a law office or a parliament. That takes place in family circles, among friends, in parks or during holiday trips and seldom has 'law' as its major theme. The multiple characters of the participants and their strong ties to everyday life situations withstand a qualification for law office or court, where 'everyone is equal in the eyes of the law'. The translation of the concept 'conversation' is therefore: 'talking' and in particular 'about law'. That reference to law broadens the field of legal semiotics. It looks very normal and even easy to do: talking about law seems one of our daily activities, and such conversations are most often solely at the borderlines of conversations on law.

But how do we know precisely? We read papers, listen to friends, listen to what is said on the train or on the street and we witness people discussing legal issues. But are they talking *about* law, or *talking law*, or *using* law as a metaphor? Are they perhaps *confirming* law or just *creating distance* from law's general impact – or are they in essence *talking politics* while talking about legal issues? They perform speech acts, discuss new laws or protest against legal rules and debate the effects of their application. All those activities lead us straightforwardly to the book's title: *what signifying effect has talking about law?* We focus on a specific part of that theme: what is the relevance of a legal conversation that does not occur within the boundaries of the profession? The question challenges our understanding of a variety of elements that constitute law and its many meanings to discover, unveil or critically discuss. Only on that basis can further research on law as a subject of social debate and its inherent signifying power take place.

The book's focus on 'talking about law' on the street and other public places illustrates in what regards legal theory and philosophy of law hitherto did not perform sufficient research. There are nevertheless important themes at stake: the gap between daily and legal language, its many consequences for understanding law and the fulfillment of legal practice, the implied thought pattern of casuistry and causality, law's language creating facts, absolutisms in legal practice and jurisprudence, the specificities of legal discourse, law as embedded in master-narratives – including the differentiation between pre-linguistic, linguistic and post-linguistic master-narratives.

'Thoughts Backing Speech', the first chapter, underlines that law depends on specific speech activities. One cannot say anything at random in law and about written laws. That is not only the case *in* law and a lawyer's profession, but it reigns also *at peripheries* of legal discourse, in a conversation on the street or other public spaces. However, legal meaning-making, which does *not* take place within the profession, is difficult to trace. That does not take away how our understanding of law is determined by what is talked about, accepted or rejected, thought or neglected *beyond* the domain of law institutionally declared valid.

Thoughts that back this type of speech confront us with major components of law's discourse such as our *evidence* of thinking and judging when we discuss law in public. They regard *interactivity* and *interaction* as constitutive in law practices. What unfolds *outside* the legal profession is often linked to concepts such as '*nature*' and '*natural*'. '*Legal consciousness*' is therefore intensively reconsidered. The sign character of laws and their meaning reintroduce the semiotic relevance of human *expressivity*, of our understanding the *multilingual* character of reality in law, and of the basics of *human rights* – altogether issues that constitute every *legal conversation* anywhere.

The second chapter develops perspectives on legal practice and concentrates on three major subjects: the citizen's mindset, the structures of law's practice and its discourse embedded in a master-narrative. Tendencies in modern law focus on the mind of a rule-following citizen in parallel with activities resulting from modern brain research and therefore not as an issue of morality. Law's practice becomes in that light a special form of brain stalking. The structure of legal practice depends today more than ever on the case and its speech character. That is highlighted in the frame of e-communication, the many uses of smart phones on the street and of the cyber-story as its recent history. Legal discourse is, not unlike all professional discourses, embedded in a master-narrative. Features of that narrative are anchored in a post-modern mentality. A comparison of three narratives delivers insight in often-conflicting attitudes, which stem from one discourse that engenders in more than one signifying narrative.

Law is generally understood as a harmonious and concordant discourse. At levels of language, social sciences, legal theory and jurisprudence an opposite viewpoint will be developed. All those levels mark one specific center of interest in law: its requirement of obedience. To obey the law is not a simple affair: law changes quickly in modern times and is varied in its past; it requires a specific mentality and brings special types of conversation to the fore, which differ in accordance with the place they take, either in law's institutional boundaries or outside them. The well-known slogan 'law without State' is discussed in this context since it profiles the 'talking about law' on the street and marks semiotic perspectives on legal meaning at the same time. The theme 'law and conflict' is often debated and closely connected to the slogan, and emphasizes the central role of harmony in law and life. That role also underlines the urgency to determine the place of conflict in law as understood at a distance to ethical viewpoints and traditions.

The earlier underlined constitutive power of a master-narrative suggests an obedience to law that reaches beyond traditional ethical motivation although it remains classified as a verbal, *linguistic master-narrative*. The archeologist Bednarik's 1993 introduction of the *cupules* implies that non-verbal master-narratives also exist, which could be qualified as *pre-linguistic*. But imagine computers hacking computers to obtain data, which must be provided to still other computers of which nobody can know whether these will hack again others – no matter where, and nobody knows where they are located on the globe. Are such events an act of terrorism or do they indicate a new obedience enforced by a *post-linguistic master-narrative* in which the concept of property has fundamentally changed?

The book finally returns to 'the street' as component and localization of all 'talking about law'. Democracy and citizens met on the street in Ancient Greece's fifth century BC, and we still know names of those streets and occurrences connected with them. The God Hermes played a central role. Modern times experienced the street as a composite of literary nature before the concept was again closely connected with citizenship, public meaning formation and the scale of public policy. Indeed, there is no 'talking about law' that is not closely connected with the street, its local and cultural dimensions, as walks on the streets of Athens, Paris and New York unveil. The entire text invites you to join that walk. We thank Mr. Ben Booth, Edward Elgar's Senior Editor, for his challenging invitation and support to bring this unconventional guide to readers who like the walking and cherish the talking about law in the meantime.

Jan M. Broekman
Frank Fleerackers

1. Thoughts backing speech

1.1 LAW

Talking about law engages in a complex language with plural levels of signification. Consider how the distance between *what is said* about law by citizens and *what law means* in the mind of law-makers, judges, politicians or arbiters appears immense. So there is every reason to concentrate on the often-neglected phenomenon we give the name: 'talking about law', which is at the borderlines of 'legal conversation' and remains a neglected field of meaning and speech in legal semiotics.

1.1.1 Signification Plurals

One notices differentiations. We often acknowledge the specificity of our daily talking about law as a need for each citizen and therefore, perhaps in an indirect manner, as a major contribution to democracy. Citizens experience a huge gap between their *talking about law* (what they daily do) and the *meaning of law* (which they cannot master). Both create a different effect and maintain different language patterns in the life of citizens and society. That distance, often a breach, between *meaning* and *saying* is always at issue when law is operative. The close connections between *saying* and *meaning* are an important theme in all regards: signs are exchanged and significations engender during those processes. Semiotics apparently does not only determine signs and reconstruct meanings: the path from sign towards signification is followed and understood as an important social process: ask the citizen on the street!

> Fundamental to the explorations of this book is that *law in its entirety* is continuously at issue. That is the case in any *talking about law* of citizens as well as in the process of *meaning-making* of lawyers in society.

There are several outstanding components that function as a subject in our investigations. We mention the *socio-legal* position of the judge, the emphasis on *speech performances* that even characterize legal texts, the need to *master, fixate and generalize* meanings that characterize the approach of each lawyer, his many contributions to maintain the *uniqueness of law's discourse*, the problematic understanding of the link between words spoken *on the street* and words uttered *in the court* or in comparable professional settings.[1] Comparable importance must be given to social issues related to law: in the first place *citizenship* in general, *civic participation* and *street level interpretations* subjected to socio-political debates, among other themes of law and modern society. The fact that they all have a dominant *linguistic* component directs our focus on *talking about law* towards a *semiotic* view regarding the predominant *law-language* relation.

1.1.2 Law-Language

However, the differences or even the breaches between what is uttered on the street and within the professional framework are *not* solely a matter of a sociology of the street nor solely an issue of the professional activities of lawyers, law-makers or those who otherwise apply the rules of law in our society. *Law is in the first place a matter of language.* What does this mean? The distance between saying and meaning, articulation and intention, expressivity and mind is a major topic in the philosophy of language since the early years of the Occidental, in particular Anglo-Saxon, twentieth century. And, we must underline, with language goes an interest in the quality of life – law being one its major components.

That broad notion of life energizes any focus on 'talking about law'. That special type of talk unfolds from sign to signification, and the latter is in itself a rough but rather efficacious indication for life in its many social dimensions. However, laws and legal rules *are* not signs but are *articulated as* a sign. They always show ties with more encompassing significations. This dynamic should be mentioned and studied intensely. Lawyers seldom embrace this feature while debating law and its multiple meanings. Any 'talking about law' is not their preferred theme: they *just do* law; they cherish the impression of performing law by means of their own legal activity.

1.1.3 Talking Pre-Semiotic

However, their practice depends on language; their speech is more important than an individual lawyer's mind is prepared to grasp. *All talk*

[1] In this book, words denoting the masculine should be taken to include the feminine unless the context otherwise suggests.

is in essence 'pre-semiotic' and thus *before* a person can begin to explain law and its social function in the framework of signs and significance. Our theme: the everyday 'talking about law' will for that reason unfold in parallel to the various methodologies of philosophy and social sciences while focusing on the extremely strong relationship between law and language. Any legal-semiotic analysis is based on that special relationship. But the semiotics of law display a heavy accent on 'law as a system of *signs*' (Kevelson[2]) and not on '*signs on the move*'. The latter are at issue when the concept of legal language is perceived as a term to describe all legal activity. Activity is always combined with the dynamics of signs, which are most prominent in speech performances. Judges judge thanks to their characteristic speech capacity, which is anchored in their socially and institutionally accepted position. To be a judge is the result of his (seldom explicitly considered) specific speech activities, which embrace a semiotic capacity with its shadows in pre-semiotic spheres. Only signs on the move pave the path towards signification. They move, while the talk goes on! A truly *legal* semiotics does not have the features of system-analysis but of a film: their ever-moving sign-characters fascinate.

1.2 TALKING

Law is in our daily feelings and actions spoken and written as a precious sign, and often unconsciously present in ways we are not aware of – even when signifying occurrences are manifest. The policeman carries his sign-characters publicly, the tax officer hidden – even if he enters an office, we are not able to fully read him. The cabdriver earns his money mainly in a legal world, not only by means of contracting with his passengers, for instance when they board his car or pay for the trip, but also while reading the traffic signs around him and respecting the rules and habits of the town's traffic. Are those participants aware of the impact of the law? They are normally not, and the use of an additional concept such as 'sign' or 'signification' is mostly worrisome to the citizens concerned, let alone the encompassing process of 'signifying' itself.

One of the major issues might be that once we talk about law, and use such concepts like 'sign' or 'signification', we almost always produce quite inappropriate reactions and contexts. For instance, we link the use

---

[2] Roberta Kevelson, *The Law as a System of Signs*, Plenum Publishing, New York, 1988.

of the 'sign'-word to the police officer or the traffic controller, but also to the judge or the legal scientist.

Moreover, we have uneasy feelings towards those words because we know not by reflection but only by daily life experiences in how many ways the trajectory from 'sign' to 'signification' is itself a sign of life that is more encompassing than those simple words suggest. We suggest in our daily communication and talk that deeply layered ties between *law* and *life* do indeed exist – but they do not belong to the materials of our daily lives because they seem to belong to thoughts that are not our everyday life occurrences. They seem primarily important when *social* life and its complexities are at stake.

We may experience that there do indeed exist precious ties between law and life, but we do not normally feel capable of solving the riddle of their co-existence in the midst of our life situations. Law and discussions on law are often seen as an important *barrier* for fully experiencing life in all its dimensions. But that very same experience of life reminds us, however, that many times we look for the support a legal keystone might provide.

1.2.1 Life, a Totality of Signs

Our world often looks like a totality of signs. However, the concept of 'totality' is in this context as disputable as the concept 'world' and the concept of 'sign' is as dubious as the two former words. We neither know nor master the multiple significations that guide us in this totality, and we are never prepared to accept accountability for the many meanings of the 'world' we live in. Their multitude is staggering, and deafens us when we talk about this to our neighbors. Problems and social positions determine our conversations as well as our exchanges of words, opinions or insights into reality. And such exchanges become, because of their plurality, lightweight, spontaneous and more immediately active in provoking counter-activities. In that context, adverse positions engender and a vicious striving for fixation in the middle of changes frequently takes place. All this happens long before 'significance' or 'meaning' is given the status of a mark of communication. 'From sign to significance' needs the addition 'and vice versa', because of its powerful flow of life – always, again and again: *life* is the favored expression.

We must add that our speaking about law, even in the sense of 'sign' or 'signification', is never identical to delivering a legal judgment, to any 'saying for law' or any final word of the judge. Indeed, many meanings of law's activity are at stake in a conversation about law. And what fascinates more: words and functions of the judge belong to the multiple meanings of any conversation, but they will never represent law in its totality. How is it possible, one should ask, that this remark seems necessary? And how can we understand appropriately that in Occidental legal thinking a judge's thoughts and words play a decisive role amidst all the uncertainty of signification? He or she often seems the personification of legal meaning as such, and thus the living symbol of all signs in law. The judge appears indeed as a specialist in the game called 'law'.

1.2.2 The Judge in Grammar

He or she is the very first person, which does not know a plural. But has law an 'I', a first person singular? Is the judge the 'I' of the law and its discourse? If that is the case, we understand that his entire psychological condition and his attitude are grounded upon one socially accepted statement: without him, law cannot exist! That is the burden of his existence: without him a debate, discussion or discourse pertaining to law would be impossible. All utterances would be incomplete, not correct and, above all, have no reliable significance! Our *legal consciousness* is law's central issue shared by all of us, and that specific central position can never be an empty chair! Law would be senseless without the fulfillment of a judge's functions. So the persistent question is: what is the core subject of our legal consciousness – the sign-function of the judge, or the signification of law determined by our Occidental culture? One answer will be in everybody's mind: the question pertains to a lawyer as determined by law's institutional features. When talking about law, who else determines the subject of our speech? Once on 'the street', the question seems senseless.

Who is allowed to participate in that discourse? Of course, we suggest: the so-called 'ordinary citizen'. He is entitled to vote every few years and determines indirectly (many via a choice for parliament) the laws of the land, which also institute its judges. But what is the exact value and meaning of that civil voice? Is the citizen the user of law, or does the law as an institution use him, the citizen, for its own purposes? Why does each citizen remain silent about the value and signification of law and leaves it as if it were an evidence *in se*? Does the engenderment of this evidence not end up silencing a large part of public as well as personal life, and with that silencing a loss of understanding of the significance of law in its multiple sign functions? What does the judge contribute to balance signs in social life and what is the sense of his unique grammar position?

All those considerations imply issues colored by philosophical considerations. They are relevant in discussions, dialogues and other forms of talking together, but never in a monologue because subjects of conversation are extremely difficult to change in a monologue. In a monologue no real resonance exists, so that significations lack any guarantee. That is important in the case of law and in particular in our speaking about law. Law is an important signification; it re-enforces powers in the many adjectives one can hear in conversations. They illustrate our awareness of the many dimensions of law. We argue, for instance, in a specific context that law is 'natural' and remind our discussion partners that there even exists a 'natural law'. Or we suggest that specific components of law are in our conversation 'evident', or 'just'.

Many of these conversational activities do clearly depend on our 'attitude'. Attitudes determine meanings in the exchange of ideas. Think of terms like 'prejudice' fulfilling a role in legal judgments; think of 'disagreement', 'dispute' or 'conflict' while discussing a trial – all are possible speech acts that involve law. Law cannot exist without such a treasure of meanings and acts. All touch a wealth of more complex notions and terms. While speaking about law one encounters notions such as (legal) positivism, reference, semiotics, virtual reality and the like – some of them embedded in legal theory, others in social sciences, psychology, economy, physics or in poetry, literary theory and hermeneutics. Those references ultimately find their anchor in words that are spoken and function in our thought formation on law. This observation should guide us: speech activities are our object of analysis and evolving understanding.

1.2.3 Talking About Law

Talking about law is, as far as we concluded, always, and like all conversations, a linguistic issue that focuses on meaning and signification. That specific focus will never result in a fixated[3] determination, but in a *contextual* event. Meaning and signification are always precious moments of an evolution that is itself enchained to meaning and signification.

Life itself; that means: every aspect of what we humans call life is an unfolding of meaning in which we play an undetermined role. We experience this lack of determination as a problem that reigns over the

---

[3] The word 'fixated' represents in this book a *dynamic* meaning and should be understood as: 'concentrating attention for', to gain a 'fastening' or 'locking up', 'determining finally' or 'firmly securing': all at the borderline of everyday discourse and law's professional discourse.

human mind. Who are we, what are we, what are our thoughts, opinions or attitudes in the process of signification? The question colors our experiences on the path from sign to signification and vice versa. The essence of life is contained in this question; we even expand that notion beyond the cosmos we consider as our home, and are prepared to acknowledge 'signification' in the context of a plurality of universes. Can we think about, and can we judge those meanings and create awareness pertaining to that significance?

The challenge to think beyond boundaries of the universe leads sometimes to results, which are difficult to accept seriously. Bennet[4] suggested in 2013 that we could reliably calculate how 1^{80} particles and 1^{10} atoms play a constitutive role in our region of the universe. As a conclusion, the volume of our universe (the part we consider to possibly be known) would be 10^{84} cm^3! Is this our desired awareness of reality?

Consider that we know only *one* time scale, so that we observe solely *adaptation* and *renewal*. The latter are developed in the dimensions of our universe, which is a construction of the human mind that covers only several billions of years. It surprises and even creates suspicion that we always encounter solely *one* type of significance. Our concept of science in these contexts is marked by the eventuality of an awakening and emancipation of those latent meanings. The latter illustrates the multiplicity in universes. We find that feature in each human genome: each cell has a copy of itself, so that in the human body itself, its brain included, a constant stream of renewal can be characterized by us as 'Being'.

1.2.4 Catharsis

While talking about law, we may embrace the role, function and meaning of *catharsis* in the human mind. The concept was coined by Aristotle in his *Poetica* to reflect the purification of emotions of the audience. Anxiety and fear during performances of drama and tragedy were encountered by empathy with the play's protagonists. This emotional purification would allow for a renewal and restoration of one's mind. In his seminal work *The Self Awakened: Pragmatism Unbound*, Roberto M. Unger's views on self-consciousness suggest that (judged from a pragmatist viewpoint) man's self-fulfillment should very well do away with human catharsis, or at least be able to transcend catharsis in an almost

---

[4] D. Bennet, *Intuition Pumps and Other Tools for Thinking*, W. W. Norton, New York/London, 2013.

divine fashion.[5] But it is our firm belief that the opposite is true. The need to embrace catharsis is a foundational attribute of human interaction or conflict even within pragmatism.

Catharsis in its most generic sense is implied in the differential dynamics of interaction. To fully understand, accept, and even embrace, change in contemporary society, *catharsis* functions as a counterpoint of our existential emotions of angst, despair and loss. This seems to include a deep-layered level of meaning: is our talking about law, which we consider as an average daily occurrence unfolding in a natural language, a *cathartic* event? Is this characterization the reason for the widespread influence of 'talking about law' in social life, for it being clearly 'pre-semiotic' and thus an almost natural habit, for an excoriation not to be confronted with lawyers, judges and courts? That question is by no means rhetoric. Any articulation of a human consciousness is an enriching activity in the context of meaning fields and significance. Speech, which focuses on reality, is in the first place a component of that activity.

1.2.5 Speech

> A fundamental inversion should be noticed of what we naïvely believe: *humans are not human because of their speech performance, but speech performance causes humans to be human!* Like a little child is given a capacity to unfold speech activity from the very moments in the mother's womb, a human being unfolds this capacity in a truly plural togetherness, which is ultimately characterized as a culture.

This inversion forms the basis on which the phenomenon we called: 'talking about law' should be understood. That understanding has far-reaching consequences. The subject of our analysis, an everyday conversation or 'talking', leads us to an insight into how deeply the ties between law and language are anchored. That insight is the basis of analyzing law in a semiotic perspective. Its basics are neither the product of a theory or of an appropriate insight into cultural processes, nor the exteriorization of a consciousness about how to articulate law linguistically. The phenomenon we call 'talking' is truly pre-semiotic.

But before a semiotic view on *talking* occurs, language and law (regarded as a subspecies of language) did already unfold! That is not a

---

[5] R. M. Unger: *The Self Awakened: Pragmatism Unbound*, Harvard University Press, Cambridge, MA, 2007.

matter of a strict order or sequence, but a matter of growth and change. Analyzing any 'talking about law' is in this regard an attempt to understand law and legal discourse while understanding and interpreting the 'talking'. 'Talking' is: the 'speech' component, and solely *in ultimo* the 'linguistic' component.

We underline that the expression 'talking about law' focuses in the first place on specific *speech acts* of specific functionaries in discourse. Language is a lawyer's professional domain. His talking does not embrace any specificity of legal language as such, or the particularity of legal discourse. Law in general is understood on the street through the various speech performances of lawyers, judges and sometimes also legislators, but also by the conversations that surround the life of the citizens. This has important consequences for legal theory and also for a semiotic approach towards law. The most outstanding of them is that *the 'law-language' relation* (the basis for understanding law) *requires a particular emphasis on legal speech acts* and the phenomenon of law in its entirety is incorporated in the practice of a speaking lawyer's, or a judge's, speech utterance. It is no surprise that this perspective leads above all to questions pertaining to legal thought formation, which are the foundation and social frame of law's verbal activities.

1.3 THINKING

Each particle of thought formation activates episodes of talk, in other words: fragments of language. There is no thinking without speaking, no possibility to think without a guarantee to be able to speak. The great significian who created the foundations for modern semiotics, Victoria Lady Welby, ventured to formulate already in 1911: 'Language is Thought in audible activity'.[6]

1.3.1 Language and Thought

She did not only initiate a turn of philosophy towards language, but she also tried to lay out some of the foundational structures of a philosophy of language, which remain until our days of highest relevance for the study of law. We mention some of their aspects, which will be relevant for our research into the semiotic foundations of law:

[6] Victoria Lady Welby, *Significs and Language*, Macmillan and Co., London, 1911, reprinted University of California Libraries, p. 68.

(1) The ties between language, linguistic expressivity and thought formation are never determined and forever fixated. They renew continuously and become different in each thought or experience that is formulated in words or speech.
(2) Uncertainties pertaining to the specificity of the language of thinking remain vividly alive despite our multitude of fixated, reliable and positive data in science as well as philosophy.
(3) Words on their own will never form an independent linguistic expression; they are always the product of time and renewal – as the user of dictionaries experiences daily.
(4) The relation: 'word, signification and text' is an example of connectivity, which is *not* fixated or leading to a fixated complexity.
(5) Language fragments switching from 'observable' to 'non-observable' can never be the basis for any meaning in language. In language exist linguistic fragments that are not expressible in language. That is as important as in life in general: what appears to be identical does not need to be identical!
(6) Our thought formation should be understood as attempting to fiercely embrace an awareness of the fact that all our thoughts are submitted to all possible forms of interactivity. The latter component requires special attention. Emphasis on interactivity as an inspiration for thought will also be interpreted as the 'management' of our thought formation. It places a thinking subject in context and reinforces its position in language and particularly in speech performances.

It also enables us to approach an understanding of what it means 'to be thought': not a pure passivity but rather a thinking *that befalls us* in the deepest sense of the word. This form of thought formation, which includes so forcefully the experience that befalls us, is perhaps the reason that we cannot always create distance to our own preconceived opinions. It says: there is no distancing, when distance cannot take place – because there is no place for distancing! But there could be one exception: there is a distance that does not *create* distance but *gives* distance. An expectation seems embedded in this consideration as such: an attempt to view our own prejudices could lead to a meaningful thinking. But that process is in no way objective! It only widens the grip of the subject while thinking.

Is the latter a veritable possibility? Should it not mean that one could think beyond one's proper thought process, while exactly the inverse should take place: you have to let your thoughts think themselves! Your thoughts are the subject and you are the object. That is a challenge within the more or less 'safe' subject–object relationship – it promises in any case much more than the idea of thought formation *without* a thinking subject!

The question is, however, whether there is any moment of thought that can withdraw from some form of inter*act*ivity and – what is more – inter-*subject*ivity. This seems circular. The '*You-think*' cannot create sufficient distance from the '*I-think*'. One cannot do without the other. Interactivity and inter-subjectivity are like the sea in which we swim/are adrift/live: we continuously engage in a form of 'thinking beyond thinking'; our thought formations are never the same; they are never identical but are rather like unfinished circles!

Those circles express a despair, which arises when we think and when we hope to be saved by language and in particular our speech activity. Thinking is also a matter of time, of phases, of attitudinal seconds that are deleted in the deep structure of speech and language because life itself moves on. That insight is a major issue in the philosophy of Ludwig Klages. Life unfolds beyond boundaries of a human consciousness, he said, and that causes prejudices to be ridiculous and the pronouncement of interactivity a vulnerable political slogan. The sense of meaning and of signification is like a hand extended to all who talk and all who are endangered to remain empty. Do we grasp the hand?

The question '*what is …*' seems a trap to catch the *being*, and subsequently fixate it. *Being* and *life* both hesitate to choose the right direction for avoiding the trap: for each of them a 'going forwards' is identical to a 'going backwards'; the trap seems omnipresent. What is our thinking, when and under what conditions would that thinking be prepared to think: *law*?

1.3.2 To Think is to Change

Edmund Husserl, the founder of phenomenology, included in his considerations about thinking two fascinating aspects: (1) thinking always includes a change of attitude, and (2) that change always includes a mode of distancing oneself from the omnipresent 'naïve-natural' attitude. Each thought formation of an individual/subject is primarily a form of exploration of the wealth of possibilities of the subject, and thus embraces many attitudes in innumerable moments of time.

The essence of thinking is apparently in the words 'other' or 'different', which is exactly *not* 'ego' but 'alter', meaning *change*, always becoming an *alter*, always being *different*. Any *becoming different* is a matter of *being altered*; the change which is the engine of our thought formation causes a change of our *being* that we experience in our own thinking. It means that this change always touches its own status, which is streaming rather than being fixated. Our *being* can*not* be thought or articulated as fixated.

1.3.3 Alteration

The power of the *logos* reaches *beyond* language and thought. The latter are obviously too limited, especially in legal practice. But take into consideration that subject and object change their limits continuously. Their striving for change is a vital force and should also characterize legal functionaries. This is why the famous linguist F. de Saussure defined his semiotic approach as 'the study of the life of signs in the bosom of social life'.[7] Meaning and signification change with what is signified and meant to be. They are therefore never the only and once determined. If a philosophy needs a subject and/or an object, than we must bring the dynamics of change deeply into their innermost changing selves. The consequences for our forms of linguistic articulation are immense. The value of a word will be deepened. A word is never an elementary particle of language. The latter is a process of changing and repeatedly intertwining relations, which seldom touches the dimensions of *being* but just approaches an articulation of *being*. It means that each form of interactivity is basically a change, and – above all – an *alter*ation. That *alter*ation is sometimes an inclusion and at other moments an exclusion; the one cannot exist without the other, but both are always different, so that other *alter*ations are engendered.

1.4 JUDGING

The French Revolution placed the power of legal decision in the hands of parliament because it did not seem appropriate to have individuals (i.e. judges) in that position. That was a problematic action in itself and an inherent danger for democracy.

1.4.1 Individuality and Education

This action, and the inherent problem of having a single individual in the position of the final decision-maker, resounds in daily talks about the law.

---

[7] F. de Saussure, *Cours de Linguistique Générale*, 1915, edited by Tullio de Mauro, Paris, Payothéque, 1972, p. 33: '*une science qui étudie la vie des signes au sein de la vie sociale*'.

One can hear the protests in many of the talks about law on the street. A judge's position and function, his freedom and limitations are a theme of citizens in many conversations – despite the various considerations in legal theory during the twentieth century and later. The idea of a judge being '*bouche de la loi*' (mouth/speaker of the law) and the fear for '*le gouvernement des juges*' (the government of judges) appears outdated and counterproductive today. The slogan '*summa ius, summa iniuria*' is valid for *laws* and not for *judges* – unless we see them solely as legal applicators, as '*bouche de la loi*', and we do not like that view, so one never hears such opinions in talks about law on the street.

It is, all in all, true that the *master* of the legal discourse is subordinated to, and servant of that discourse. That need not be problematic. Why should we try to be 'objective' here? The apple is falling down anyway. Darwin was also right. But human, ethical and legal activities are not completely subjected to *laws*. And it makes no apparent sense to submit or to analyze human activities in accordance. As was said: the master of the legal discourse is an essential component of that discourse while he actualizes it. Yet the position and structure of *discourse* in itself has to be revisited in many of the following pages. References to internal or external positions in view of the totality of law do not work in legal analyses. The question, whether 'matter is ontologically given' cannot be articulated by the judge; the solution of such a philosophical question is not within his institutional power. His checking is not a way of finding the truth. The Central-European term 'finding the law' is in that context also not acceptable. It would be better to introduce terms such as: 'generation of law' in parallel to 'generation of sense' or 'generation (eventually "engenderment") of significance' – underlining the feature of an 'always again' and the desire to keep perpetually 'a new case' in mind.

We touch here as an example on the difference between Anglo-Saxon precedent law and the Civil Law view on precedent. Most lawyers refer to the former in order to obtain a better understanding of *case law*. But they are not aware of the fact that bounds with cases and case law will never be the solution for Civil Law cases. But both types of law compare and qualify the case as if a case were a static substrate of its reality. Both apparently do not provide the possibility to differentiate and thus appreciate the dynamic character of a case. However, consider: what is a purely static case?

Is that also valid for our ideas about legal certainty? That idea is as difficult to understand and to apply to social life as 'social security' or 'security in a love-affair'. Only '*a*ffective', which is perhaps even '"insecure" legal certainty' makes sense. It is in this context that the judge demonstrates how he is subject *and* object, and that his position is *in* and *beyond* the legal discourse. Consider that classical thought patterns abiding objective thinking cannot explore or forward thoughts that have to do with an 'insecure security'. Relate to someone who is able to embrace and think *interactive practices*, and a new world will appear!

1.4.2 Educate Judges

Think of the many attempts to focus on the so-called human and social image of the judge. There are many doubts about the homogeneity of such an image in the mind of the judge. But they do not touch the essence of the problem. They demonstrate perhaps an enduring uncertainty when cases are decided on the basis of the judge's mind. Mind you: that image can never become explicit in any type of reasoning and will never contribute to any explication in the words of the judge. Empirical sociological analyses may suggest the existence of such an image, but the real effects are never demonstrated. So, have a new judge function, and let us educate him appropriately! But: *how*? By intruding in his speech activity? Or will we be successful by teaching him a different language, which includes many more and really different meanings of the street?

The judge is essential in our 'talking about law' and he fulfills roles of which we are not aware and cannot master. Not only the ways we think about law, but also in our conversations about law on the street and in other public places; also in talks on TV, the social media and at many other occasions there is the judge in a primordial role. It is hardly possible to understand the task of the judge anymore as 'thinking' and 'judging' in those many patterns of communication and representation. The Common Law claims therefore that a judge should in many cases only function as a *mediator* in social conflicts, whereas all other solutions are solely a matter of correctness regarding the application of the laws. In the Civil Law (as far as this distinction has a sense in our modern day) the application of laws is still understood as an integral component of the legal discourse, so that the judge remains focused.

Applied laws speak in the legal discourse like lawyers or judges, politicians or citizens. But the speech activity of a law is decidedly different from the activity of a person, and remains confined to the discourse as institutionally fixated. This way of speaking of *laws* is predominantly *rhetorical*, in so far as it confirms the perfection of a fixated and institutionally bound discourse. That creates a disputable relation with reality. Judges order reality *facts* in *categories*, *events* in *rules*, *ethical* issues in strict *contexts* – and all those moves are named 'legal'. What is individual will thus be ordered in what is general, and any inverse move is strictly forbidden. That is how the judge produces a policy, which ultimately leads to 'the dynamics of difference' of reality. But those dynamics do not always belong to the institutional boundaries of his discourse, and a judge will not be prepared to provoke any *change* because of this discursive limitation. How can an education encourage a judge to cope with the strength that binds him or her to fixated patterns of speech and behavior?

1.4.3 A Judge's Discourse

These observations underline the coherence among the many components of a legal discourse. But at the same time they make clear how limited this discourse is. It is limited because this discourse is a discourse tied up with a professional – and thus an artificial language. One always uses words that are *made* valid and words that *control* significances, such as 'norm' or 'judgment' or 'reality' or 'case'. That is most challenging: the *master* of the legal discourse is *subjected* to – and a *servant* of – the discourse, its signs and its signification. Consider the comparison: our physicists are able and are allowed to think in nano-dimensions as well as in macro-dimensions mixed with dimensions of our daily routine. Their point of tangency with ontological and even metaphysical issues is rich and complex. The question whether matter is a metaphysical datum can be posed by them and directed to them. A judge is never in that position because his discourse is far more limited. A reference to inter-subjectivity or even interactivity will seldom solve the problems and it may not even be qualified as an appropriate approach. Will a judge ever enjoy the freedom of thought a physicist has? Can a lawyer ever cooperate with a physicist? In that case, he has to leave the boundaries of his profession and step outside the legal discourse – or have the physicist acquire access to the legal discourse by qualifying his specialism as legally necessary. So, can a lawyer ever see his image and his task from another side of his discourse? *Quod non*: that would be classified as creating 'legal uncertainty'!

A judge is in all situations and talks the *subject* of the legal discourse. This remains the case even apart from any analysis of the specific properties of that discourse. His position is and will be understood as a particular subject-position. The question is whether any new type of education will change that position or take that manner of understanding away. As such, lawyers and citizens are being spoken to before they speak! Even more so, while speaking, they are the object, not a mere subject, of legal speech. Ortega y Gasset once wrote: 'the term "subject"

... stands for radical instability of the human person'. Is that not the case in our considerations pertaining to the judge and his or her legal discourse?

But there is a huge difference between a philosophical and a legal argument. The first is all too often apodictic and tends to contrast concepts without providing solutions for those tensions. Notice the adverse in what seems the same, in Bach's '*Parodieverfahren*' (procedure of parody) and his contra-punctual movements. The latter allow him to repeat the same again and again without saying the same all the time – always slightly different, at another moment and in a somewhat different context. Here one encounters 'interaction' between word and context, although the idea of interaction itself becomes vague. It is difficult to find appropriate expressions: 'respective', 'communal' or 'inter-mutual' will hardly do!

We should perhaps find a specific lemma in this context for 'interaction' or 'interactivity', and for that reason the term '*aeffector*' could become a description of those determinants which specifically effect the position and the behavior of an actor. Bach's counterpoint should be remembered here. It seems evident that the judge is not simply a subject of the legal discourse, but on the other hand one cannot claim the opposite and tell that he is not!

Re-read Ortega y Gasset: both counterpoint positions (subject/non-subject) are useful to approach that instability. Describing or fixating is not! The '*Parodieverfahren*', perhaps the only way to unfold a philosophical activity, continuously initiates a form of interactivity with counterpoint character. It is useful to experience the difficulties that are inherent in all attempts to articulate. But here one focuses ultimately on the *o/Other* or *someone else*, or *other human abilities*.

1.5 INTERACTIVITY

The question has been posed several times: is interactivity a valuable and acceptable term to discuss a judge's social position and reflexive standing? Should judges no longer work, speak, consider, and decide *solo*? In the framework of such a generalization, it must be researched whether interactivity among judges is better for legal judgments. Or do we have to differentiate between collegiality and interactivity, mutual respect and cooperation? This does not only pertain to civil or management lawyers and not only to alternative forms of conflict resolution, but to judges, above all to magistrates.

A philosophical remark embraces the idea that interactivity is mainly understood as a preferred form of togetherness (Latin: *inter-esse*) of acting subjects. But how can interactivity exist without the predominance of the subject? Any view on the position and socio-legal structure of the judge produces solely a repetition of this difficult question. It relates to the legal thought patterns dominated by cases, which raises the question how a legal understanding of a case evolves, and how important that insight is for the personal view of the judge. It could be illustrated that active panel participation creates distance to personal prejudices. That emphasizes a concordant functioning in, for instance, Courts of Appeal and at lower levels where appeal cases could be reduced. A quote seems important here: In order to deliver a highly valuable judgment, the judge should conclude in cooperation with other judges, so that prejudices are reduced or less effective. If three judges do not accord, they vote by majority. That is interactive jurisdiction.

1.5.1 Interactive Jurisdiction

We are, like the majority of readers, victims of a centuries-old tradition to see the judge, as the crown of legal thought formation and legal power in society, as an individual. Is that correct? What then about the law-maker, what about the parliamentarian, his political party and his citizens? A legal discourse does not provide a clear profile in that regard. It only reinforces the pinnacle position of the judge and focuses on his or her extraordinary function, position, role, name or fame in legal practice as reflected in legal theory! That has many implications. They relate to *interactivity* among themselves as well as with citizens on the basis of a subject-centered thought pattern. The question is how far that offers a new profile for the professional behavior of judges, and relates in that light to law's discourse as a basic concept in the study of law and jurisprudence. In the end, the question 'what is, and how does talking about law function?' seems at stake. Hence the following remarks on interactivity, despite its limited meaning and subject-driven approach in law:

(1) *A New Dogma?* If interactivity becomes the new dogma in law and jurisprudence, one should critically research in connection with that proposal how far the '*super subject-position*' of the judge can still be accepted within the legal discourse.

Of essence is the consideration, whether a discourse supports such a position within its own boundaries and philosophical profile. In other words: is a *super speaker* in a discourse acceptable, and is such a speaker position tolerable in our everyday talking about law? The answer is to be found at various levels of a theory of spoken language and of speech acts. Those theories are somewhere on the path from *sign* to *signification*, and vice versa, as we explained above. It implies that *the acceptance and understanding of the role of the judge is ultimately a legal-semiotic issue*. But semioticians will agree that their discipline does *not* unfold once a sign is produced (a word spoken) but only while outlining the entire path from sign to signification. It is clear that we already begin to outline a signification once we determine the *sign-function* of the judge. The semiotic dynamics of the two interfere with the *interactivity* requirement pertaining to a third component. There is no other answer possible than this *triadic* answer, which just outlines the structure of meeting the suggestion to accept interactivity as a decisive feature of the judge.

(2) *Sharing v. Power.* The interactivity proposal is not without consequences for our socio-political thought formation and is in fact not solely a proposal for the functioning of judges. That concerns the downgrading of the majority of thought patterns in which the subject plays a decisive role.

Keep in mind: it does not concern our *subjective* thinking and speaking, but rather the *power* position of all thought formation, which centralizes a subject. That position is in its highest degree specific for law and legal discourse. Legal power is in the maintaining of the subject: the subject as speaker, as judge, as thinker, is always engaged in producing power. The *interactivity* proposal downplays the power position law mirrors in its discourse. It is therefore to remind that the legal discourse is generally understood as the discourse of the legal profession, of law and jurisprudence, of legal practice and legal theory – not the discourse we are engaged in when we 'talk about law'. In essence should interactivity replace subjectivity: *sharing should replace power*! That is in law only possible under the condition that interactivity remains a legally valid and thus a legitimate position. Interactivity will be a feature under the command of the continuous structuring of legal discourse itself and will therefore fulfill the role of a legal term. Only under that condition will a judge be able to perform interactively. Does that performance bring him to any outside position of the powerful discourse we call 'law'?

(3) *Multiple Languages.* There is an important feature to consider in the case of interactivity among judges: the latter should be studied as a specific *form* of behavior and thought formation.

Lawyers or judges do not play soccer together, they are not interactively gardening but they *must* speak and write together. Their interactivity is above all: a *textual* affair; their attitudes and knowledge will be expressed in exclusive words, sentences and texts which all belong to their professional language – even when those expressions are sometimes commentated in daily language. They are not comrades but colleagues and thus are obliged to restrict their means of communication to their professional language.

Any interactivity proposal is a matter of language. In this light, one should understand the earlier remark that outlining the role of the judge is in essence a semiotic affair. So we highlight the distance between the language on which that interactivity focuses and the everyday act of 'talking about law'. One of the major characteristics is *not* in the grammar or vocabulary of those two languages (the daily and the professional language) but in the necessity to understand the function of the judge as a speaker-function and not as a listener. Even legal theoreticians do not pay attention to what messages a judge has to *receive* but solely to his *utterances* resulting from his professional speaker's viewpoint. That illustrates in what regard *speaking law* embraces another language than *speaking about law* – despite all the interactivity between citizen and lawyer or judge.

1.5.2 Dimensions in Legal Discourse

The multiplicity of language and its related social patterning seems of central interest here. Interactivity unfolds in a professional language, which *must combine* the language of the law/jurisprudence with the language of everyday. Both types of language describe reality, and its consequences are of interest.

Predominant is the fact that language (a) can be described, commentated, outlined and structurally analyzed in language (b), but that the inverse is impossible: (b) can never be described in (a). This is a problem, because functionaries are supposed and want to be able to present 'reality' (language (b)) in their own language (a) – and cannot. For the sake of clarity: lawyers and in particular judges have their conversations in a mixture of languages (a) and (b) but their final conclusions and judgments are entirely in (a) and thus difficult to translate in (b), which are levels of language we characterize as 'talking about law'.

What judges say and write is ultimately determined by standards of jurisprudence, which are prescribed in handbooks, special websites, precedents and specific sections of legal language that remain under control by internal system requirements, procedures and possibilities of appeal. The *interactivity* among judges is linguistic, safeguarded, obligatory and preformatted, not knowing of any crisis of meaning that reaches beyond a court decision or judgmental conclusion.

Legal speaking and writing does not embrace any risk of an unexpected confrontation with an existential abyss of meaning or societal signification. That only happens in language (b), a language in which *interactivity* has definitively other dimensions. One should be aware of those differentiations. The effect of prejudices can be reduced through clarifying exchanges in the parts of language (b) that play a constitutive role in language (a). We often call that 'interpretation', 'weighing', 'hermeneutics' and the like. They cannot, however, be grasped in the heart of language (a) and interactivity cannot for that reason find a place in the linguistic framework of institutional legal language (b). Everyday language (b) seems the most important means of communication to transfer and effectuate professional language concepts, views and judgments (a) – prejudices and related views of the professional included. The standardized and controlled terminology of the latter makes the language of the judge inaccessible for interactivity. The latter finds a place in a natural language (b), but not in a profile of legal concepts that characterizes law's discourse (a). The two languages remain separated even if they do occasionally intertwine. Their separation forms a *social* problem of *legal* discourse.

Law as a discourse that exercises an immense influence in social life can only continue its existence thanks to a rigid pattern of prescribed, repeated and continuously refined terms and concepts. But how free is the language of such a discourse? How free is its speaker? Is a mutual expressivity of language and social function possible? Those questions mirror a complication: can words, concepts, texts, laws, procedures, functions, and roles fit to a stable social pattern of narrowly described, fixated, precisely determined functions and residences? They might enable and stimulate us to analyze the implications of a socially desired discourse. The suggestion that interactivity is a reality within the boundaries of that discourse has extreme relevance in that regard.

That is, however, determined by *limits of law* itself. Introducing interactivity as a behavioral feature in the case of judges creates the impression that issues, which are in essence *philosophical* issues, can be tackled by means of an *organization* of legal functions and institutions. Can interactivity in law be *organized*? The question implies particular views pertaining to language and knowledge. Major elements are:

- specificity of the legal discourse and its institutional anchors, which result in attempts to define that discourse;
- subject-directedness of all law and the questionable ideal of interactivity;
- relations between language and sociability; and
- relations between philosophical views and socio-organizational measures.

Those elements not only characterize the complexity of relations between law, language and knowledge, but their presence in this complexity is also a sign for the urgent need to focus on the concept of discourse itself when legal discourse is mentioned. Ideas on interaction and interactivity appear to relate to qualities of law's discourse – an observation that should be appreciated correctly.

1.6 LANGUAGE

It appears that emphasis is on the *pragmatic* character of a legal discourse. It is a discourse serving specific practices (legal practices in social life) by means of a language that embraces a mainly fixated terminology. But there does not exist only *one* language! Practice and terminology are both major features of a professional language, and there is no discussion about the contrast between the language of everyday (mostly a natural language) and the language of law – itself the proof of the *plural character of language*. A legal discourse is not exceptional. There are many professional languages that function in Occidental culture: the physician, the historian, the linguist, the chemist, the archeologist or the astronomer, illustrate this function when they articulate their observations via words and texts. One particular situation in legal discourse should, however, be seen as an exception. In law's professional discourse a special position is foreseen for a non-legal specialist to contribute to the legal discourse (referring in his own language to opinions, providing data, etc.) within legally defined procedural limits *as if* they spoke legal language. The outcome of such a contribution is important and can influence the totality of a final judgment. That position can be a lively presence of another specialist in law's discourse, either in words spoken or by means of quotations of important non-legal texts.

1.6.1 Language of the Profession

There is often an identification of law's professional language and legal education. Students should in the first place 'learn the legal language': they are taught to think, speak and articulate professional meanings of specific expressions. They perform that in their mother tongue and are trained to harbor legal meanings in the everyday language of their social life. This process of positioning meanings in a significant context seems dominant. To 'be a lawyer' is often identified with a perfect mastering of law's language.

A philosophical analysis of the features of the legal profession unveils, however, much more than just this mastering of the specialized language. It means that the philosophical view on language appears to be rooted in other philosophical dimensions than language alone. These focus on the speaker activity and the speaker (social) position in discourse and – more generally – on those for whom the language of a discourse is an important *sign* that refers to articulation (speech) processes entwined with language as such. All lead to transcend a solely linguistic expressivity and embrace the process of signification in its cultural and even 'life'-context. At the end, reality as such is at stake. The discourse of law colors an outstanding form of social life. Such coloring is a matter of *total attitude* embraced by subject and object alike. The term total 'attitude' has to be explained.

1.6.2 Attitudes

A mother tongue, at home in our everyday life-world, has been characterized as different from a professional language, and that is basic in legal discourse. The natural language/mother tongue, in which the professional language is articulated, conceals the difference. It may be helpful to refer to a fundamental distinction between two positions or attitudes, introduced by Edmund Husserl, founder of phenomenology, in the first decades of the twentieth century. His primordial qualification pertains to the difference between a *naïve-natural* and a *non-naïve-natural* attitude/position.[8] In each of those two positions, reality is constituted. That seems a true challenge for law and for lawyers: how

[8] Edmund Husserl, *Vorlesungen über Bedeutungslehre, Sommersemester 1908* (edited by U. Panzer), Husserliana, XXVI, Nijhoff, Dordrecht, 1987; Edmund Husserl, *Ideen zu einer reinen Phänomenologie und phänomenologischen Philosophie*, I, Halle, 1913; Jan M. Broekman, *Phänomenologie und Egologie*. Series Phaenomenologica, Bd 12, M. Nijhoff, The Hague, 1963,

does a lawyer reach my reality? And: all this includes a distance to psychological as well as other types of interpretation of this world-changing position of each individual.

Views on reality are at stake in law and legal judgments, and they are often understood too narrowly as prejudice, lack of neutrality and objectivity, deviant or asocial behaviors and the like. Those classifications of *attitude* do not meet the challenge of our understanding of reality: a key argument for us as it already was in the days of Husserl's phenomenological approaches. *In law's language reality is already interpreted before any legal position or judgment is taken.* There exists no point of reference in view of which a prejudice can be profiled: all reality is 'interpreted reality', and law's share in this is overwhelming in Occidental culture. It implies that every legal interpretation is the interpretation of an interpretation. This motive challenges us (who live a life of observations) to search for the touchstone of a lawyer's epistemological position, for his or her point of exploration and understanding of the range from *sign* to *signification*, which is a range that is in itself a continuous *sign* of life.

Husserl introduced two concepts, which are until our days underestimated in phenomenology and Continental philosophy: one that indicates the entirety of life as a whole, and one that establishes distinguished and various positions in life. The common denominator is called *naturalness* and the distinctive denominator brings a difference between the *naïve* and the *non-naïve* position/attitude to the fore. A mother tongue, the language of everyday life, is, as was already said in this context, a *naïve-natural* language whereas legal discourse is *non-naïve-natural.* The breach between the two, important in all regards, is difficult to grasp. If a mother tongue is a language articulated naïve-naturally, the language of the lawyer is the mother tongue (indicated as (b) in the above pages) *entwined with* the professional language (which was indicated (a) in those pages). Notice that any professional language needs a mother tongue as its contextual discourse. Also law cannot do without a native, or naïve-natural, language! But is that very special awareness the result of considerations within our mother tongue, or do we in that case appeal to a professional language (such as philosophy, psychology or any other)? A naïve-natural attitude hardly provides reflective power. How then do we know about its character?

p. 109ff; Jan M. Broekman, *Meaning, Narrativity, and the Real*, Springer, Switzerland, 2016, p. 50ff.

That question brings us to the stage of reflection/knowledge and its limits. A naïve-natural language can be performed but apparently not lead to knowledge about all components of that performance. It means that awareness of any feature of linguistic performance never equals the *use* of a language, as many analytical philosophers of language fail to consider. If one reflects upon the naïve-natural character of one's mother tongue, one has already changed attitude, and unwittingly encapsulated a non-naïve dimension. In such cases, one really explores 'another language'. It is as if a naïve-natural position exists beyond any possibility of articulation. That particular naturalness exists but cannot be formulated in any language, word or expression. What we *know* is expanded wider than we articulate! One conclusion is far-reaching: there can never be a secure 1:1 relationship between word and thing, language and reality, or mind and matter! That is the basis for a pre-semiotic approach of law, and of reality *tout court.*

That sounds radical and mysterious at the same time. It focuses quite intensively on our concept of 'knowledge' and our activity of 'knowing'. Should one not consider the mystery of *re*flection as a preferred form of legal thought formation, which one can call 'bending back'? Is legal practice not a form of 'responsible bending back' to earlier words, considerations, laws and decisions? How far does law, and strict legal thought formation, reject your view and its 1:1 implication?

1.6.3 Reflect and Bend Back

All considerations pertaining to language and law, to reflective dimensions and the human mind, are important in our considerations about law's practices. They are altogether involved in a continuous looking-back, a repetition, mirroring and bending back. It is clear that the above-described *naïve-natural* is *not* solely the reality of everyday in which law is bringing order and perhaps even justice. And legal discourse as well as jurisprudence are *not* exclusively *non-naïve-natural* issues. That contrast would be too simple, and we underlined therefore already their contrast in the light of their intertwining: opposition and intertwinement belong together – is that indeed a riddle at the basis of our knowledge?

Mind you: this consideration is already a proof of the unacceptability to see a *fixated* contrast between the two positions. It appears that the awareness of the two embraces a gradation of intensity of knowledge. Legal thought formations could not exist on a sole naïve-natural or on a sole non-naïve-natural level. 'Being' can be experienced on each of them but is never articulated at only one of these two levels. Any judgment pertaining to a specific life-quality requires an intertwining of the two. For instance the concept of 'justice' is for that reason never qualified as a strict legal term. Practitioners at any level of law's exploration and application do *not* talk about justice as a technical term. The concept belongs to an intertwined position of thoughts and practices accepted as legal, not to any specific level of legal technical knowledge or to a level of naïve-natural language.

It is important to underline that only different levels of *intertwining* can be effective as a means of articulation. In other words: a professional language cannot represent a profession on its own but is always needs to be entwined in an everyday language. That gives the citizen a feeling that law belongs to her/him and should be spoken on the street. However, the street can, as already often formulated, *talk about law* but not speak law, nor make any judgment legally valid in its proper language. The speaking on the street is only a part of language as a human reality in its entirety. A *legal* semiotic approach can only unfold when the intertwining of everyday language (the so-called 'natural' language) with a level of specific *legal* expressivity (the artificial, or professional language) has taken place – semiotics never concerns a professional/artificial language separated from daily language, but it cannot concern solely a natural language either. We have to come back to this observation in other contexts. There are different levels of signification in the simple advice: 'reflect and bend back', especially where the relation between language and law is concerned. The 'talking about law' is indeed an issue to 'reflect' upon without certainty whether a 'bend back' will ever be possible or useful!

1.7 CONSCIOUSNESS

How can an exposé of the main semiotic components of 'talking about law' as a pre-semiotic field of events, introduce the theme 'consciousness' *after* the 'language' issue? Does that not lacerate the observation about legal conversation as signifying power? In other words; should consciousness not be mentioned *first* because it is the source of language, and would the order of this chapter not better be reconsidered in that sense? The question is heavily burdened in philosophy and certainly more than solely a basis for understanding law. The concept of *legal* consciousness is very particular and incomparable with, for instance, psychological, physical or physiological consciousness. It is an outstanding theme in Occidental culture, although not many legal theoreticians embrace the theme.

But one should understand that the problem is absolutely not reduced to decisions about the level of articulation of legal consciousness. It is an illusion that citizens in a specific period of Occidental culture possess a specific consciousness about law while they speak, act or reflect. This exceptional and specific type of consciousness changed in the course of European history in various directions and socio-political contexts. Law remained the major component of that consciousness without, however, precisely defining or describing its properties and social determinations. The theme changed considerably; it was in the center of political and legal interest during the last decades of the nineteenth century, whereas a very different image was connected with it in the twentieth century. Whether it is equally important in the twenty-first century is difficult to decide.

1.7.1 Socio-Legal Consciousness

The twentieth century in Western Europe displayed indeed a worrisome image of legal consciousness. One can roughly say that this type of consciousness was, approximately since 1933 until the final days of the Second World War in 1945, dominated by the idea that law represented a reality created to conform to the will of the people. De Haan's problem about the gap between a lawyer's words and those that were audible on the street changed into the predominance of a political party, which was said to be acting on behalf of the volition of the people. A party thus decided the character of law and ultimately destined the features of reality. The same political forces were in effect in Eastern Europe in the aftermath of the Bolshevist revolution and the years of the Soviet Union deeply into the Second World War and until the fall of the Berlin Wall in 1989. A Marxist legal philosophy was already in the 1920s the servant of political views of the party, and legal consciousness was determined by that dictatorial interpretation of law and reality. The latter was in hindsight and roughly speaking effective from the Bolshevist revolution until 1989: a dark period in European culture in which a differentiation between facts of daily life and facts of law was suppressed. In that period an eventual distinction between legal facts and facts of reality/everyday life was an exclusively *political* issue. One of the consequences is that the distinction between those two is not without memories of a political dictatorship and war when it is introduced as a theme of legal theory.

It does not surprise that after the Second World War in Western Europe and before the fall of the Berlin Wall the concept of *freedom* dominated in discussion about law and reality. That was the case in the many attempts to renew the pre-war designs of a (transcendental) phenomenology, in later drafts of structuralism and in attempts to outline deconstructivism. A citizen's experience of freedom, or the concept of freedom as such, was in the forefront of all those considerations. The latter became the context of studying the role of consciousness and in particular of *legal* consciousness as the source of constructing reality.

This short outline indicates an important problem. It illustrates that the relation between law and reality belongs to the most important factors in our understanding of our consciousness pertaining to the real in its totality. That relation becomes clearly visible in the patterns of behavior of our citizenship. It remains important in all considerations pertaining to Law, State and Society to keep an eye on citizen opinion and behavior as a major component of social life. In that light is De Haan's view on the gap between legal and citizen speech of utmost importance for us today. The concepts of freedom and consciousness fulfill a primordial role while no longer under a twentieth century political pressure.

1.7.2 The Historical School of Law

The two concepts were essential in the works and political decisions of Friedrich Karl von Savigny (1779–1861)[9] and his inspirations during the unfolding of the German 'Historical School of Law'. Von Savigny, impressed by the discussions and views of Immanuel Kant on law and citizenship, focused in particular on the *foundation* of the practice of a lawyer. His opinion was just the opposite of the social and political situations that occurred nearly a century later in Central Europe. The practices of a lawyer, he states, should never be based on political and ideological constructs of the mind. Law should unfold as an important social phenomenon that embraces values, norms and goals of a society and its citizens as profiled in the '*Volksgeist*' (the spirit of the people).

Von Savigny does not envisage law as the work of social specialists but rather as a system inherited from our ancestors and their culture. It is clear that his attitude did not concern law in its empirical quality but emphasized its signification. That semiotic reference culminated in understanding law in parallel to the existence and actual worth of the classical Roman law: a system in its uniqueness. It will be clear that the name 'Historical School of Law' was based on that reference, and not on eventual applications of Roman law during his days in his society.

---

[9] See M. D. A. Freeman, *Lloyd's Introduction to Jurisprudence*, 7th edn, Sweet and Maxwell, London, 2001, p. 903.

His appeal to Roman law includes a variety of constitutive elements. The Historical School emphasized that law should always and under all circumstances be understood as an *event*. It means that law is for Von Savigny an evolutionary process. Our entire history should be understood as evolution and the law one encounters in every moment of that evolution is always the result of a *becoming* and never of a political or economic *decision*. Commentaries pertaining to the Historical School portray Von Savigny for that reason as a 'social Darwinist before Darwin'. But whoever envisages law as an evolutionary process, will also underline that law aims at *articulation*. In the 'becoming' is the semiotic component, the flow from sign to signification. In that regard has the Historical School a unique function in Occidental legal thought formation. Whoever understands signification or meaning as the product of a historical evolution, interprets at the same time *consciousness* as a meaningful evolvement.

This view causes a distance between the empirical reality of law and the idea of a real law. This was documented in his famous 1814 essay *Vom Beruf unserer Zeit für Gesetzgebung und Rechtswissenschaft* (Of the Vocation of our Age for Legislation and Jurisprudence) when he suggested that 'the real law is not the same as the empirical reality of law'. We cannot read that line as if it concerned a historical fact far beyond our world of today! It means the opposite that the meaning of law should be expressed according to its full evolution – a task that is truly difficult to accomplish!

The Historical School appeals for that reason to the '*Volk*' (people) as the preferred partner to create such a process of meaning-making. Its role is exquisite: being a concept of important economic and political signification, it is now given a new role through the creation of a new field of meaning, called 'law'. '*Volk*' implies that a human consciousness is challenged to unfold new constitutive powers, no matter whether they pertain to an individual or a collective consciousness. '*Volk*' indicates a will to create a meaning, which empowers law to be effective in all regards.

1.7.3 Legal Consciousness

A very special aspect of the philosophy of the Historical School of Law is that the '*Volk*' (the people) is understood as the 'bearer of a legal consciousness'. That is inherent to the expression '*Volksgeist*' (spirit of the people), an expression that was given a central position in the semiotics of law, which was explored in the work of Von Savigny. This expression gave the German jurisprudence in the midst of the nineteenth century its flavor, its power and its cultural significance. Since that period, the term 'legal consciousness' acquired a key position, until it was oppressed by totally opposite political practices. That key position was not only important in Western Europe, but also in Eastern Europe. One must conclude that the understanding and use of the term 'legal consciousness' was for some decades at the end of the nineteenth and the beginning of the twentieth century a common basis for German and Russian jurists.

Hegel already observed that a well-understood concept of consciousness would solely be effective on the basis of a capacity to move in our conceptualizing mind from the individual towards the general and from there back to the individual. Neither of the two prevails in any thought formation pertaining to consciousness. An example is in the majority of European languages: in German, French, Italian, Spanish and Dutch, one can distinguish between '*Recht*' (law) and '*Gesetz*' (laws) but not in English. This had its consequences in English and US jurisprudence. The links between *law(s) as* a scientific/empirical concept on the one hand and *law* as justice or an ideal situation, in which *law* can flourish, is essential. An insight in legal consciousness is only possible on the basis of convergences. The concept of 'legal consciousness' remains dubious in meaning but also actual in politics, even in our days of semiotic approaches and analyses of consequences of what is said about them on the street!

Von Savigny understood this when he claimed that each right became acceptable and understandable by means of its fixation in language sustained by the life styles of the people, the community or the street – to mention more recent denominations of the German expression '*Volk*'. Do not forget, he would have said, that people need that fixation, that unity of language and life style, to find an expression for its many ways of life. Three different aspects come together in the life of people: the German expression mentions '*Volksrecht*' (legal consciousness of people) expressing directly the feelings of citizens, the law of *laws*, the prescriptions of the law-makers, and the *lawyers' laws* (German: *Juristenrecht*) that originate in legal science. This triad was the most important in the days between Von Savigny and the outbreak of the First World War in 1914. The idea of legal semiotics, under the guise of what then was called 'legal significs', was formulated only a few years before that catastrophic 1914 war.

1.7.4 Russian Legal Philosophy

The concept of a legal consciousness was widely spread in Europe by the Historical School, but its influence also reached far to the East and a Russian philosophy of law. We mention in this context the work of the Russian philosopher and lawyer Ivan A. Il'in (1883–1954) that dominated the Eastern-European legal world. He not only underlined the importance of the concept 'legal consciousness' but also tried to acquire access to law in its entire semiotic relevance via this notion.[10] He therefore did not give any meaning to the differentiation between law of the people (*Volk*), law of the lawyers and law of the law-makers, because law should be understood in its totality, which is a cultural domain of first order importance and signification. One can understand that this approach became very near to the centuries-old concept of *natural law*. The latter does, however, suggest universality, which is a contrast to the reality of law in every cultural setting one can observe. The human mind, even expressing itself in a legal consciousness, is never a universal datum and never unfolding beyond boundaries of understanding and interpreting reality. This viewpoint brought Il'in to distance himself from natural law and yet recognized that law often strives for power and articulation beyond boundaries.

A background issue here is whether an individual or a collective consciousness should be regarded as the ultimate constitutive power. This was a most important consideration until the beginnings of the First World War. Its inner dynamics were expressed in the almost omnipresent question whether one can determine the notion of 'people' on the basis of the individual citizen. No wonder that in Il'in's days of the Bolshevist revolution, Socialism, Marxism and the Communist Party regime around the 1920s, the relation between individual and society was the central issue for understanding the signification of law and legal discourse.

But *what* individual was envisaged? Does this focus the individual as a participant of 'the people' or the individual which functions as a legal subject, the individual that empowers the law? The years after 1924 in Russia, evolving towards the Soviet Union, and after 1933 in Germany, gave a clear insight. We remember the German slogan in the 1930s and 1940s: '*Du Bist Nichts, Dein Volk ist Alles*' (You are Nothing, your People is Everything). This emphasis on the people has been a leading

---

[10] Ivan A. Il'in: *On the Essence of Legal Consciousness*, 1919, 1956. Translated by Philip T. Grier (edited with commentaries by William E. Butler, Philip T. Grier, and Vladimir A. Tomsinov), Wildy, Simmonds and Hill Publishing, 2014, pp. 113–373.

political principle in European culture. But Il'in's texts aimed at the law and a legal system with individuals after the Soviet State and the Nazi German State in a later period of the twentieth century. It may be regretted, in the light of today's European Union life, that Il'in's words were not judged relevant when the foundations of the Union were formulated. EU law was outlined in treaties which embraced forms of legislation that focused on a perfection of democratic nation States through reinforcement of the four so-called 'fundamental freedoms' of a citizen instead of new forms of law, which could reach beyond thought patterns that embrace any possible form of State.[11] And Il'in's works were not widely known until recently, thanks to the translations and interpretations of Philip T. Grier.[12] However, Alexey and Stanislovas underlined not long ago (without taking any semiotic relevance into account) that:

> Russian scholarship at the end of the 20th and the beginnings of the 21st century was based on a well-developed sense of legal consciousness, the key ideas of which were the dependence of the content of popular legal consciousness on the dominant socialist ideology, the domination of public interest over the personal interest of citizens, and the citizen's predominantly secular (atheist) perception of the world.[13]

Their words underline (1) the importance of today's concept of legal consciousness and (2) a recent focus on the ongoing tensions between individual and society. For Il'in, the modern rule of law was more or less identical with a healthy legal consciousness in social life and society. For him, a true patriotism had everything to do with the performance of a State – a performance mirrored in a legal consciousness that aimed at a common desire and strong will to realize the Good. It is clear that a socio-cultural life is in this context understood as the life of human individuals that is based on psychic independence and a consciousness of one's proper dignity, respect, trust, reliability and justice.

Has Il'in foreseen and prepared the life of modern man in the twentieth and twenty-first centuries with these ideas? Hesitations to answer that question in a positive sense relate to the critical view of legal and social

---

[11] Jan M. Broekman, *A Philosophy of European Union Law*, Peeters, Leuven/Paris, 1999, p. 279ff.

[12] See the bibliography in Il'in, *supra note 10*, as well as Ivan A. Il'in, *The Philosophy of Hegel as a Doctrine of the Concreteness of God and Humanity*, edited and translated by Philip T. Grier, Northwestern University Press, 2010–11 (2 volumes).

[13] T. Alexey and T. Stanislovas, 'Interaction of European and Russian Legal Consciousness' *BRICS Law Journal*, No. 2, 2015, p. 33.

explorations on the classical idea of a *natural law*. Il'in's ideas were embedded in that type of legal thinking. The latter remains a problem in modern jurisprudence and legal theory, which overshadows legal semiotics as well. It is present in all considerations pertaining to the foundation of law and society. The heritage of Von Savigny and Il'in does not seem to be dissolved in a post-modern culture. Emphasis in legal positivism on the importance of written laws did not diminish the attractive character of natural law ideas. But it also did not delete an interest in the values and traditions of the concept of legal consciousness either. Alexey and Stanislovas highlighted the concept of legal consciousness in European and US thinking, especially in their comparison with the US Critical Legal Studies Movement as a form of critical awareness of law in society.[14] However, a semiotics of law preserves traces of insight in the foundations of law as formulated in proximity to the concept of natural law, and honors Il'in with that view. The latter focuses on a legal consciousness based on citizen participation, which contributes to a legal system that provides a just and balanced society, as will be critically explained in the final paragraph of this chapter.

1.7.5 Expressivity: Visual and Verbal

The title of this chapter 'Thoughts Backing Speech' implies serious philosophical considerations. The 'law-language' relationship is their basis. If legal consciousness backs speech, then legal articulations (conversation belongs to articulation) will have to be regarded as the outcome of legal consciousness efforts, which are mediated by language. That is basic for all perspectives on law's widely explored expressivity. Hence an omnipresent interest in the speech acts of lawyers in general, and judges or legislators in particular. But one should not forget that this is only one of the many possible perspectives: there is not only the view that consciousness constitutes the basis for linguistic utterances, but also the inverse, which emphasizes that acts of consciousness are formatted and kept alive by words and other forms of linguistic activity. There seems to be no other choice than honoring both viewpoints at the same time – and even that appears to be insecure! We meet here one of the central questions of legal consciousness: is a signifying force in law (which this book accredits to legal conversation, i.e. to 'talking about law in non-legal settings') *solely verbal*, or is a legal semiotic approach possible *beyond* the boundaries of linguistic expressiveness?

---

[14] Alexey and Stanislovas, *supra note 13*.

An example directs us – again – to *the street*: modern roads, in city life as well as in rural surroundings, are filled with *signs* that characterize the landscape as if it were totally mastered by signifying forces. There is hardly any countryside in the Western world that escapes from this semiotic grip. Yet, there is one condition, which should be revisited and reconsidered: are traffic signs *legally* effective because of their *visual* quality? It is beyond doubt that the almost universal traffic signs aim at the regulation of individual patterns of behavior and a collective following of legal rules. But are those rules followed because of their functioning in the world of visual expressivity? Or are they effective because of an implicit link of visual signs to an inherent verbal expressivity? In other words: are *legal* signs always connected with *linguistic* expressivity or is their visual property accepted in law on an equal basis?

In her 2006 study of 'The Rules of the Road', A. Wagner suggests verbal- and non-verbal expressivity to be equally valid in law and legal discourse:

> The interaction between signs and institutional context is at the core of this analysis. The production and diffusion of images tells us a great deal about the meaning attributed to these signs … By their simplicity in meaning, the Rules of the Road show how simple and unconscious these rules have now become. They are good substitutes for textuality (i.e. written formulas) and reveal the fact that legal knowledge about traffic road regulations are known and visually codified.

She further explains, how 'the perception of meaning of road signs, road markings and traffic lights' is, in the words of Umberto Eco, 'under the domain of meaning-making operations of the human imagination literally the ability to make and remake images and the feelings they evoke in the mind' so that 'absence of textuality is shown' and demonstrates 'what the consensus of the symbolic among the society is and how pervasive its message can be'.[15] The example in this study aims at a disputable conclusion. They want to illustrate an equivalence of the visual and the verbal in law. At the end, it would lead to a 'seeing is speaking; a view equals a speech act' in law. Do I really pay my fine when the police officer *shows* me a ticket like there was a traffic sign *shown* to me at the roadside? Is there not a distance between a *quality* and a *faculty* of

[15] Anne Wagner, 'The Rules of the Road, a Universal Visual Semiotics' *International Journal for the Semiotics of Law*, Vol. 19, No. 3, 2006, p. 312ff.

expressivity? Is the emphasis on non-verbal dimensions in human behavior not a challenge to perhaps widen but certainly not abolish the power of language in law? Does the law-language relation always prevail?

Richard Mohr suggested in the same issue of the quoted journal the opinion that 'everyday life is continually reconstituting the meanings of law and state'.[16] If that is the case, then this reconstituting force is *linguistic* or *language-bound* by nature, one should underline. This appears to be extremely self-evident, so that it is often forgotten to consider it. Mohr gives an example near to several others in this book: 'Even if a person', he remarks, 'has been duly sworn as a judge, the opinions she expresses over dinner do not have the force of law: the judge must also be in an authorized place. The power of the law is projected from the bench where the judge sits.' But no attention is given to the difference between the *quality* of expressiveness in legal language and the *faculty* of the bench. Even when this place is indicated by appropriate symbols, which confirm 'the judge's authority to give diction to the law (juris)', there should be attention given to language as the semiotic means to 'give diction to the law'. Also in this example the link between law and language prevails, which puts the distance between visual and linguistic expression into perspective.

That link represents a cultural challenge on its own. The challenge focuses on our understanding of consciousness in general and legal consciousness in particular. It brings us to deeper anchored notions of language than those of just a communicative power, and it illustrates in how far law – despite its immense social relevance – is one of the many discourses in modern life. The phenomenon of language reaches other levels of life than those of a pure exchange of expressiveness: it represents a continuous reach of an individual or a group of human individuals for transparency in relation with reality. A speaker is most often characterized by the desire to articulate a world around. It is often said that the more gifted and inspired the speaker is, the clearer reality will be expressed. Unfolding that talent is indeed not a strictly individual gift; it engages generations and a cultural era that stimulates such capacity. The latter is most probably an essential component of human consciousness, which leaves purely individual features behind. This was one of the motives of the Historical School of Law, as well as the work of the Russian jurist and philosopher Ivan Il'in. Legal consciousness

[16] Richard Mohr, 'Living Legal Fictions: Constituting the State or Submerging the Signifier?' *International Journal for the Semiotics of Law*, Vol. 19, 2006, pp. 237ff, 245.

illustrates that a human consciousness is not a more or less passive force-field in which human activity can hardly be profiled other than with an unclear concept of 'people'. It is, on the contrary, a primary force of expressivity in its relation with reality.

Indeed, law and language are closely tied for legal philosophers in the twenty-first century, and these ties are beyond doubt an important part of the cultural heritage of the Occident. Law's expressivity is dominated by the scope of linguistic possibilities of articulation. That became a weighty issue of the era. Never before were plurality and the multicultural so evident as in these days. The fact that TV programs and smart phones bring varieties of mother tongues into one and the same daily life at one and the same moment is only a sign of that new complexity. Can law still limit its expressivity to one tongue? Do single-language legal problems still exist? Law's variety of valid meanings suggests the opposite. Any single meaning of a written law will be surpassed by its multilinguistic context despite all positivisms hidden in the mind of the modern lawyer. This simple observation touches the concept of legal consciousness. The latter must be understood in its deep dependence on the tongue of individual and society. Legal consciousness is no longer seen as a private attitude, the will or inner force of a '*Volk*' or nation, nor of a political body of any type. The question came to the fore whether a legal consciousness fits to the new complexities of articulation that characterize a twenty-first century. The emphasis changed from mastering a socio-legal system and its political consequences into the mastering of an unheard complexity of expressivity related to law, which is honored as a human potential.

1.7.6 Significs and Human Rights

An understanding of legal consciousness as the foundation for human expressivity and in particular for articulating the language of law was already targeted in the first decades of the twentieth century. Law was, next to sciences, mathematics, literature and logic, a field of discussion and research of the Amsterdam Signific Circle in the years from 1892 to 1926.[17] During the time the Circle was active, the First World War had

[17] H. Walter Schmitz, *De Hollandse Significa: Een reconstructie van de geschiedenis van 1892 tot 1926* (The Dutch Significs), Van Gorcum, Assen, 1990; H. Walter Schmitz (ed.), *Essays on Significs (Papers presented on the occasion of the 150th anniversary of the Birth of Victoria Lady Welby [1837–1912])*, J. Benjamins Pub. Cie., Amsterdam/Philadelphia, 1990.

not ended and a desire to broaden the notion of legal consciousness in daily life and law was a shared, legitimate and fully understandable desire. That attitude can be read in often important philosophical texts from the famous Dutch author Frederik van Eeden or the mathematicians and logicians L. E. J. Brouwer and G. Mannoury – all more or less inspired by the English Victoria Lady Welby, who, close to the US philosopher Charles S. Peirce, had introduced the idea of *significs*. A generally debated problem in the Circle pertained to the disturbing distance between reality in the words of the citizen and reality expressed in the words of a lawyer. And the concept of a *natural law* played a central political role at that time: patriotism, counter-revolution, Bolshevist revolution, criticisms pertaining to State and Church were alive. We still wrestle, a century later, with that problem of the gap between what we now characterize as two types of language!

The foundations and developments of a *legal significs* (later documented as 'legal semiotics') unfolded through the work of the Dutch author, poet, politician and lawyer Jacob Israël de Haan (1881–1924). The signific approach of De Haan is important for us who live after the 'linguistic turn' in philosophy. However, De Haan already accentuated that law is definitively connected to the power and uses of language, and thus embraced the 'law-language' thesis.

Our everyday *talking about law* appears to embrace a secret: *the secret of the non-naïve in the midst of an everyday language discourse*. In how far may the artificial change the significance of words spoken on the street, change the intentions of participating groups or even change the purposes of politicians? The question is never solved, but pertains to a particular understanding of a general concept called '*legal consciousness*', which is used on streets as well as in courts. De Haan already formulated the issue in his 1916 inaugural lecture at the University of Amsterdam.[18] He underlined the gap between our everyday language and the language of the law and its functionaries, which is caused by a gap in the multiple uses of signs and in the many meanings embraced in those two worlds. As a consequence, he was hesitating whether lawyers can express in words what happens in reality. For him, it was a matter of

---

[18] Jacob Isaël de Haan, *Wezen en taak der rechtskundige significa* (Essence and Task of Legal Significs), Van Kampen, Amsterdam, 1916. The text is also published in G. C. J. J. van den Bergh, *De taal zegt meer dan zij verantwoorden kan. Een keuze uit de verspreide rechtskundig-signifische geschriften van Jacob Israël de Haan* (Language tells us more than it can account for), Ars Aequi Libri, Nijmegen, 1994, pp. 48–72. See also Jan M. Broekman and Larry Catà Backer, *Signs in Law – A Source Book*, Springer, Switzerland, 2014, pp. 51–89.

communication between two languages, a natural and an artificial language – the latter embedded in the first, and the major question was formulated in his lecture: are lawyers able to bridge the gap between their language and their speech acts and the language spoken on the street? That issue fascinates until our days: is our legal consciousness a *natural* feeling or the expression of a sophisticated *artificial* language? We always operate one or another form of artificial language in daily life, for instance when using our computer or our smart phone – so why not the language and consciousness of law?

A basic signific slogan was: 'better law through better language'.[19] De Haan claims in his PhD thesis that a 'better language is a better thought formation. And better thinking is better law.' A first focus is on the language of law as a means to develop a legal system that is just and socially relevant. Whoever wants to complete that task, depends on language. Particularly laws, as texts that should initiate specific patterns of behavior, must be formulated in clear terms. 'The insight that the language of law should be reinforced is important in the eyes of those who apply laws and the law in general as a truly social science', De Haan writes.[20] That challenge to lawyers and the law is also heard in our days. The interest in the linguistic dimensions of law has been enforced by legal semiotics, also by those who were first fascinated by the idea of a *signific* approach of the task. De Haan, Victoria Lady Welby, Frederik van Eeden and even Martin Buber were (among others) united in embracing that idea and receiving that message. Their ideal was in the construction of a language in which all lack of clarity vanished. A better harmony among citizens and their law – in fact a harmony of two cultures – should result.

There is a remarkable link between the signific/semiotic ideals and early developments leading towards the *human rights* concept. They expanded via multiple interpretations of the concept of *natural law*. Several anchors are in the publications of Victoria Lady Welby, in particular her 1903 book *What is Meaning?: Studies in the Development of Significance*, and her *Significs and Language*, 1911. Both publications

---

[19] Jan M. Broekman, 'Betere Taal is Beter Recht' (Better Language is Better Law), *Wijsgerig Perspectief op Maatschappij en Wetenschap*, Vol. 20, No. 2, 1979–80, p. 48ff.

[20] Jacob Israel de Haan, *Rechtskundige Significa en hare toepassing op de begrippen 'aansprakelijk, verantwoordelijk, toerekeningsvatbaar'* (Legal Significs and its Application to the Concepts 'Liable', 'Responsible' and 'Accountable'), Versluys, Amsterdam, 1916, p. 69. See also Broekman and Backer, *supra note 18*, pp. 73–89.

share an equal disposition, an interest in the concept '*legal consciousness*' and the gap between multiple types of language that is inherent in both. Their ties with the German Historical School and Russian Legal Philosophy on the one hand and the Amsterdam Significs Circle are stronger than we ever knew. It impresses to learn about common insights in the texts of Ivan A. Il'in and De Haan. The latter must have known the Russian legal philosopher, who was also close to Von Savigny, and the philosophical/political discussions about natural law. However, the works of Il'in were not published when De Haan visited Russia a few times in and around 1912. He visited, analyzed and highly criticized Russian prisons, while using the methods that are still used in our days: visits, document analyses, reporting conversations, interviewing prisoners. Humanitarian questions and criminal law practiced in prison camps were the topics of his investigation. Peter Kropotkin had sustained this activity when De Haan and Frederik van Eeden visited him in London in 1912. The visits to Russia were in later years never researched, neither in relation to significs nor to forensic semiotics. De Haan's 1913 Dutch publication *In Russische Gevangenissen*[21] did not play a role in his later semiotic publications. Political interest in the life and thoughts of De Haan dominated and was enforced by his often changing Zionistic attitudes as well as the fact that he became the victim of the first political murder in Jerusalem, in 1924.

However, a signific/semiotic approach and methodology is surprisingly effective in that book. That approach is backed by a general impression of the author's attitude in the entire text. His book does *not* seem consciously critical of a State, a government or even a political system but is dominated by a *deep concern*. The latter has a broad sociological intuition as its background and foundation. One of the components of De Haan's view is that a State always has a *substance*, which is primordially its *population*. It fascinated that De Haan describes in how many ways the government has nominated its population in smaller and smaller groups, which are given even more detailed names. That name-giving and specific determination appeared to have become a totalitarian means of governing – an act and attitude creeping even into the prison floors and cells, which were divided in correspondence with those names.

More important was De Haan's explanation of one of its semiotic effects: the dominating legal system in the country did not know or recognize any *legal subject* anymore, but only *groups of subjects*. In

---

[21] J. I. de Haan, *In Russische Gevangenissen* (In Russian Prisons), 1913, 2nd edn, Wereldbibliotheek, Amsterdam, 1986.

other words: the procedure of highly differentiated *naming* caused *individuals* to disappear in law and the legal system! Where individuals are absent as the result of a system of naming, other names come up: 'the people' will oppose 'the government', and 'politicians' as well as 'intellectuals' unite in that action. The vocabulary of political activism, which one encounters in modern public places, has its roots in the Russian system during the second decade of the twentieth century.

Where the people contest governance measures, private persons and private organizations take over. That was especially the case in the field of youth welfare work while no special juvenile courts existed.

> That is the reason why in Russia an initiative of private persons is more effective than elsewhere. One does not try to become supported by the government. A juvenile criminal is to a large extent a matter of private care and perhaps of a few liberal councils of large cities. One strives in general, to keep the government at distance. What is in the hands of the government seems hopelessly lost. The power and dedication of non-revolutionary Russian citizens working at a neutral level causes Russia to surpass other countries in many regards ... That is in particular the case when the care for juvenile criminals is concerned.[22]

The latter was progressive in socio-legal as well as in political regards through the exceptionally important and effective participation of care-taking psychiatrists. That work primarily took place in pavilions, which were systematically in a rather loose contact with the rigid police-guarded prison system.[23] But notice that these pavilions *socially* organized juvenile criminality long before any juvenile laws were conceived and in power! Those social forms of living together were understood as a *sign* of a new and eagerly desired type of law. De Haan acknowledged that sign during his analyses and his subsequent visits. We venture to formulate the opinion that De Haan's interest in *legal consciousness* in parallel with his *humanitarian attitude* was fruitful in the framework of his views in legal theory and legal-semiotic practice as it was decidedly in his socio-political observations.

His ideas and interviews were given importance in Russia as well as in Amsterdam and in signific (semiotic) circles. Once he returned to Amsterdam during the beginnings of the First World War, he founded an influential Social Democratic Labor Union (SDAP) Committee in which Frederik van Eeden and the Dutch poetess Henriette Roland Holst also participated. It is essential that De Haan understood the positions of the

---

22 J. I. de Haan, *supra note 21*, p. 31ff.

23 See J. I. de Haan, *supra note 21*, pp. 29–31, 39.

Russian prisoners as a *sign* of a more complex signification process – as Lady Welby would have done. *Legal consciousness* became in that manner defined at the borderlines of legal discourse and thus approximated an enormous political relevance. It implied the development of a new and different concept, which received only decades later, in the work of Eleanor Roosevelt in 1948, the name '*Human Rights*'. Importantly, De Haan's legal significs broadened the meaning and significance of a legal and rights consciousness. The concept reached from natural law to human rights.

His visits to Russian prisons, his discussions and reflections on that issue, were inspired by the need of this extension of legal conceptuality towards deep layers of political consciousness. No wonder that his attempts were honored in naming him a precursor of 'Amnesty International' and a predecessor of the 'Human Rights Watch'. It fascinates that the recognition of the multilayered character of language, a specific theme of semiotics, leads to such globally relevant conclusions. De Haan's thoughts illustrate that the move from a simple *sign recognition* to complex *systems of signification*, and vice versa, have implications that also reach beyond the boundaries of law.

1.7.7 Multilingual Consciousness

The system of signification in which we are all enveloped is a system of multiple languages; the multiplicity of those languages does not only function as an expression or communication but is also a sign of our speech performance and thus our abilities and qualities as *a speaker in plural cultural contexts*. Words and cultural differentiations correlate, and those are often a problem for a lawyer or a judge. Streams of migrants in Europe and elsewhere make visible that a legal decision pertaining to a subject that is anchored in one religious and cultural set of norms and values is difficult to realize in another. Today, geographical locations change more quickly and easily than cultural roots. Basic values, norms and human rights interpretations are at issue once a multilingual consciousness becomes objected to a monolingual consciousness. Languages and cultural patterns function as a *sign* of differences that are often troublesome to bridge within one generation. Sociologists concluded this since the 1950s while analyzing the world of Polish peasants in the US. A standard example in the European Union of today is the gap between traditional Christian and Muslim notions of life and norms. What is 'normal' or 'desired' in the one is 'absurd' or 'unjust' in the other. There is no way to decide between one or another system of values being 'wrong' or being 'just' – a view that many politicians try to achieve in vain.

This discussion, itself an example of the implicit difficulties of a multilingual approach and life style, is an important *political signifier*. The law-language relation is a central issue in politically critical situations. Tensions among them do not dissolve by legal or political means. A possible clue, semiotic by nature, is the insight that *language does not describe, but evokes reality*. Only an impossible form of positivism formulates the question *which person* will be able or entitled to solve the conflict. The actor of an evocation in this context is not personalized or dependent upon an acting subject – the actor is an impersonal power active in the field of footing, of human relations, and in particular in being receptive to the appeal of an o/Other. Are law and legal discourse able to take this dimension into account?

The question is the more urgent since the Occidental culture became roughly confronted with the capacity to master more than one language instead of exclusively one particular mother tongue. The clash between this post-modern requirement and the deeply engraved monolinguistic features of law and legal thought patterns (law is the law as expressed in one particular language; law expressed in another language opens the gates of 'international' law) is understandable. Legal jargon has focused on that clash by referring to the eventual *plural features of a legal consciousness*. This does not, however, solve the issue legally or politically.

A legal consciousness will always and in all its cultural and legal forms be appreciated and regarded as an asset of all of us: citizens on the street, in parks and other public places as well as participants in a law office or a court. That view is basic for understanding a consciousness as a footing or a relation, and not as a possession. De Haan already remarked in a 1917 publication that semiotic views on law must differentiate between layers of meaning and first of all focus on the dynamics of *materialization*, which endangers law as well as language: 'Think of legal expressions such as "having", "acquiring", "losing", "transferring" a right. Those treat a right as an object and not as a relation. A legal language, which treats a right as a relation, would liberate the law from its materialist character.'[24] In other words: *laws are*

[24] J. I. de Haan: 'Taal en Rechtswetenschap' (Language and Legal Science), *Weekblad van het Recht*, No. 10103, 1917; also published in G. C. J. J. van den Bergh, *De taal zegt meer dan zij verantwoorden kan. Een keuze uit de verspreide*

not things, but human relations. The malady of modern culture is in De Haan's eyes the Occidental fascination by possession and the vision of reality as if it were a cosmos of commodities.

But that malady is a *sign* of a deeper problem in Occidental culture. The sign pertains to our understanding of law and legal discourse as a major force that serves society. If the essence of law is in relations among human individuals rather than in the ownership of properties, then those relations are understood like linguistics understands relations: as relations among separate individuals. Theories of language and legal theory focus on 'speaker–hearer' relations; those are law's model for sociality. Dimensions of a legal consciousness are by consequence also determined by such one-to-one relations. 'So speech, so justice': good terms are terms among individual parties. The need to speak the same language is rooted in this view of man and society, and reminds us that this view of relations was already the basis for the social contract theories of Hobbes, Grotius, Descartes and others. The way language is understood (as an instrument to relate individuals) has since those days been fundamental. Inter-subjectivity and interactivity were names for individuals and independent parties, which were created by a relation-producing apparatus. The latter is the ultimate *corpus* to understand and analyze by means of legal semiotics – an approach with great critical potential. There is in this light more than one critical consideration implied in the concept of 'legal consciousness', although it has disappeared from legal theory and philosophy since the midst of the twentieth century.

First, the dominance of the 'speaker–hearer model' has suppressed in which dimensions a legal consciousness is a power of articulation. The latter is *incomplete* in any 'speaker–hearer' relationship. The appeal of the o/Other is silenced when law remains to be the language of two. Even the discussions with Martin Buber and his dialogue philosophy in 'Ich und Du' in the Amsterdam Signific Circle did not entirely overcome this implicit restriction in our understanding of law's potential to fully understand human relations. Second, the semiotic approach illustrates that law and legal consciousness as a cultural and historical phenomenon should lead to a broad understanding of law's inherent power of articulation. Law and legal discourse are active in the history of a collective human consciousness: the two participate in modes far beyond individual initiatives or party interests. Third, our considerations also result from semiotic analyses of the 'legal consciousness' concept. It

rechtskundig-signifische geschriften van Jacob Israël de Haan (Language tells us more than it can account for), Ars Aequi Libri, Nijmegen, 1994, p. 69.

suggests that if the first person, the speaker, dominates the way law enforces that exclusive position, then there is no understanding possible of any access of the o/Other to a common pattern of speech and language. In other words: the road to signification by means of an active *legal* consciousness appears to be blocked by our (materialist) understanding of law.

A conclusion must be formulated.

> What originated a century ago but vanished in our modern understanding of law should be restored: a renewed appreciation of the concept 'legal consciousness', in which the language of law's inner logic and the language of law's logic of relations unite in appreciating the otherness of the other.

The two languages can perform this task through strengthening the experience that law can speak the language of *appeal* instead of *claim*, including an 'appealing to the other' without losing one's *self* – a challenge that can loudly be heard on the street and is definitively the expression of a multilingual consciousness.

1.8 NATURALNESS

'Nature': the word, the concept, the notion presents itself as innocent, without many complex consequences and useful for everyone in every type of language. Above all: everyone knows what should be articulated by the word, without further ado. And the latter is the problem! Many of the above pages tried to make clear that even a mention of the word 'nature' (in particular when used as a legal concept) has its problems. Do we not utter the word 'nature' to underline that in this case we do *not* think about any reflexivity? Of course: we pronounce 'nature' most naturally. The problem is that even this type of expressivity indicates a particular complication, since it embraces a naïve-non-reflexivity together with varying degrees of reflection. What is 'nature'? And: what is 'natural'? Is it 'Mother Nature', is it 'Evidence' – or is it 'a matter of course'? How does one know? We often disregard any answer and include the word along the lines of the many traditional ways of performing speech. In other words: the expression 'nature' entices us to maintain a certain naïveté in language.

1.8.1 The Natural, and Reflexivity

Modern forms of life illustrate the need to unfold and understand more encompassing forms of reflexivity. Differences between Occidental culture in the sixteenth and the twenty-first centuries illustrate this need very clearly, but the means to achieve more insight remain a philosophical problem. In law, jurisprudence and legal sciences 'the natural' is a genuine problem that has hitherto not been solved by philosophers.

That leads to one of the central issues of legal philosophy: *in how far is 'legal conversation' or 'talking about law' a matter of a specific level of language, and can that specificity be determined as the 'natural' or 'everyday' language?*

Basic to this approach is the recognition that language is a multileveled phenomenon with many and often very different features. A natural language is layered at a pre-semiotic level, a level at which signs are taken as natural and significations as evident. That characterizes the expression 'talking about law' and the predominant motive for underlining the non-naïve-natural character of legal language and its discourse(s). Do not forget: the leveled character of law's language is a *sign* of the multiple implications of knowledge formation. That sign situation embraces the 'natural' as one of its basic notions.

Our talking about law on the street meets our ability to reflect upon law. That reflection allows more subtle insights in law as a linguistic phenomenon. A major condition is in the shift from naïve-natural towards non-naïve-natural positions or attitudes, and vice versa.[25] The shift must be understood as a shift in the *innermost regions of the natural* itself. Any unfolding of human knowledge – be that knowledge religious, philosophical or scientific, be it in relation to nature and natural facts or to society and social facts – begins with the introduction of fragments of non-naïveté. This process is neither a simple negation within nature nor a shrewd dialectical move in science and thought. It is in itself a fragment of cosmic dimensions and its most powerful component is the human capacity to *articulate* linguistically. Language plays a major role and a simple speech act illustrates the ties with body movements, looks and movements. All are present in stories we tell or narratives we reproduce – and all are distanced from the naïve-natural position.

There is, however, more to register than a simple shift from naïveté to non-naïveté. The natural's naïveté can never disappear completely; it is

---

[25] Jan M. Broekman, *Meaning, Narrativity, and the Real*, Springer, Switzerland, 2016, p. 45ff.

already articulated in the fact that no artificial language and also no discourse of whatever discipline can exist without an encompassing natural or everyday language. Although it cannot disappear, it can change. The major and all-determining change is from naïve to non-naïve, as has already been underlined several times. But the naturalness remains natural during the first steps of that change, a non-naïve-naturalness does exist and is often heard in public when an 'uh …' is uttered. With that sound, a certain uncertainty arises: a second thought that will be followed by a third, which is an interruption of evidence with deeply rooted consequences. First steps of the non-naïve are filled with naturalness. But they already support a distance from the naïve. Naturalness appears as an unfolding balance between the two. A long way towards signification seems ahead. The balance will always be represented in language. Our speech acts are witness to the degree of balance and thus live from the progress made towards signification. 'Am I clear'? That question always indicates a phase in the unfolding of meaning: 'do you understand'?

1.8.2 Understanding Law

It would be understandable if law in general becomes categorized as a clear form of absolute non-naïveté. From that legal viewpoint, reality would then be completely naïve-natural and law its ruling force. The difference would be a solid ground for law to manage and thus to intervene in the stream of everyday reality. But this view does not honor the differentiations in the heart of the natural, which are also relevant for law and legal discourse. A philosophical remark, which is never discussed in legal theory, will come to the fore: *law can only characterize itself as 'non-naïve' in social reality if it accepts the 'naïve-natural' in itself as an articulation component.* The latter is the essence of the expression 'talking about law' and of our conclusion that *there exists on the street a 'pre-semiotic' field of understanding law.*

As explained, roots of that viewpoint are in the complexity of the natural as a cultural concept. Indeed, it seems undeniable that 'nature' and 'the natural' can be terms loaded with a different meaning and signification than the Occident provided. But the center of our reasoning remains the term 'natural'. The latter will never evaporate under the pressure of a non-naïve positioning; changes in naïveté do not annihilate the nature concept. The opposite seems true: *'the natural' changes its character where non-naïveté develops; it opens up to reflection, it creates perspectives on a new path from sign to signification and to new thought formations with a deeper understanding of law.* This has far-reaching consequences of a philosophical and cultural character. Changes in nature take place in the stream from naïve-natural to non-naïve-natural attitudes, positions and viewpoints, their vice versa included. Those changes are cosmic, and thus are ours: they include man although they are not man-made. New attitudes and positions are components of the unfolding of nature and its history in which the human mind is enveloped.

Understanding law is not a matter of a subject–object relationship, but in the first place of a participation in the unfolding of natural processes and the recognition of otherness of the other.

It has always been a problem to understand the role of the subject when the need to understand law becomes an urgent issue. Now we can see that this problem is characterized as a different type of holism: not man creates the whole but the whole creates human creative positions. Law is a sign of that new type of holism, and its signification a facet.

1.8.3 Holism, Naturalness

Emphasis is not on the creative powers of human consciousness as an autonomous source of knowledge, but rather on the inclusion of those powers in nature as a process. Law has a surprising feature in common with a work of art: artwork and law appear both as man-made – a feature that leaves naïve-natural positions behind while striving for articulation as a specific concept takes place. But one remembers the famous considerations of Kant on the question 'what is law', including the fact that the question will never be correctly answered. That lack or difficulty to answer is engendered by the 'man-made' dimension, which is often connected with the 'I know' scheme used in all those cases. In the expression: 'I know what; I know how' knowledge is involved, and human knowledge is in our minds determined by a subject–object relationship. Because that is the case, one must expect that law's essence (which is a concept) could be perceived as a sensible object within the domain of a traditional subject–object relationship. It is to Kant's merit to have concluded that this cannot be the case.

The seminal question for 'knowing law' in parallel to 'knowing an artwork' is in the consideration: how can the concepts of art and law be present in the world of signs and sensations, meanings and significances? Their presence is beyond doubt a matter of a more transcendental character: what logic makes this presence knowable? What logic is at stake when the view of a painting, a water color, an etching, a statue, the sound of a harp, an orchestra, a disc, the reading of a text, a poem, a law or an ingenious construction plan has entered human life and the human mind as a sensory event and eventually an object? It is evident that the answer refers to the logic of life, of which logic as a philosophical consideration in the tradition of human thought formations in a certain period of humanity and within a certain culture is a component. The 'I know' expression is solely a phenomenon within the broader context of the latter – a phenomenon that is certainly not able to construct a 'whole' or a 'universality' nor a 'naturalness' *tout court.*

1.8.4 The Self

The same is true when we regard any 'talking about law'. One often encounters a complaint in conversation: 'as an individual, you feel very much alone and completely powerless in law, despite the support of lawyers'. In other words: what do loneliness or powerlessness mean here? It requires traveling a long distance and a walk on various philosophical byways to find fragments leading to an answer on that question. All of them touch the logic that backs the concept of presence, and all refer to that presence in the form of some type of perception.

How do we perceive a concept in life? Not with our eyes, but we perceive in the first place through organizing life in such a way that a perception can and will be realized. This organization requires *the presence of o/Others* in various forms: others in the form of the natural, other persons, but also others in the form of cultural histories, habits, institutions and phenomena, as well as others as stories, narratives, eventually discourses, and others as conceptions with a logical character. The majority of these forms of o/Otherness are called: language. Every detail of what organizes presence, is in need of, or is: language. Is language the ultimate form of the *Holon* in human life?

That question has multidimensional consequences. It would mean that loneliness and powerlessness – the abovementioned complaint in much talking about law – is *not* an issue that could be solved by social measures, by financial remodeling of the encounter with a lawyer, by being more clear in the reasoning of judges, in more accessibility to sources and thought patterns of jurists, or by filling in the gap between a natural and a professional language. The answer is in the positioning of the Self.

An 'I' that does not consider itself to be a component of a larger totality is condemned to be left on its own, because it seems unable to accept the meaning of 'receiving' and 'otherness' in human life. In other words, a subject–object relationship is never the final instance to decide about inter-individual relations. And what is an obvious consequence: if an 'I' or a 'Self' is *not* able to see itself as a component of a larger totality, then it is also not able to engage in a conversation or any speech act.

To take the steps of a discourse in our stride is normally an act without awareness of spatial components of our speech or the limits of our language. A multilingual consciousness does experience this challenge, although it often withstands the influence of the o/Other and otherness, which is in essence a rejection of its belonging to dimensions reaching beyond the 'I'. The Latin expression '*discurrere*' indicates the roots of the word 'discourse', and an enlargement of speech dimensions is incorporated here: one can 'walk through' speech dimensions and encounter others speakers! Such language dimensions are *not*, however, determined by the speech quality or capacity of an individual. Solely an attitude towards the plural defines a speaking human individual. This invites one to rethink the speech act in the frame of talk and conversation. Each speech act (also in *legal* conversation) engenders a *presence* that is larger and more encompassing than the speaking subject envisions in its singularity.

Speech is a sign of freedom and presence. It does not determine *what* is said, but regards the act of speaking itself. Do not forget that the latter, as Jacques Derrida underlined in many of his texts, occurs solely amidst others and otherness. However, one has to consider that this insight is formulated in a particular context: the predominance of speech. The speaking seems more important than any form of silence, the writing and the emergence of texts and discourses more than holding one's tongue. That predominance can apparently not be abolished. Presence articulated in speech cannot be dissolved, annihilated or elevated – not even by silence. Speaking is a form of presence that cannot be denied.

The power of speech and the power of presence will ultimately become identical in all human linguistic activity. A *Self* does not recognize or know *it-Self* in silence! The natural character of language and speech in Occidental culture is the key to understanding reality. Even if a jurist were able to hold their tongue, that silence would be powerfully embedded in law's speech. The question whether silence is an interruption of speaking, melts down in the predominance of speech. This dominance of performance illustrates the limitations of a legal consciousness. The latter has normally been understood as a capacity to perform speech acts – an uninterrupted activity that does not appreciate silence. The professional speech activity of the lawyer does not allow any interval. A lawyer's mother tongue, which will be experienced as a specific discourse, is in essence a continuum. Any threat to break this continuum down (even by moments of silence) will be qualified as an attempt to damage the legal certainty a society badly needs. The *Self* of a lawyer is a *speaking* Self.

1.9 INTERACTION

Interaction is one of the pillars of the shift towards the non-naïve that characterizes the path from sign to signification. We already highlighted the multiple meanings of interactivity and their in-built difference between collegiality and cooperation. But if the emphasis is on interaction, a specific meaning comes to the fore when law is at stake. Close ties between *nature* and *interaction* are basic for legal articulations from streets to courts. But one has to understand that the non-naïve is a matter of nature (in the sense of reality naturally given) *and* of the social (in the sense of preparedness to accept the o/Other) – an insight particularly precious for lawyer and judge alike. All positions in law and social life are by definition 'shared positions'. So there are two foundational contexts of the *interaction* concept: first is the specificity of legal *discourse* and second the *institutional* character of law. Both, *discourse* and *institution* are understood as thought patterns that support legal speech activity in a specific manner.

1.9.1 Dynamics of Discourse

Law has principally to do with a shift from naïve-natural towards non-naïve-natural languages – their thought patterns and influences on patterns of behavior included. The dynamics of law seem to have their foundation in continuous changes from naïve to non-naïve views, positions and attitudes. These are culturally anchored phenomena at a distance from any psychological or psychoanalytical restriction. To be a skilled lawyer or an experienced jurist implies insight and mastering of those shifts from naïveté to non-naïveté, and vice versa. To be knowledgeable in legal practice thus implies mastering a shift from one to the other as well as from the other to the one continuously. It thus means that with regard to thought patterns, traditions of explanation and understanding, legal practice is first of all a matter of mastering social dynamics.

The word 'mastering' is used in its most powerful meaning; the balances to be mastered in legal practices are subtle, complicated and require the mind of a pioneer. Legal security and legal certainty should not do away with renewals, changes of view or adaptation of the mind with regard to new techniques, to new data, or to political or economic interests. Naïve and not-naïve are continuously on the move. Nothing seems so challenging in law as the evident, the normal, the given, the traditional and the safe! Those dynamics are in law represented by the challenge of the shift, which is in itself a beginning and a finality of dynamics. Interaction is in this view an omnipotent requirement within legal discourse. The latter dominates all phases at all moments of law's proper unfolding. Law is by definition an interactive occurrence because of its dynamic character that focuses on a plurality of participants. The position of various speakers in the discourse of law reflects this necessity of interaction as well as the need for a dynamic unfolding of speech, thought and action.

1.9.2 Managing Meaning

Interactivity may belong to the potential to define law; interactivity is always encapsulated in a broader context; the latter is in the first place the mastering and management of meaning. Lawyers are professionals in meaning-making, and it is interesting that their task is often understood as a most powerful mastering of non-naïve-natural positions. However, there are limits to this activity, even if one agrees with this characterization. Interaction and interactivity among participants of a legal discourse can never be *completely* non-naïve, because its opposite (the naïveté) remains an important force. This does ultimately mean that jurists, who indeed do manage meaning, can unfold that management only within boundaries. The many cases of *repetition* in a lawyer's discourse illustrate this observation. A repeated term, a frequently used expression, a word in various contexts repeated in law's discourse, focuses on stages within the evolution and inner dynamics of law and its language.

We speak, for instance, of a 'victim' in the language of the street. Someone is a victim of aggression in traffic, of a car accident or plane crash, the victim of a company's incorrect behavior or the victim of an illness. A lawyer repeats the word but handles the context of that word in connection with the situation in which he wants it understood. The meaning of the word victim in his or her discourse will without further clarification be specified and managed through its proximity to concepts such as 'suspect', 'accountability', 'injury' or 'reimbursement'. A field of meanings is created, often qualified as belonging to a professional language, and mostly at a distance from the everyday articulations we regard as our life-world. There is no need to explain: the lawyer's speech, in particular when it demonstrates his mastery of meanings, creates a degree of alienation. This is the most important issue in the context of interaction and interactivity in law's discourse. Meanings brought to the fore should meet that fore; they must have a communicative base and serve understanding and commonness. That view implies *restriction* in so far as the management of meaning is concerned. All interactivity needs a frame of expressivity, of meaning management, of applicability – and only within those frameworks can a lawyer's word be (inter)active and a value to society. This *restrictive* component is called 'institution'. It was said before: law is *institutionally* anchored in Occidental culture.

1.9.3 Institution

It is not simple to answer the question what this expression 'institutionally anchored in Occidental culture' means as a component of legal discourse. Its formulation refers to important parts of legal philosophy, at least in the last two centuries, and there is equally important research from the second half of the twentieth century. All have in common that 'institution' and 'institutional' refer to strong ties to a State or comparable organizations, to (often international) corporations as well as to deeply engraved habits, uses, prescriptions and other cultural values, which have an obligatory character for their participant citizens. The major obligation in the concept 'institutional' is to develop a strong identification with the dominant features of the institution, so that the recognition of an identity, a view, or a form of participation and thought formation, can easily take place. The State's virtue and interest is to offer powerful frames for thought patterns and social behavior, which unite its citizens, make them identifiable and create conformity, so that questions about the quality of interactivity do not even come up. States and corporations are in many regards identical, and interactive commonness is one of their major conditions for surviving.

Do not forget that the concept 'institutional' is a *thought pattern* and a *social organization* at the same time. No wonder that Law relates to States: the two are sublime and complex thought patterns and effective social organizations, and both reinforce each other in every decision or judgment. Occidental law has, for at least four centuries, determined that the legal concept of *contract* is one of the most outstanding manifestations of *freedom*. The latter is institutionally anchored, so that Western concepts of freedom, legally determined, do in essence lack freedom. The philosophical discussion about differences between 'freedom to …' and, for instance, 'freedom from …' mask the foundational ambiguity in the concept, caused by its roots in institutional thinking.

Words in law are signs of freedom, but institutions limit their meanings and socially modeled expressions repeat vested State structures and suggest that judges judge in courts, that courts are privileged supporters of the democratic State and the latter supports the rule of law. Institutional requirements determine the meaning, the value, the evolution and evaluation of the constitutional State in a mixture of terms and codes, which illustrate the necessity to intermingle law and politics. Even a democracy is a *cratos* (power) founded upon a *legally codified* interactivity of its citizens. Notice that even voting rights are limited in the US as well as in the European Union, and that these are determined and managed by States and State interests – not to mention corporate interests.

A conclusion fascinates: a repulsion of the naïveté and a legally refined activity to further the non-naïve in speech, thoughts and practices within a democratic society creates abundant space for the realization of institutional dimensions to regulate major dimensions of life. This insight makes the *anarchist* position clear – a position that wants to create freedom from institutional dominance. But what happens after that freedom is acquired? A lack of possibilities to answer that question again leads us to embrace the fixations of institutional thought patterns.

1.9.4 Legalism

Legalism is an example of such a path. It is often regarded to be one of the most conservative spearheads of legal discourse. To 'take the law literally' is a leading slogan in this context. If applied, legalism seems to make the change from a naïve to a non-naïve attitude superfluous. To follow the letter of the law implies following the spirit of the law!

Why is *legalism* still an issue in times of mass (im)migration, political instability and terrorism – and even in times of the rapidly progressing power of electronic communication? The question seems ridiculous: it is evident that following the letter of the law offers social as well as emotional, communicative, State and political security. Legalism does not need any interpretation: act in accordance with what is laid down on paper or with viral means! It thus delivers a maximal limitation of meaning, reduces signification to a handbook-security and inspires citizen behavior to (inter)activities as if a dictatorship reigns. In that case, law in the books suffices to direct law in action, as Roscoe Pound accentuates.[26] Is it feasible that law books are dictators? Pound, initiator of applying the term 'sociological jurisprudence', wanted to integrate the

---

[26] Roscoe Pound, *Social Control through Law*, 1st edn, New Haven, CT, Yale University Press, 1942.

Common Law pragmatist approach and the European social traditions to create an interdisciplinary research and theory program that leads to large scale possibilities of a social engineering through law. But legalism and its strong positivist attitude do represent an extremely strong desire for security, which initially should be delivered by lawyers and particularly by judges.

One should not forget: legalism's cultural context is not limited to Western history and democracy. It is generally known that one of the schools in the ancient period of Chinese philosophy lasting until 221 BC was the Legalist School. The name was never in function before 90 BC, but the basic idea(s) lasted nearly five centuries. That is most remarkable to remember. The concentration of power was the mark of the School, and law was, with statecraft's power, the main instrument through those ages. The system blossomed because of a rigid manipulation of power, a strict and perfect balance of reward and punishment influencing politics, and because a stable ordering of social levels could express the total involvement of citizens. The latter did not possess freedom, but they were hardly aware of it. It is interesting that an implicit image of a human being was based on the assumption of the evil nature of human character and thought patterns. Only a rigid system of rule-following could prevent social life from being a disaster. State-laws and law in general should balance the ineffectiveness of moral values that guide social conduct. It is evident that this School brought feudalism to an end and initiated a new dynasty.

However, early Chinese legalism did not completely embrace authoritarian views and practices without further reconciliation. Taoists around 220 BC affirmed already that rulers should act in accordance with nature but foremost with the talents of the people. Legalists interpreted that insight with their own preoccupations and furthered *legal* control of the State. Law should perform as a good neighbor: good relations as well as enforced and respected rule-following and a sense of peace. That is in harmony with the insight that education should be the basis of law and State. Moral and legal consciousness, the legalist confirms, must be acquired through education. Modern psychology and education theories confirm this viewpoint.

1.9.5 From Anarchism to Legalism

Legalism is not overtly present in legal theory or jurisprudential considerations. But it is omnipresent as a thought pattern in the Western world, and its closeness to legal education (and education in general) is a brute fact. It is fascinating how legalism displays the genius of *differentiation*.

It takes the distinction between public and private law as a natural fact and draws lines between law and non-law rigidly. While differentiating between law and non-law, between itself and others, law distances itself from all other domains of social reality. As a consequence, law's inherent legalism causes legal theory to differ fundamentally from other sciences and from other social theories. Law's heart is legalistic, because it engenders a 'minimum of positivism'.[27] Legal facts will for that very same reason bear *rights* before any semiotics can elucidate their significance. Rights are a dogmatic form of representation. They contain a binding opinion about how reality is, without considering time, place, character or culture.

The problem remains nevertheless the absolutism in accepting those forms of non-naïveté. When considered in the above-outlined specter of meanings that reaches from *anarchism* to *legalism*, 'talking about law' in one of them is consequently a different discourse about legal thought formation and practices. The first revolts against almost all aspects of the second, and the latter cannot imagine any form of society on the basis of the first. Disorder and order are opposites in this legal span; lack of values and absolute validity a complete contrast.

'Talking about law' occurs at both levels, and both can be found everywhere, but legalism and its institutional meanings put the relevance of those ways of talking in perspective. It will be clear that law itself, especially in the form of legalism, suggests that presuppositions of jurists and judges are natural. Citizens share them (for instance, enforced in a dictatorial State) or oppose them (in anarchist opinions and small communities), but *all* are continuously confronted with this feature. A *sharing* darkens the legalistic *differentiation*, which accepts certain biases of jurists to function as a mark of the profession. Law is inevitable: if jurists' biases weigh heavily, then these will be presented as democratically generated – a reasoning that reinforces democracy as a contract, that is: as a legal issue. Can it be done differently? The institutional features of law make one hesitate to suggest a positive answer to that question. Yet one remembers the expression 'Law without State' which is almost neighboring those considerations. They forcefully select, differentiate and fixate meanings that belong to natural languages into a professional language: meanings that bind, suppress others and leave no choice, direct meanings autocratically and argue as if law's grammar is a *natural* phenomenon.

---

[27] Jan M. Broekman, 'The Minimum Content of Positivism' *Rechtstheorie*, Vol. XVI, No. 4. 1985.

1.10 NATURAL LAW

References to nature and/or naturalness are significant in anarchism as well as in legalism; so why not interpret law as natural? The distinction between a 'naïve-natural' and a 'non-naïve-natural' position is not specific for law and legal discourse, but the expression 'natural law' has existed since ages past and is an influential way of thinking in law. Reaching beyond the boundaries of Western culture, natural law is a concept related to various religious traditions.

However, this form of understanding law does not specifically represent a particular religion. We rather think in this context of Aquinas or the seventeenth century Renaissance with Grotius, Pufendorf, Locke and others. The key of that thought pattern can be found in an argument that is astonishingly near to anarchism. It suggests that the power, the intentions or practices of a State can never be the origin and the justification of law. Another power has to be acknowledged, as, for instance, the protagonist Antigone suggested in Sophocles' tragedy that 'unwritten laws of God that know no change … live forever'. One cannot, however, suggest that these laws are of no importance for humans and for human society. The question whether normativity is the key and the beginning of any engenderment of law, posed by Hans Kelsen, illustrates the opposite.

1.10.1 Nature and Validity

In the field of legal thinking named 'legal positivism' one encounters the burning question whether an 'unjust law can be a law'. The formulation of that question leads to a hidden semiotic component. If unjust law *can be*, or *cannot be*, or possibly *ought to be* law, the expression 'law' does not articulate what legalists consider as the most important dimension: law is regarded as *valid* only when this consideration is brought to the fore in a legally correct form. Change the words and one has another position: may valid law be immoral or unjust? If such law is valid *and* immoral, then the validity sustains its character articulated as 'law' – although legal practice will hesitate to appeal to such laws. But substantive moral criteria are not criteria to decide legal validity: law is law because it is acknowledged as: being law.

Law is law because of *legal* criteria.

So natural law is a form of law in which legal criteria decide about its being law. Since the Ancient Greek period, but in particular since the Renaissance in Western Europe, we focus for that decision on *human nature as rational* and as the basis for *reasonableness in justification.*

The necessary context is, however, outlined by a set of *natural goods*, which are substantive values that are not marked as ends but as means for law and legal practice.

1.10.2 Human Nature

Natural law may defend the thesis that any reference to the *nature* concept brings a maximum clarity about the position of the *naïve-natural* in the entire field of meaning. Also *non-naïve-natural* positions will come to the fore while doing so. The important tradition of natural law is based on its pretension to articulate and to position law (mostly represented by the State) in a cosmic order. That pretension does not, however, clarify the crucial bound between 'nature' and 'the human mind', which seems always presupposed.

An important aspect is not considered: each concept referring to 'human nature' is a cultural phenomenon. The contrast between nature and culture appears decisive in its clear implications to defend a natural law as such: *nature* is independent from the human mind and its abilities to articulate, whereas culture is its product! Ultimately this leads us to the question: can *nature* be thought of while separated from *culture*? Is not each thought needed to articulate each component? The same question pertains to the *factual* character of those components. Are facts decidedly: *facts*? Or are they ultimately the result of human articulation? It fascinates when we take into account that Italian natural philosophers first used the term for 'fact' in its contemporary meaning in the 1570s and that only after 1660 did it acquire more widely spread attention in English and French.[28] Is *nature* a fact? Is the *human mind* a fact? Do *legal facts* exist, and if they do, what is their nature?

Tensions between the naïve-natural and the non-naïve-natural rose in the politics of the first decades of the twentieth century, as we mentioned in preceding pages. The Bolshevist revolution, the dominance of the Communist Party and the establishment of the Soviet Union, developments rising to National Socialism which later led to the Second World War in the middle of that century, are altogether linked to the nature–culture debate and to the political dominance of selected fragments of ideas about the State and the basic features of mankind being anchored in natural law. The relation between, and coherence of, 'nature' and the 'human mind' was an essential point – even in discussions, theories and

---

[28] David Wootton, *The Invention of Science: A New History of the Scientific Revolution*, Penguin, London, 2016; see also Nicolas Popper, 'Period Label', *Times Literary Supplement*, No. 5908, 2016, p. 3ff.

research in physics, with Einstein's theory of relativity or Heisenberg's uncertainty principle as eye-catchers in modern history. Phenomenology underlined in the same years that the 'I-think' mode contrasts importantly with thought patterns that regard the 'I' as a philosophical solo-instrument. Indeed, an 'I-think' mode transforms the divergences among the naïve and the non-naïve-natural into components of the dynamics of the human mind. The latter dominate our theory of knowledge, and put the concept of natural law into perspective. Does that concept represent, or even articulate, the naïve-natural in law and legal discourse? Is it a valid legal concept although it is not a valid law?

1.10.3 Natural Law Re-Positioned

While considering the many meanings and roles of the natural law concept in legal discourse, one is surprised how skilfully it positions the 'naïve-naturalness' in its proper theory of knowledge. But to what level of language does the naïveté of the naïve-natural in these positions belong? The question at the background of this entire chapter becomes visible again. At issue is again the gap between a natural and an artificial language.

Are meaning and significance of the natural here a legal language issue or an everyday-natural language issue? Has the concept 'natural law' been successful in counterbalancing all naïveté and is it therefore understood as a pure non-naïve, *legal* concept? The difficulty of that position is, and has been in that case, that a reduction of naïveté – the demand of every artificial language – is required for such a natural law concept. But does it meet those demands?

We change the formulation of that question and remember (as has been concluded in the above pages) that *every professional or artificial language needs a context of natural language in order to safeguard its special power of articulation.* This insight guides us in the case of understanding and (re-)positioning the concept of natural law properly.

Once legal discourse operates as an artificial technical discourse (as a practice) and has diminished the naïve-natural and its manifestations, it needs to determine precisely the naïve-natural remains in itself as well as in its proper context. These remains are baptized 'natural law' and in that regard legal discourse is a truly unique discourse. The naïve-natural is determined in legal terms. That is the reason that Occidental jurists spoke about 'natural law' for centuries and the streets continue to talk about law in approximately the same terms. Notice that this region in law's discourse is *not* valid positive law: it will never be the language in which judges are allowed to formulate their decisions, but it remains rather the language in which legal conversations can be articulated.

1.10.4 Legal Knowledge

Law's discourse has this particular feature: it has (a) diminished/reduced the naïve-natural in its discourse, and (b) kept a place for the remains of natural naïveté. That feature is itself a clear *sign* with regard to a general insight in the basic structures of human knowledge. All discourses with the task of unfolding scientific insights and transferring scientific knowledge focus on non-naïveté. While performing this task, they reduce meaning and re-scale signification. This reductive dimension can be understood as a general feature of knowledge. It also occurs in law and legal knowledge. But here the concept of natural law, with its longevity and its trans-cultural history, is significant.

The concept is a *sign* for meaning (the naïve-natural) and a *sign* of a specific feature of human knowledge in general.

Knowledge is always a matter of a complex articulation of reality, as the implicit tensions between mind and body, matter and mind, reality and perception illustrate. Emphasis on these *signs* is characteristic for the knowledge process in its totality; it unfolds, as it were, beyond cultural specificities or periods of history.

We must underline again that law and legal discourse have a very special position in this context of knowledge creation. Knowing law (a particular feature in 'talking about law') implies a positive position/attitude in view of the tensions between the naïve and the non-naïve-natural dimensions of knowledge. The concept of natural law illustrates that those tensions are not solved by a violent reductive attitude or by silencing phenomena of their existence.

Natural law understood as *a sign for the complexity of human knowledge*, coming from a particular discourse – the legal discourse – bears the burden of the continuing plurality of discourses through which knowledge engenders. 'Legal conversation', even in the form of 'talking about law', has occurred already during many centuries and in various cultural settings. Many of them sound identical but demonstrate different meanings in the languages of judges as their tools. Relevant thought patterns, and those having law as their major subject, unfold in many fields. And philosophical reflection appears to move above limits and boundaries like a drone.

REFERENCES

Alexey, T. and T. Stanislovas, 'Interaction of European and Russian Legal Consciousness' *BRICS Law Journal*, No. 2, 2015.

Bennet, D., *Intuition Pumps and Other Tools for Thinking*, W. W. Norton, New York/London, 2013.

Bergh, G. C. J. J. van den, *De taal zegt meer dan zij verantwoorden kan: Een keuze uit de verspreide rechtskundig-signifische geschriften van Jacob Israël de Haan*, Ars Aequi Libri, Nijmegen, 1994.

Broekman, Jan M., *Phänomenologie und Egologie*. Series Phaenomenologica, Bd 12, M. Nijhoff, The Hague, 1963.

Broekman, Jan M., 'Betere Taal is Beter Recht' *Wijsgerig Perspectief op Maatschappij en Wetenschap*, Vol. 20, No. 2, 1979–80.

Broekman, Jan M., 'The Minimum Content of Positivism' *Rechtstheorie*, Vol. XVI, No. 4, 1985.

Broekman, Jan M., *A Philosophy of European Union Law*, Peeters, Leuven/Paris, 1999.

Broekman, Jan M., *Meaning, Narrativity, and the Real*: *The Semiotics of Law in Legal Education IV*, Springer, Switzerland, 2016.

Broekman, Jan M. and Backer, Larry Catà, *Signs in Law – A Source Book*, Springer, Switzerland, 2014.

De Haan, Jacob Israël, *Rechtskundige Significa en hare toepassing op de begrippen 'aansprakelijk, verantwoordelijk, toerekeningsvatbaar'*, Versluys, Amsterdam 1916.

De Haan, Jacob Isaël, *Wezen en taak der rechtskundige significa*, Van Kampen, Amsterdam, 1916.

De Haan, Jacob Israël, *In Russische Gevangenissen*, 1913, 2nd edn, Wereld-bibliotheek, Amsterdam, 1986.

De Haan, Jacob Israël, 'Taal en Rechtswetenschap' *Weekblad van het Recht*, No. 10103, 1917; also published in G. C. J. J. van den Bergh, *De taal zegt meer dan zij verantwoorden kan: Een keuze uit de verspreide rechtskundig-signifische geschriften van Jacob Israël de Haan*, Nijmegen 1994.

De Saussure, F., *Cours de Linguistique Générale*, 1915, edited by Tullio de Mauro, Payothéque, Paris, 1972.

Freeman, M. D. A., *Lloyd's Introduction to Jurisprudence*, 7th edn, Sweet and Maxwell, London, 2001.

Husserl, Edmund, *Ideen zu einer reinen Phänomenologie und phänomenologischen Philosophie*, I, Halle, 1913.

Husserl, Edmund, *Vorlesungen über Bedeutungslehre, Sommersemester 1908* (edited by U. Panzer), Husserliana, XXVI, Nijhoff, Dordrecht, 1987.

Il'in, Ivan A., *The Philosophy of Hegel as a Doctrine of the Concreteness of God and Humanity*, edited and translated by Philip T. Grier, Northwestern University Press, 2010–11 (2 volumes).

Il'in, Ivan A., *On the Essence of Legal Consciousness*, 1919, 1956. Translated by Philip T. Grier (edited with commentaries by William E. Butler, Philip T. Grier, and Vladimir A. Tomsinov), Wildy, Simmonds and Hill Publishing, 2014.

Kevelson Roberta, *The Law as a System of Signs*, Plenum Publishing, New York, 1988.

Mohr, Richard, 'Living Legal Fictions: Constituting the State or Submerging the Signifier?' *International Journal for the Semiotics of Law*, Vol. 19, 2006, 237–58.

Popper, Nicolas, 'Period Label', *Times Literary Supplement*, No. 5908, 2016, p. 3ff.

Pound, Roscoe, *Social Control through Law*, 1st edn, New Haven, CT, Yale University Press, 1942.

Schmitz, H. Walter (ed.), *Essays on Significs (Papers Presented on the Occasion of the 150th Anniversary of the Birth of Victoria Lady Welby [1837–1912])*, J. Benjamins Pub. Cie., Amsterdam/Philadelphia, 1990.

Schmitz, H. Walter, *De Hollandse Significa: Een reconstructie van de geschiedenis van 1892 tot 1926*, Van Gorcum, Assen, 1990.

Unger, R. M., *The Self Awakened: Pragmatism Unbound*, Harvard University Press, Cambridge, MA, 2007.

Wagner, Anne, 'The Rules of the Road, a Universal Visual Semiotics' *International Journal for the Semiotics of Law*, Vol. 19, No. 3, 2006, 311–24.

Welby, Victoria Lady, *What is Meaning?: Studies in the Development of Significance*, Macmillan and Co., 1903.

Welby, Victoria Lady, *Significs and Language*, Macmillan and Co., 1911, reprinted University of California Libraries.

Wootton, David, *The Invention of Science: A New History of the Scientific Revolution*, Penguin, London, 2016.

2. Legal practice stalks the brain

INTRODUCTION

While thoughts back our speech, legal practices stalk the brain. Are law's practitioners involved in legal conversations with their clients or just 'talking about law'? No, they do talk about *legally valid law*, move their thoughts in this field of specific meanings and want their clients to adapt to that language in order to provide solutions. No more, no less. Indeed, thought formation in legal practice unfolds at the same time in various fields and formats a client's expectations and expressive potential most powerfully. All of us cherish the feeling that this is what legal practice has to offer.

Reducing meanings make interaction between lawyer and client possible, although the alienation of the artificiality of law's way of articulating reality remains an issue. Lawyers who bring law to practice do not worry: their consumers listen to their words and take any possible misunderstanding as a price to pay for their activities. Clients attach great importance to each word the lawyer utters on the case. However, they are hardly aware that this interest is not their free choice. It is rather the result of a subtle form of law's stalking the brain (or consciousness) of its subjects. The power of the inherent structure of law is so overwhelming that legal concepts and meanings are *evident* to each form of citizenship. Yet the abyss between the two languages remains yawning. How can a professional language, perhaps because of its artificial components, create submissive forms that provoke legal formats for life?

That question dominates in each consideration of the legal practitioner's activity, but only a semiotic approach understands the power of stalking in this regard. It leads to an almost continuous critical consideration of the social function of the law in deep layers of understanding. This seems so radical, that the question arises whether legal practice is from time to time not identical to social misunderstanding in its most general and generalized form. And, in another light one could argue that legal practice mimics misunderstanding at a large social level, because divergence in opinion and interest is part of any drive towards a legal intervention.

2.1 STALKING THE BRAIN

The legal practitioner does not speak about law's practices because he focuses on *legally valid* law. The term 'practice' is an expression of a realm of meanings in which he is not at home. There is too much theory involved in the term for a lawyer, and not theoretical ideas but the client's *interests* are at stake. So the practitioner talks about *cases*, but the fact that cases are a theoretical construct will not influence the goals she has in mind.

The mind of citizens must adapt to the formats of legal thinking and legal practice. As a participant in a society's legal system no citizen is *free* to think or act the way she wants to explore life. Legal format stalks the citizen's brain, which is imprisoned in the thought patterns that manage the architecture of law's practices.

Stalking your brain: does the power of metaphor make us stop short when we read that phrase? What do we do when we continuously reconsider the function and physiology of our brain, whereas we are used to considering our consciousness as the source of our mind, its actions and attitudes included? The final decades of the twentieth century displayed an all-embracing fascination for consciousness and the human mind finally being rooted in the brain. Philosophy focused on consciousness in Freud's dream interpretations, Bergson's exploration of time, Husserl's phenomenology of the ego, Merleau-Ponty's understanding of perception or Sartre's exploration of social relations. Indeed, 'a questioned consciousness' seemed to unite culture and science in that period.

2.1.1 The Brain Questioned

At the dawn of the twenty-first century, the brain as a neurophysiological organ plays the role we once ascribed to consciousness. Do we thus widen our understanding of the mind–brain relationship and live in a period of 'a questioned brain' and thus leave 'the mind' to social sciences, philosophy or even metaphysics? Indeed, methods of investigation changed; analyses and research replaced speculative reflection almost entirely. And so did the object itself: the belief that consciousness and the mind form the greatest riddle in human life faded away, whereas technically achieved knowledge and mastery of what was called 'brain' took over. Philosophical ideas about the essence and function of basic human concepts changed with that turn. Pedagogues reformulated their task: education is the art of forming the best possible brain of each individual.

But one should not forget, in what regard inter-textual notions (to which such concepts as 'brain', 'consciousness' and 'mind' belong) remain elements of language and speech. Roland Barthes underlined already three decades ago that the wealth of linguistic components seemed immeasurable in that semiotic perspective.[1] Not only philosophical ideas changed, also law and medicine are changing continuously in their ever-close relationship. However, they never unfold outside of language as a general semiotic category. Speech has in common with the more general concept of language that it embraces all systems of signs, including those belonging to neuro-scientific and other systems of communication. A particular system functions in view of another always as the *other scene of signification*. That is also the case in the most modern views on the mind–brain problem, and the position of the brain as a mainly neuro-physiological complexity with unknown or even unknowable psychological and spiritual implications.

An independent science of 'text' is missing, despite all implications of hermeneutics and other text-related insights. The liaison between text and signification is *one-sided*, unfolding in studies of language and meaning, linguistics and semiotics. That is important in view of neurological brain research, law and electronic technology – a bewildering combination that will be more and more important in the years to come. In that field, in which the human *brain* seems to be of major importance, three elements are combined.

The *first* is the indeterminacy of perceiving and defining reality (including virtual reality) in relation to legal, psychological and sociological problems of identity. The *second* is the intertwining of legal and medical discourse. Both undertake to change indeterminacy into determinacy, security and comprehension. The *third* is the semiotic insight in the dynamics of signifying processes. Those dynamics result from a general application of the concepts of language and speech during which socially dominating discourses unfold. Their dominance leads to the expression 'stalking' as a term, which fits in this regard to brain as well as mind.

An example of 'socially dominating discourses' in the context of law and neurology is in their entangling during the early years of the twenty-first century. Special attention was in that period on the 'brain fingerprint', a brain scan technology based on the fact that the brain emits characteristic electrical wave responses when stimulated. That test

---

[1] R. Barthes, *L'aventure sémiologique*, Editions Du Seuil, Paris, 1985, p. 28ff.

was admissible for US Courts under the condition that the scientific result was tested, peer reviewed and published, accepted and proven accurate in the scientific community. Law's practices were recognized as valid on the basis of the recognition of the fact that information was provided about what *a person has stored in his brain.*

The latter expression is remarkable: as if electronic wave research discovered the human brain as piggy bank. The storage story is a matter of mother tongue – the expression belongs to ordinary language but is suggested to be in use as a technical term in neurology and brain research. Focus on parts of the terminology are of interest, and concern (1) the semantic implications of 'stored', (2) the naïve use of 'in', and (3) the lack of an appropriate definition of 'brain'. Are all three terminological issues? No, they are a semiotic pitfall. An ordinary language cannot replace the language of neurosciences and brain research; one artificial language discourse cannot simply substitute another non-natural language discourse. Yet the suggestion is accepted by US Courts that also in cases of a brain what is inside should be outside, so we can deal with the brain as a box being a box: in terms of yes/no, inside/outside, and other binary images with their space-metaphors. In law, brain scan technology must function as a high-tech lie detector, encroaching on a suspect's private memories and consciousness. What about the US's Fifth Amendment or European Union constitutional parallels?[2]

One of the key questions that fascinated scholars and school kids alike during the final years of the twentieth century was whether a computer has consciousness. Then followed the question, whether the division we use to explore between natural and artificial intelligence is still acceptable in the light of our supercomputers, space travels, deep universe explorations, subatomic experiments and observations, not to mention our GPS systems and handheld devices, which reach beyond the boundaries of feeling, perception and orientation. The latter differ already considerably from the devices we possessed when the question was formulated: has a computer consciousness? As a consequence, natural and artificial intelligence will be understood as belonging to the same language we explore while speaking about the differentiation between an 'I' and a 'Me'.

The flow of conscious intelligence from which each individual is a particle, emphasizes the 'I' as belonging to artificial as well as natural

---

[2] Jan M. Broekman, 'Trading Signs: Semiotic Practices in Law and Medicine' *International Journal for the Semiotics of Law*, Vol. 20, No. 3, 2007, p. 223ff; also: Jed S. Rakoff, 'Neuroscience and the Law' *The New York Review of Books*, Vol. LXIII, No. 8, May 12, 2016, p. 30ff.

intelligence, and the 'Me' as being entangled in all possible interrelations. This gives birth to a more precise consideration about the linguistic character of legal language and discourse, where we compare its artificial language with the many natural language-forms of expressiveness. The transformational features of the two languages fascinate, are often determinative – and yet it remains unsolved to what type of expressiveness, intelligence and thought formation they should belong.

A further consideration would underline that the separation between the 'natural' and the 'artificial' intelligence serves the fortification of a more cultural and scientific background. Semiotics will underline that the name giving of the two regions of intelligence produced a *sign* rather than any scientific or philosophical factual *articulation*. So the question arises whether the concepts 'mind' and 'brain' are a *sign* – or are they an articulation of reality? In a semiotic light, the two forms of intelligence are neither separated autonomous entities nor entities with a set of specific features that justify the question, which of them has the character we in earlier decades called 'consciousness'?

A first glance at the Google N-gram analysis of the concepts of 'Artificial Intelligence' and 'Natural Intelligence' shows for the period 1980–2000 a curve in which the two types are nearly identical. For the period from 2000 on there is a curve indicating a considerable deviation: one is for 'Artificial Intelligence' downwards and one for 'Natural Intelligence' upwards. The deviation between the two thus makes clear that Natural/Artificial Intelligence terms function as building bricks of a discourse based on a flow of 'I'/'Me' variations. That discourse seems a more and more accepted component of our so-called 'natural life' discussions and their attempts to enhance intelligence in daily life.

2.1.2 The Metaphor 'Stalking'

Deciding about the use or prevalence of the term 'consciousness' or the term 'brain' is indeed not a simple issue; in particular in the context of law and legal science. The one will never become completely identical with the other. Yet in recent days – in social as well as neurological and other behavior research – the human 'brain' became a central issue. That step from understanding 'brain' as a neuro-physiological organ towards appreciating its social importance leads modern thought. The metaphor 'stalking' has a clear sense in this context, although the word has, in daily life, a considerable variety of meanings. However, an expressed dynamic is undeniably applicable in the case of the brain as a dominant concept. More than fifty thousand neuroscientists in the world write on the subject in more than three hundred journals! When criminologists tell us that in most cases stalking does not rise to extreme levels of violence despite high numbers, we note how our scientific industry displays a comparably high activity that also never rises to a level of alarm or harassment. So what about the metaphor?

Stalking is primarily a matter of social behavior, in particular of how to maintain and manage social relations. It became only recently overshadowed by legal and in particular criminal dispositions. That concerns the structure and effects of a conscience. Recent developments in criminal law exhibit enhanced attention to the way the human brain relates to social activity. But if the stalking really begins to replace publicity and related commercial activities, we have to consider several issues which also play a role in the recent dominance of the e-culture.

First, rational thought formation seems no longer maintained in that type of culture. Rationality is recognized as only a part of human experience and wellbeing, and this should straightforwardly lead to a more encompassing view on the total position of the human brain.

Second, what is offered to play a role in relations should explicitly *not* look rational but awaken empathy; it should show a baby-face rather than an earnest intellectual expression; it should provoke compassion at first sight and not awaken feelings of incompatibility. An important component of that newly developed position is that all relations awakened or vested are *in se* addictive. The latter is an obvious goal in the frame of the brain stalking. Socio-political decisions, including macro-economic considerations, determine whether these addictions are openly initiated.

Third, we mention an important implication, which is closely connected to the omnipresent e-culture. Most of the decisions made, or politics designed, focus on the personal data of the player/citizen. Those data not only became a commodity but also a major object to deal with and to use as material that can be sold/bought and can bring profit at an hitherto unimagined scale. Facebook is a good example.

One's identity thus became the most recent merchandise. Protecting one's identity and all goods (also e-data) that carry data to which this identity belongs or which represents it drives the new market. Selling and constructing new e-plays is not for the social good of creating new joyful dimensions for citizens, but for creating new trap-nets in which the player will not be aware how he or she plays the role of a new commodity. That is technically perceivable: a player can only play the game when everything about him or her is known and can be transferred to other networks in all languages that offer to buy it.

All this pertains to individuals who exploit 'normal' social relations. Law's attention goes mostly to one specific pattern of conduct that needs correction through legal intervention and perhaps psychological therapy.

Law's scope coincides with what is considered as 'normal' and 'acceptable' social behavior. Psychology tells us how stalking corresponds to established clinical pictures, which show strong delusions or delusional fixations. Stalkers target strangers all around, desire personal contact with them and seem insensible to the maintenance of their personal opinions and actions.

Brains feverishly research brains today. This fascinates and shows again the forceful dynamics that were altogether expressed by the metaphor 'stalking'. To stalk means: to approach a target, to move gradually, quietly and as nearby as possible with the intention to submit that specific target to the desires, dreams and delusions that drive the stalker. It is not beyond interest to highlight that the existence of such a target is the main condition for the vehemence that characterizes stalking. And it is not evident that the target is always a natural one. How many times is the object of the stalker a phantasm, a construction of the mind, or the product of scientific construction, often resulting from logical or experimental deductions?

The Other and Myself should be two separate individuals, so that a balance of rights and obligations can form the major frame of knowledge, any lawyer would say. An inappropriateness of the balance is provoked in the process of stalking, as it is often in the process of scientific research and epistemology. It means one has to clarify the phrase of the paragraph: brain versus brain – what does it mean?

To stalk the brain means: to gain insight in the brain, not spiritually but as a reality perception, which can eventually, yes, most preferably, be imagined. We do not want the brain as a specific piece of material in our hands, like Hamlet, but we do want to perceive the brain precisely as it functions – and make extensive use of it! The latter is perhaps a major problem: if advertisements do not work anymore in the eyes of corporations, would the application of brain research replace them? And is that the way we wish to become facilitated by legal provisions of all kinds, or would that be a wrong message?

2.1.3 Stalking and Application

It is the case that makes the practice, not the law in the books or related legal-theoretical aspects of what comes to the fore – that is a well-known but widely discussed opinion. It dominates in all layers of a lawyer's activity and his applying law in social contexts. But are cases not also theoretical constructs? The gap between application and activity is often translated in a conflict of interest: the interest of the client is a lawyer's interest and the function of law in social settings is society's interest. Do these really clash, or is this clash a theoretical construct as well?

The first word we hear on the street as well as in law offices refers to a basic concept of law since Roman practices: the word *applicatio*. It is up-to-date in Common Law as well as in Civil Law, and has been used even in Marxist law practices and legal practices supervised by Chinese Communist Party officials. Many of us consider that any legal system in any cultural circumstance is a matter of decent and appropriate application of laws and their implicit rules. And who says *application* does also say *interpretation*. The two expressions are pivotal for our talking about law, they can be heard on the street, in political debates, in law schools, and be read on many Internet sites. They specifically balance on borderlines between naïve and non-naïve attitudes. This balancing act is evident. Any spoken language is in every possible situation a medium of inter-subjective footing. Words mediate always and everywhere and are only effective when they are not transferring solely *one* meaning.

But the power of words is more general and forceful than we are aware of in daily life. Law, in particular modern law and its multiple access to IT issues, Internet and e-communication, has the tendency to be *everywhere* and *always* powerfully present. It is possible that the daily streams of advertisements with seducing images of products and producers do not have the effect of creating our behavioral patterns. But we cannot make an appointment, buy something, rent a house or a car, promise a payment or pack a suitcase without becoming entangled in legally structured behavioral dimensions. We are not aware of it, because the powerful non-presence of these dimensions is the result of our brain activity, we discovered. That is an immense difference to our traditional belief about our consciousness being the source and master of our behavior. Today, advertisement and behavioral consequences are more subtly researched and changed under the guidance of neuro-scientific insights. Brain activity and consumption are, as we already mentioned in the above paragraphs, directly connected and transformed into legal acknowledgements. Our cognizance of the brain is based on the closest possible observations by means of all kinds of electronics, from scanners to internal observation instruments. The latter surpass simple observation: the brain became the targeted object rather a vague notion of consciousness. 'Stalking' appears to be the correct expression for mastering human behavior, lobbyists can tell us.

What is more: words spoken or written, remembered or just engendered, are always mediating. The special mediation between a speaker and a hearer has become its most studied form in Western philosophy, named the subject–object model or also the speaker–hearer model.

The consequence is that *words of law should not command* (an opinion often formulated on the street) *but mediate, and thus create commonness.* That modification introduces the concept of 'stalking' on a broader basis than ever before. Mediations enforced are elements of a culturally determined discourse, and in the special case of law closely related to texts. It may sound strange; the stalking (as an extremely global and forceful type of mediation) underlines that law's language is textual and spoken words in law are governed by texts. Wherever a jurist functions, he or she does so on the basis of, and is at the same time limited by: texts. That basis is the major composite of law's practice. A lawyer may not cite those texts loudly but she speaks, thinks and acts accordingly. The same is true for citizens: all participate in legal interaction, but this activity is seldom only *legal* activity. Words are signifying this observation: they never transfer solely *one* meaning, but always mediate bi-directionally – in an active as well as a passive sense. The managing of *legal* concepts is in that regard a *political* affair.

Notice that texts are no longer only written or published on paper or written as e-communications in their traditional forms, but they also reign in forms that at first sight have little to do with what we normally consider a text. Rites, quotations, procedural behaviors, orders of speaking within a session – even robes and other forms of clothing – play a text-determined role. In a deeper sense are all those textual phenomena manifestations of the institutional character of law. In law is 'text' an institutional element. One should take care to understand this specificity of legal speech acts: those acts are always determined by law's institutional power: the text.

Indeed, this textual identity surpasses a mere presence of legal texts in all appearances and articulations of the law. Lawyers think law in a textual fashion, and this propensity reflects on the way their thinking evolves, as well as on the way the law positions itself. Textual thinking offsets the occurrence and plausibility of non-subjective, or less subjective thought, yet it is recognizable as a constituent to the law's focus on legal certainty.

This insight has consequences for legal practice. Any practice of law is a manifestation of the institutional/textual interpretation-bound features that prescribe a lawyer's professional speech acts and activities. Even the laws of a land do not form an exception here. That specificity of legal practices embeds all facets of the classical *applicatio* in the life of a lawyer. One should never understand him or her as a subject that solely applies laws! Each client of a lawyer, as well as each citizen 'talking about law', is in the embrace of *applicatio* as a mode of being – never as a preferred instrument. This purports to the seriousness of the situation.

All language in and of law is governed by an inherent attitude called 'application', canvassing all of (social) life as a world waiting for and posited towards (legal) application.

2.1.4 Hermeneutics

We should venture one more step in this same direction. The existence of texts, often appreciated as the basis for *hermeneutic* approaches (which include applicative steps everywhere and are specifically located in religious studies as well as literature and law) forms a foundational feature of Occidental civilization.

It could very well be that, for instance, our contemporary fascination with 'intellectual property' as a legal discipline relates to this basic feature. Consider the ways our electronic communication (Google and others) treat associated rights. In every quotation there are legally determined values at issue, they become readable in the modes of writing and they vibrate those legal conditions in book publications and at Internet sites. Hermeneutics reign, intellectual properties accompany them, and legal semiotics clarify their complex meaning relations.

'Talking about law' is in this regard exceptional, as it belongs to *pre-semiotic* fields of meaning and sense. Semiotics focusing on law or hermeneutics paid no attention to this subject. It embraces a precarious position of the citizen who talks – a position that is at least characterized as an in-between attitude among naïve and non-naïve speech acts. The latter is unknown in traditional hermeneutics. That observation illustrates the dominance of binary thinking (represented by subject–object relations) when *application* of texts (fragments) or their *interpretation* is at stake. Yet we have to notice that the talking about law also has its forms of interpreting law and in particular legal texts. The role of textual writing in law cannot be overestimated. In most legal systems a written piece of evidence trumps any other in such a manner that for many legal acts proof in writing is considered an absolute prerequisite: no text, no proof. In essence, the textual determines the real in law, or at least, the non-textual is considered non-essential in legal reality.

Is the difference between the everyday level of speech and the level of professional legal speech in the accepted *degree of naïveté*? It would mean that what a citizen is allowed to say is not always allowed to be said by a lawyer – part of that allowance being the social situation in which the two speak: the street being again confronted with the law office or the court. The first is barely, the second is entirely determined by institutional features, which society and culture embrace.

Lawyers read with interest the philosophical attempts to a deeper understanding of the newly revised discipline called *hermeneutics* in order to find the means of understanding their practices. They read the famous *Wahrheit und Methode* (Truth and Method), a 1960 study written by Hans-Georg Gadamer in Heidelberg, Germany. Jurists recognize immediately two aspects which relate to their work: (1) the identity of basic thought patterns in law, literature and religious studies, and (2) the role of language in their efforts. They were informed (which they experienced in a non-philosophical manner) that *application* was a knowledge move at the crossings of language and culture. Neither is evident to understand or to accept as a field of change, reflection and management of conflict, in behaviors or psycho-social attitudes.

2.1.5 Hermes

Hermeneutics became classified as 'the theory of interpretation'. But it is a theory of *understanding* rather than a theory of *interpretation*, because it contains more, and other, elements than a fixation pattern such as: if 'a' is 'Y', then 'b' must be accepted as 'X'. Its logic and its socio-logic are more dynamic and complex. The Ancient Greek figure of Hermes illustrated this feature. The Greek word '*hermaion*' denoted piles or even pillars of stones positioned on hills in the countryside and in the city streets as marks belonging to the houses. Hermes lived in those stones to guide walkers and wanderers on the street. The messenger of the Gods protected travelers as well as merchants, and thus heralded the Roman *pater familias*.

Interpretation is never a skill for one person alone – it is a spiritual force that could inspire the lawyer in his social context and in his task of interpreting occurrences in a way that makes o/Otherness prevail. Hermeneutics concern a *total* occurrence, and this totality may be one of the most powerful challenges one encounters in a lawyer's practice. Indeed: Hermes is alive in legal practices of the twenty-first century.

Is that a *sign* of its full *signification* for the idea of democracy? One cannot deny the scope and importance of this consideration. Gadamer explained that a text has an overpowering effect on all of us, on artists as well as on theologians but on lawyers specifically. Any interpretation or application of a law is *not* a form of power, mastery or stalking but rather a form of serving, of public work called *applicatio*. The latter should be cherished in law and fully accepted by lawyers in their activity, because it carries a very special idea with it: a view on the commonness of cognitive and normative functions which our words exercise.

Words of a law express *only*, in terms of our reading and understanding, those words that are the innermost signification of the case at hand. The dominance of the text, as outlined in the above pages, is, in hermeneutic perspective, *not* a matter of exercising power but of understanding to bow to the superiority of the text.[3] The signifying of Hermes' stones fascinates again. Are they symbols of the signs that are composites of hermeneutics? It remains clear: the *applicatio* correlating with language and culture dominates our conceptualization of culture itself – and, at the end, of ourselves as a Self. The stones are neither Hermes' private property nor the result of an indifferent ramble or its opposite: a careful engineering. Hermes' stones were a text, a tag, an index, or a sign. Who knows?

2.1.6 Voices, Speech

The self of a lawyer considers stones: words are like stones, words appear important but they are in essence unimportant, they are not effective when single and they impress only as a pile. They fit together, in each other, in one hand altogether; when thrown up against all forces of gravitation; they never fit into each other when broached all in one. This is how we throw words in social complexities, as if we throw them in a river. Some sink immediately, others bounce, some make noise and others disappear in silence. With them we live, and we always interpret them in the course of life. Every stone has a voice; our hearing and understanding varies daily, hourly, every moment while moments appear as grasping irregularities. Everyone contributes one's might. Platitudes are effective when we throw stones, or words. They are never qualified as objective values thrown in the water. Voices will never be neutral, judges should consider this. But together they are a rock, they always beam forces of gravity and demonstrate the force of sound, balance and purposefulness together in: a stone, a word. That is our level of interpretation. We simply cannot escape. We hear voices. We cry, regret, shout, and reverse.

2.2 CASES AND CASUISTRY

The many vows withstand time and history. Each fragment of understanding legal practice will legitimate the sentiments of law's

[3] H. -G. Gadamer, *Wahrheit und Methode* (*Truth and Method*), J. C. B. Mohr/ Paul Siebeck, Tübingen, 1960, p. 294.

practitioner: 'I cannot *say* what I do, I can only *do* that!' It is a sentiment in the innermost feeling of judges as well as lawyers, and gives birth to the enormous importance given to the *case* in law.[4]

2.2.1 Code and Case

One should not forget, however, that just as the Napoleonic codification brought the concept of the *code* to the public fore, the *case* is at that same place, bearing the same accountability and the same cultural weight. However, the case is and remains a *legal form.* Cases suggest that a naïve truth in life exists and with it a naïve level of knowledge. The names of cases, we will find, are powerful suggestions about their naïve evidence – although there is no such naïveté. On the contrary, cases are often treated as *dogmatic* principles (in particular in Common Law) and as a *sign* of a justification for mastering complex fields of knowledge and signification – both as fields of *legal* meaning.

All this implies that the case is *not* the appropriate instrument to understand the legal practice as a coherent whole – neither in theory nor in practice. And it is a widely spread misunderstanding to see the case as the catchword of coherent legal practices. So we propose another path. We underline that law's practice is a path to a commonness of language, leading to the creation of a common 'view'-point, which is a common point of articulation, and ultimately the path to accept legal practice as a commonly acknowledged field of *constructing facts.* Those constructions are the central task of the lawyers, the jurist or the judge.[5] The factual character of their arguments, the fact-based components of their discourses, or the facts that bring the client or citizen solutions for life, are his or her construct. That is a motivation to provide a series of features linked to the *case* and its many implications. There is every reason to consider the following features inherent in any mention of 'the case'; they are: the *dynamic* character of the case, its relation to a *social structure*, its *authority*, its basis in *social experiences*, its *institutional*

---

[4] R. M. Unger, *The Self Awakened*, Harvard University Press, Cambridge, MA, 2009. See also: F. Fleerackers, *Affective Legal Analysis: On the Conveyance of Legal Awareness*, Duncker and Humblot, Berlin, 2000.

[5] Compare this view to Richard Posner's outcry: 'Lawyers should make a greater effort to present facts to judges, not so much the facts of the case, the adjudicative facts, which most lawyers do emphasize, but rather the background or general facts that influence a legislative decision.' R. Posner, *How Judges Think*, Harvard University Press, Cambridge, MA, 2008, p. 11.

features, its *time and time-complexity* and the role of *names* in considering the case.

2.2.2 Characteristics of the Legal Case

(A) Cases are dynamic and differential

The phantasm that the stream of live events can become objective knowledge by means of using fixating elements of language is mirrored in the case. To unfold that phantasm, one has primarily to suggest that cases are dynamic *in se*. But for a lawyer the qualification of the stream of life events by means of calling that stream a 'case' is meaningful and often sufficient. The dynamics of life are, for a lawyer, implied in the case; any case of law makes the stream of life ready to be fitted to all legal grips or determinations law can arrange. In this case, the dynamics will be accorded legally valid names that originate from naïve-natural occurrences in everyday life. Those names are family names (of persons involved) or names of specific events (contracts, political statements, treaty names) or major procedural steps in law. It means in essence that legal language suggests another reality and another world than everyday reality while using the term 'case'. There are no corresponding cases to any legal case. Words of the case imply meanings and their consequences that are unknown in reality.

In other words: the breach in naturalness that leads from naïve towards non-naïve meanings is decisive. Legal facts are legal – non-legal facts, which belong to constructions in everyday life, decidedly differ. Are legal facts: 'facts'? Yes, indeed, in so far as both are social constructs. No, not at all, in so far as legal facts are constructs of the legal meaning complexity and, added to that, a construct in naïveté. However, the two meanings of 'case', and their semantic implications, are not only opposites, they have their constructive character in common: law's cases stem from a *double* force of reduction whereas everyday cases stem from a single reductive move. This commonness of their constructive nature implies that both – legal and non-legal cases – are forms of expressivity in view of a specific reality or of reality as such. The latter is the origin of the dynamic character of any construct called 'case', underscoring its differential stance, since cases are predominantly governed by similarity and comparability. Any construct in naïveté is founded on preordained membership, correlation and closeness. This kinship of cases carries the burden of legal as well as non-legal thinking. Expressivity in 'talking about law' and of 'saying law' strives for unfolding meanings in common, which should balance the most influential powers in society.

(B) Cases profile a social structure

Cases depend on specific social structures, and they contribute to their balanced functioning. There are no cases beyond a recognizable social structure. A comparison between law and medicine is very illustrative of the issue.[6] Both disciplines relate to different social contexts and are instigated to contribute to different structures. The lawyer–client relationship differs from, and is yet identical with, the physician–patient relationship. The identity, which creates a well-determined social structure, is anchored in the text. Medical as well as legal texts are meant to allow the formulation of a diagnosis and the latter is an implicit instruction to the lawyers and the physicians how to act. Those texts are indeed scientific documents, but do not forget that they also mirror a pattern of accepted truth and values in society, which lay down the prescriptions for action from physician as well as lawyer. This complex situation of the case expresses how a culture should unfold. This profiling occurs at the basis of rigidly fixated restrictions of meaning.

But notice that those ground lines of cultural fragments embrace *the voice of all* who are participating in that pattern. The voice of all is a basis for medicine or law, their practices included. No wonder that in order to gather the voice of all, conditions must be fulfilled. One of the major conditions is that an *actor* is detectable, whose *activity* can be clearly traced. As a consequence, legal practice involves discussions about the characteristics and idiosyncrasies of the subject in law.

That consequence often regards a person in the legal sense of the word but it also concerns a living individual with specific properties. In both are subjects involved who are forced into one legal category (for instance 'accountable' or 'not-accountable') so that they do not disturb the pattern of thought or application. This habit will be maintained, as Jonsen and Toulmin suggested, even where legal case patterning includes moral issues.

(C) The authority of the case

Any case, in medicine or law, shows a most remarkable mixture of order and disorder. The order of the rationality that functions as a basis for the concept and the connected conceptual thought patterns meet the disorder of all social interests and diversities of a cultural pattern in which the case should function. The '*sans frontiers*' functionaries experience it

---

6 Jan M. Broekman, *Intertwinements of Law and Medicine*, Leuven University Press, 1996, p. 121ff; Albert R. Jonsen and Stephen Toulmin, *The Abuse of Casuistry*, California University Press, Berkeley/Los Angeles/London, 1988, p. 231ff.

every day. But the latter, disorderly patterns are fought and will lose rights as well as claims 'in the name of order' so that the authority of the case will be reinforced. Social behaviors will ultimately result from that twosome: whoever follows the order will be provided with a solution to his or her problem, will be socially accepted and will be allowed to follow outlined patterns of behavior.

Whoever does not follow the order of the case will not succeed. To accept what is implied in the case has a *social* effect. Why? It is because the case is never the case alone: in the case of the treasures of a culture, its values, norms and expectations, are packed. To deny them makes life impossible. Cases represent an image of social order that lawyers put forward. They are themselves not entirely secure about the content or effects of that image, but they are (in all regards like the citizen) obliged to internalize and follow the case. The case, engraved in (legal, medical, theological, psychological but also chemical, mathematical, physics) texts represents a framework of cultural determinations. They are, in that regard, to be accepted as a meaning *in se* and as a halting-place, a '*caesura*' on the path that leads to signification. This is not merely negative. Without halting-places, social order would succumb. However, one could argue that the absence of any *caesura* entices reawakening, or at least *catharsis*, and thus movement, as the Latin origins of dynamic coincidence or *casus* illustrate.

(D) Cases are experience based

All cases are based on experience – not on an experience in life as a general phenomenon, but on experience in a specific discipline, a particular field of meaning that relates to the dimensions of an individual life. These can concern all sorts of disciplines, among which law and medicine belong to the most frequently appealed. The Self-experience of the individual often determines the casuistry initiated in life. That experience will not appeal to totally unknown discourses or practices, because all human self-experience is ordered along the main lines of a culture. So *Culture*, so *Self* and thus so *Self-experience*. Decisions encapsulated in cases are socially relevant and all-accepted patterns; cases do not revolutionize but confirm the effect of vested thoughts, interests and views.

That conformity is powerful and a generally experienced and accepted mode of unification. It conceals conflicts in views and volitions. The natural naïveté is far away, because cases are – one is surprised to conclude – *signs of conflict*. The case is useful and valid as long as the disharmony of interests, values and norms is not uncovered. The case covers conflicts. It is this concealment that makes the case such an important component of social life: cases cover and uncover conflicts long *before* they function in a solution-based decision or diagnosis. The authoritative structure of cases makes them indispensable in human life.

Unveiling that structure makes the non-naïve character of the case visible. That is an important issue to consider. The subject in the case, no matter whether the case is medical, legal, psychological, or of any other discipline, is formatted along the patterns of that discipline. The patient, the legal subject or client is medicalized or juridificated before that subject is given a role in a case and thus will be categorized as the material components of the case. Disciplines format patterns of specified knowledge, which include the *self* that functions in and appeals to the special discipline's knowledge presented. *Cases mirror Selves* – that slogan offers a valid representation of the case's authority. The latter represents the relevance of a *case* for social inquiry as well as for a dynamic understanding of human interaction. Any analysis of a case must therefore apply *difference* and *dynamics* as a constitutive component.

(E) Cases are institutions

In Chapter 1 we outlined the character of social institutions as a defining power for law and legal practice. Legal discourse in particular appears as a preferred instrument of institutions and institutional thought patterns. A case is an important component of that general feature. Cases serve institutions; their authority derived from and remains tributary to them. What does this mean? Their task is primarily semiotic: they have to function as *signs* that indicate the institutional character of legal discourse. Their sign character, however, remains hidden in their central functions at all levels of the discourses of law, technical as well as theoretical. Cases will become exchanged (via their names in standardized ways) in legal discourse so that they often function as a word with specific features! While functioning in that manner, cases are in the first place components of a legal language that fulfills a signifying task in democracy.[7]

A consequence is that cases connect different social dimensions while integrating them in the story they offer. For that reason, cases are often understood as *social miniatures* – even when they pertain to large sections of society. They focus specific, selected and fixated fragments of

---

[7] See the interconnections between Marxism and psychoanalysis, in particular in France, and the publication of C. Castoriades, *L'institution imaginaire de la société*, Du Seuil, Paris, 1975, Part II (translated by K. Blamey, MIT Press, Cambridge, MA, 1975). For law and legal discourse, see: Neil MacCormick and Ota Weinberger, *An Institutional Theory of Law*, Springer, Dordrecht, 1986.

social behavior that are apt to the creation of an *image*. They are a means to focus on social complexities and as such preferred by lawyers. Here is a remarkable difference as compared to physicians: the latter use the case-construction to create a diagnosis and seldom to understand the roots of an illness as a social problem. In this light, one should consider that cases in law determine the patterns of meaning of law's practices. This connection between *case* and *institution* leads back to Max Weber's famous introduction of the concept of 'Idealtypes'.[8]

(F) Cases, time and time-complexity

Time is studied in a Weberian *Idealtype* and its conclusion is remarkable. Time is *folded* in the Idealtype and thus becomes *a moment that can be repeated infinitely*. This is a respectable force in legal discourse. Time folded is also meaning folded. The fold characterizes the case. The latter never deals with a complex story-function in the creation and practices of legal knowledge. It leads to law's world: facts are offered *as if* they were naïve-natural components of legal thoughts. Who is brought to accept law, must accept the fictions implied.

Time and the plural are closely intertwined. They form the *here and now* that makes the case so powerful. Castoriades referred, as many before him also did, to Aristotle: every move is a stream, and so is time. At every moment, time is itself and as such the same, as it is in essence *now*. Only time's relations with the world around are different. The *now* remains identical and it is continuously different because of its infinitely varying functions in what we call the past and the present. Aristotle suggested that the *now* will follow the always moving object, that we only know in its 'before-and-after', that is in its move. That is exactly what we perceive, and what leads us to the concreteness of the objects in the world around us.[9]

The suggestion of these considerations is important: as if complexity is a matter of time. That is specifically interesting for law. Already Plato dealt in his *Timaeus* with the issue. What is the word 'always' expressing, he asks? In essence it seems a *misuse* of the language; its inner dynamic moves against the course of life, against each becoming as if a concept of language that is not committed to time were possible. It is not. But exactly this controversy is feasible in the legal construction of the case.

---

[8] Max Weber, *Wirtschaft und Gesellschaft*, Mohr, Tübingen, 1914, Ch. 1.

[9] Aristotle, *The Physics, LOEB* Harvard University Press (translated by Wicksteed and Cornford), Vol. IV, Book IV, xi, 219a[20-30].

Identity of what is *becoming* and what *is* was in the case enforced by the *fold*. The latter enables legal discourse to maintain the concept of the case as expression of an extreme independency. Its next step leads to strong and stable positions of disciples like medicine or law. Each case appears in this light *exemplum vitae*, a pattern of interaction in life.

(G) Cases and names

It was already mentioned that cases in law were objects of a specific nomenclature. In Common Law as well as in Civil Law most cases bear a given name. What does this mean?

Notice that the essence of cases that they should fulfill the task to assist the required clarification of occurrences remains hidden in the name of the case itself. Cases bear a meaning before they help create meanings in the discipline. The bearer of a meaningful name has a secret to keep: the sense and meaning of that name, which is clear for insiders of the discipline only. The name is in this situation a *sign* that the case hides its central meaning, its character and its purpose and hides its relation to social reality. Cases are presupposed to create stability in life and science, but they perform that task in an alienating manner: they hide meaning to propose and discuss meaning. In doing so, legal casuistry illustrates that law must refer to institutional powers in order to achieve a functional (re)construction of reality. The latter is for law the field to explore and solve conflicts and irregularities. In addition to this insight, it is clear that law's patterns of knowledge also display this structure with the case as its center. The latter pertains to the structuring of legal arguments as well as the legal interpretation of non-legal texts.

Names of cases refer to encapsulating processes of personification. The latter is an interesting philosophical issue. The name of the case conceals that this name is also the name that legal discourse will suggest as if it were an acting subject. Proper names and names of institutions, corporations or other entities that are repeated as the name of the case, mark the thought pattern as well as the totality of social relevance, political and economic interest given to the case. It is often difficult to indicate the borderlines between the names that refer to components of the case and the names or related interests. No wonder that rigid rules try to determine accepted borderlines in those cases. It remains concealed that all this mirrors the fundamental structures of law and in particular the structural determinations of law being valid law.

All this becomes clear if one consults the websites of, for instance, the 'Legal Information Institute' or the 'Oxford Standard Citation of Legal Authorities', or the US 'Historic Supreme Court Decisions'. Once one reads those sites, one is once more placed at the borderlines between everyday and professional language. All proposed names give the impression that they belong to a natural language, but in a more concealed manner they possess a precisely described function and meaning of the legal discipline. The higher a court's ranking, the more frequent the use of names of persons, firms and corporations. No wonder – there are lower numbers of cases, and the authority of the cases is augmented with the ranking: a truly first class institutional mechanism. Names of cases are signs of the specific features of law and legal discourse and of law as an institution. All three determine the many ways in which those names should be used legally. Relations between names and cases are encountered at many layers of language and knowledge; they are illustrious servants of law as an institution.

2.2.3 Law's Casuistry

The characteristic components of the case are also characterizing law in its entirety. It means that one of the most profiled concepts of legal practice has a decisive theoretical signification. Structures of law, legal thinking, legal application and thought formation appear in the dimensions of its practice in society. This observation will please jurists who are used to extralegal criticisms in politics and social sciences as well as in theoretical considerations. Their constructs called 'cases' fit to legal discourse and its language. But the *coherence* of all mentioned features is and remains a problem if we consider the many ways of 'talking about law' and their implications!

Essential seems the question *how* those hallmarks relate, are brought together and operate, and *who* is entitled to master that great pattern. One can at least say that all of them serve a specific purpose: to create a (legal) meaning with which the professional can operate. This has important links with a more general observation: the evidence of what was observed is based on the fact that human life is always anchored in meaning. Legal and all other scientific as well as practical discourses depend on that basic insight. Where there is no meaning, there is no fact. This seems foundational in all regards, and underlines the importance of interpreting life as the development from sign to signification, even *before* any interpretation (of texts: the basic fact of law) can occur.

Hence the pre-semiotic importance of the expression, which has been designated more than once as the point of departure for any insight in law, the utterance: 'talking about law'. In that expression is a secret drive to unveil which is called the semiotic perspective that is hidden in each conversation and leads to our major forms of reflection – even those beyond the distinction between naïve and non-naïve thinking. Each case embraces these dynamics. Each case is a text and as such a con-text. Jurists presuppose that we are able and willing to understand reality and the social world along those continuously changing perspectives on meaning. That is the dynamics of what we call 'legal practice'.

2.3 CASUISTIC AND PRACTICAL

Multiple definitions on various websites describe the Latin word *casus*, and several refer to law and legal discourse. The expression is even heard on the street. Is the derivate from the Latin expression typical for law and medicine, or does that word belong to scientific disciplines all across the globe? *Casus* is an originally linguistic term, but it is firmly anchored in law and medicine. The reason for that specificity is that both disciplines are designed to reach out immediately to everyday life situations. Hence their importance for life in general; modern life in our Occidental culture cannot be imagined without legal and medical practices. The pattern of applying general insights to individual situations is apparently one of the most general and thoughtless moves of the mind. A specific feature of that mindset is that texts and their static character deliver a safe catalogue of actions to take in emergency situations – a truth that seems essential for legal as well as medical options. Dynamics and casuistry form a contrast in many situations.

2.3.1 Casuistic Rhetoric

Rhetoric is, since the Ancient Greeks, an art in itself. It concerns motivation, meaning proposal and politics of word powers all in one. No wonder that legal rhetoric became monopolized by institutional powers, by political, governmental, corporations – all alike. All of them try to master and manage the open road from sign to signification, and are thus semiotically relevant. That activity is powerful and inclusive in so far as it pertains to the inner dynamics of speech and language. Those forces direct our everyday talks, our expressivity on all occasions and our living concepts such as health and justice. The latter illustrate that *there exists no static language at all.* As a consequence, legal meaning is never *by its nature* identical with itself and meaning is always different as it focuses on change. Goodrich concluded: 'Law, which reasons explicitly by images, analogies, associations and other narratives or metonymies similarly represents or dissimulates the invisible affects or unconscious desires of legal custom, judicial intention or sovereign will.'[10]

But we do not accept this. Our daily experience yearns for stability, fixated identity, ethical stability and scientific truth. Nobody wants to perceive him or herself as different; everybody wants to feel continuity and sameness as a means to fight time and its continuous change. This is what colors the rhetoric of law, and that very same argument suffices to convince the walkers on our streets to appeal to law. Jurists concentrate on what appears at the surface of life, of texts, of understandings, of perceptions – in short: they focus on everything that could establish certainty, identity, continuity and safety. Jurists will take each text as a final word, and each delivers a stable set of interpretations, recommendations and conclusions. This is how law makes itself acceptable even on the street.

Although this may fit our attitude and intention, there is a problem to encounter. Our positions in life are never an exclusive matter of steady surfaces and surface structures. Even the generally accepted idea that life and texts are surfaces leads to the conclusion that there also exist deep structures, in-depth regions of meaning that direct our understanding and appreciation of such crucial disciplines as law and medicine. The French semiotician Algirdas J. Greimas (1917–92) proposed a name for the *surface* of texts and behaviors, which he called *phenotexte*. This designation explored the idea that language is a layered phenomenon.[11] As a consequence, deep structures of language also received a name – they were called *genotexte*. In the 1960s, Julia Kristeva focused on the indispensable function of the text in all types of language, and studied both levels as a representation of the dynamics *in* language.[12] The latter approach brings the flow from sign to signification (studied by semiotics) in language to the fore. The opposition between *speaking* and *writing*, which one encounters in the linguistic theories of J. Searle, is no longer of essence,[13] because the two take an equal part in the engenderment of

---

[10] Peter Goodrich, '*Jani Anglorum*: Signs, Symptoms, Slips and Interpretation in Law', in C. Douzinas, P. Goodrich and Y. Hachamovitch (eds), *Politics, Postmodernity and Critical Legal Studies*, Routledge, London/New York, 1994, p. 107ff.

[11] See Thomas F. Broden, 'A. J. Greimas: les anneés de formation' *TEXTO! Textes & Cultures*, Vol. XX, No. 2, 2015.

[12] Julia Kristeva, *SEMEIOTIKè: Recherches pour une sémanalyse*, Du Seuil, Paris, 1969, p. 278ff.

[13] John Searle, *Speech Acts: An Essay in the Philosophy of Language*, Cambridge University Press, Cambridge, 1969.

meaning. Where the textual surface relates to occurrences and meanings in everyday life and its observations (what you 'normally' see), the deep structure leads you to 'other thoughts' and probably also to 'a second opinion'. There will be no doubt that this insight, and in particular the proposal for understanding a phenotext in contrast to a genotext, seems most important for legal practice.

2.3.2 Dynamic Language

The distinction is a first step in structuring language as such, and in understanding language as a dynamic phenomenon. A lawyer cannot deny that such insights are important for his practice. Words, expressions, texts and other linguistic issues are the materials of that practical activity. They concentrate on one particular datum: the text. The cases he or she constructs are meanings; they are derivates composed of those materials. There is no way to deny the true character of the lawyer's practice: meaning and its instrument: language, play the most dominant and socially accepted role. Jurists say what words mean and their complex signification obliges another person or an entire institution to act accordingly. An entire political philosophy is concealed in this form of obligation.

A Self that answers this obligation is grown in a field of meanings, which presupposes its participants to fulfill a number of specific profiles. It must unfold an identity, it has to cultivate a stable awareness of social networks (in fact: a whole and sound power named 'sociability'), it has to grow a sense of citizenship and of understanding what it means to live the life of a legal subject. Words do more than communicate! In the midst of them, and with them as a preferred means, words create meaning, create reality – is 'reality' more than a word? It is: for lawyers words are the pillars of their profession. But words are always embedded in other word-complexities and ultimately in meaning. The latter is the center *and* the ultimate borderline of a word. Language is always dynamic and never an ensemble of static data, as we explained before.

In the light of this observation can any meaning in the hands of a lawyer be understood as a *reliable* datum? What authority can law via its institutional power impose on words spoken by a lawyer? No wonder that we restrict ourselves to the surface of words and their texts, even to the evident appearances of the phrases in legal language that oblige us to act, when we are 'talking about law'.

2.3.3 E-Communication and the Street

What is the function of those words, while spoken on the street or comparable public places? Is the street limiting their meaning or is the street an unknown dimension of human communication and its words? The latter seems an odd idea, because already in the fifth century BC we find reflections on what is said on the street and its relevance for a democratic society. But in any case, today one feature is relatively new amidst what occurs on the street: streets became fields of electronic communication, and certainly no longer just between one person and another. Interactivity is on the street, but not solely between those who are just walking there! Modern e-communication systems and the smart phone as technique and symbol of that communication enrich, deepen and intensify the dimensions of togetherness and solitude within spaces hitherto disregarded. They do so despite all hesitations and philosophical cautions in view of the virtual world and the basic features of e-media.

The intensity and multiple forms of e-communication on streets are a new and surprising phenomenon. The street as index for everyday experiences also changed, and we will therefore deal elaborately with the features at issue. For considerations related with casuistry as a dominant character of legal practice, the language of the street seems to be of immediate interest. Does the language, which manifests itself on the street and should be described analytically, include its e-communication? In other words: did smart phones change the essence of language we encountered in its multiple forms on the street? Is 'word' no longer a word, and 'sentence' or 'text' no longer what they used to be? The theme that unfolds here before our eyes does not seem to be studied thoroughly. Indeed, smart phones and other electronic media instruments are overwhelmingly present on the street, but there is until now no research that convinces us to think in terms of revolutionary changes in the use and understanding of language, and certainly not in so far as the language of law and legal discourse are concerned.

2.3.4 Casuistry and Communication

Consider a number of aspects that touch the outlines of casuistry as a dominant feature of legal practice. What occurs if these aspects appear to be linked to new fields of social and scientific research on the basics of IT, e-communication and their multiple uses in modern life?

If changes in the profile of the street can be determined at all then those changes concern *the behavior* of people on the street, and certainly not their language as such. Walking around with a smart phone also changes, for instance, the walking itself as a physiological phenomenon. In short: neither the language nor the walking seem at issue, but the interactive behavior. The mass of 'selfies' taken on streets and plazas, in parks and at riversides as well as in thousands of other places and under different conditions is a symbol here: 'I was at that moment with you and looked at …'. Conclusion: if there is a change in the modern street, then that change pertains in the first place to people's behavior and behavioral attitude.

A consequence is that changing profiles and patterns of the street today can be caused by changes in techniques of communication, but the latter are an (often determining) factor in the entire process of change, and solely that process itself in all its social and technical views should be studied to profile our twenty-first century culture. Everyday life and its language patterns are a component of that issue. To research 'what communication is today' is apparently a multilayered and complex theme. Even its shadows on legal activities and procedures, judges' behaviors and victim responsibilities are parts of that totality. Do not forget that the capacity to experience occurrences in life could be reshaped by the intensity of e-communication in society. The latter could become an element of law's casuistry.

The question of e-communication on the street and its impact on law and legal practice focuses again on the multiplicity of languages which are at stake. It has been remarked before that any non-naïve-natural, often artificial language pattern is in need of a natural language to be framed, and only on the basis of the latter can it contribute to understanding and communication. That is also the case with e-communication and its linguistic means. Even if the street would communicate solely in e-languages on Twitter or Facebook, perhaps in e-mails, the street would need to submit itself to a natural language to express its means and clarify its communications. Try to explain a mathematical formula without using a natural language, and you experience what is meant here. Any non-naïve-natural language needs at least fragments of a naïve-natural language in order to articulate and transmit meanings. That is the leading thought that has guided us until now and this guidance imports also in the context of e-communication. It also illustrates that our remarks on language, word, text and speech remain valid for any consideration of law and of legal issues.

2.3.5 Smart Phone Streets

An unfolding critical literature on e-communication suggests a variety of items to consider when law in its relation with an e-loaded communication technique on the street is at issue. The main question pertains to the compatibility between legal thinking and the thought patterns of life in an e-world. Those concerns are serious: *can law in view of fundamental changes in communication on the street still be perceived as a social power and a mediating force in a conflict-loaded society?* To formulate only the beginnings of a meaningful answer to this question, one must focus on various in-depth themes. Their keywords are: body, presence, and language. Those concepts function primarily in the context of law's power being accepted in a society driven by e-communication, and do *not* pertain to questions whether IT and wider e-communication issues can be or are regulated by law.

Until the recent global development of e-communication, the streets were populated with persons whose *bodies and corporeal properties* were not questioned. An absence of such consideration endured through the ages, and the human body was seldom an issue during the centuries in Occidental culture in which one discussed its legal bearing. That changed in our days. While entering the twenty-first century, the cell phone had already become a substantial part of a citizen's hand. But the latter did not connect to the Internet. The cell phone caused an expansion of talking – but talking implied the possibility to provide and receive further information on the whereabouts of the participants in conversation. It proved to change more than just the contexts of conversation: the later smart phones developed global information, data provision and GPS positioning. Those features enriched the hand and made it into a new body part: hand *and* smart phone webbed, as if they were a virtuous component of human anatomy. Indeed, they became indispensable for modern life and did more than a laptop to challenge the borderlines between the artificial and the organic, the non-naïve and the naïve attitude in social life. It should be underlined that this view is completed by the fact that numerous artificial agents developed in the last decades. They made social life more *situational* while multidimensional and even global; they made it more *smart and unpredictable* while organic and natural, and nobody knows when *robots* will replace or become integrated in the culture and application of smart phones.

The *legal* dimension comes down to the question of compatibility. What does it mean that in view of those new dimensions of human body and mind, law's language (and thought patterns) remain limited to categories like 'accountability', 'causality' or 'liability' – presuppositions which are limited to subject and/or object of law in a traditional sense of the word?[14] Be aware, this critical philosophical consideration does not refer to eventual qualities of any branch of law named 'IT law', 'Mass Media Regulations' or '(Big) Data Protection'. At issue here are the limits of expressivity one encounters in legal discourse and the dimensions of the image of man in law. Are the basics of a non-naïve-natural legal language, which the 'subject–object' model represents, still effective on streets populated by smart phones?[15]

2.3.6 Presence

The major suggestion of all types of e-exchange is that with the smart phone at hand or that phone *as* hand, a life in multiple dimensions persists: a daily and naïve life on the basis of observing concrete issues, and a virtual life that unfolds virally at any moment. There is no consciously operated switch between the two. That situation is most clearly experienced when the presence of people on the street is questioned. 'Were you there?' will be clarified by a *selfie* as well as by a *story* – by an *image* and by *words*. The virtual environment expanded at the moment the smart phone and related electronic means were introduced and blurred the clear lines between 'mine' and 'yours', 'here' and 'there', 'now' and 'then'. Asking for a precise identity equals the introduction of alienating considerations. How can I know? Were we present in a virtual world, did I follow my Facebook friends, or did I look at all the 'likes' I wanted, or did I walk that street – why should I know or be aware of all that? An utterance of such feelings illustrates the expansion of my world of experience far beyond the range of our senses. A virtual environment, a Web presence during a walk in the woods or on the street no longer creates awareness about the dimensionless extension of my capability to see, hear and touch data that can only be digitally accessed. Why should I wonder whether my smart phone has become an organ just like my fingers?

Such enriched touches, which reach out to more than one dimension, give an immediate visual, audio or even haptic feedback. Are those

---

[14] We mention these, because they were already the subject of semiotic analysis in the PhD publication of Jacob I. de Haan, *Rechtskundige Significa en hare Toepassing op de Begrippen 'Aansprakelijk, Verantwoordelijk, Toerekeningsvatbaar'*, Versluys, Amsterdam, 1916.

[15] Parallel questions pertain to law and legal discourse. See the nineteenth Internationales Rechtsinformatik Symposium IRIS in Salzburg, 2016 in: *JUSLETTER – Die Zeitschrift für IT und Recht.*

touches not the best for orientating myself? Why then this talk about *presence*? I am chatting whenever I want to, find friends on Facebook and learn about and am informed about their behaviors, plans and ideas. I seem to be everywhere at the move of my fingers, with the recognition the instrument delivers via my eyes or my voice, which is kept in the memory of the phones of all who populate my world. That is a very special form of presence. It is an interaction with the world that is mine, and with the immanent feelings of being immersed in that world. But together with that immersion comes a sense of presence, which is not necessarily only real, yet, even perhaps, predominantly virtual – but has the same value for what in earlier days was called a 'real' experience. Presence has indeed many faces, but the sense being shared dominates in presence. All e-dimensions illustrate the silent presupposition of sharing. Walking the street is a scene of sharing, and the multiple dimensions of a togetherness, being a mixture of real and virtual, present and timeless, challenge law's self-images.

A lawyer would indeed raise questions that concern the compatibility of modern law and modern e-exchanges. What sense does it have to require an identity of those who populate our streets with hands that move smart phones? Can an ID (a piece of paper, or a card – in any case a written document) still be legally required? What should a lawyer or even an average police officer tell a person whose life dimension is mainly a matter of Facebook? All today's presences awaken the impression that different modes of presence are realized *at the same time* as well as in hitherto unknown forms of togetherness and sharing: what has law to say – can legal discourse remain compatible with that language?

2.3.7 Data

In addition, we consider the (in)compatibility of e-exchanges and the world of data, which is at first sight a truly new world and language phenomenon. What about its features and its relation to law? The question can hardly be answered because of its complication and novelty but the issue must be brought up in this context. Do not forget how law is physically and mentally incorporated in modern life, and so are all forms of e-exchange in our days. Borderlines between the natural and the artificial are no longer standing; they rather became instruments of social practices and the consideration whether law can be maintained in this complexity of social elements may be essential. Many characterize our modern data-industry as a new evil in society, which is above all transforming individuals into slaves. Who has feelings in the field of Big Data? What IT-functionary can incorporate his or her feelings and emotions in the work? Who is able to produce public utterances that meet the secrets of the data-industry? What role does an individual, or an acting subject, have in the large frameworks of global data provision and their macro-deals?

One of the features that characterizes the modern cult of data is that the data flow is never effective in a world populated by individuals operating on their own. On the contrary, the most persistent ideology of the data trend is that everything can be broken up into and thus represented by data. All data correlate – their correlation does not ground in individual decisions to create such an effect. Consider the fact that nobody is individually held responsible for data because service providers and other parties are always involved. Hence the multiple attempts to develop adequate legal data protection. That legal form of protection is not based on the desire to protect the data-producing individual consciousness of the citizen. The voice of an individual is hardly given a chance to be heard; institutions offer individuals a balanced and legally stable situation in cases of contract, sale or other responsibilities in which legal certainty plays a role.

One of the philosophical considerations about this field pertains to the fact that data are *not* equal to information or knowledge. What do we know when data are provided? That is a question which politicians meet almost every day. But keep alert: data interpretation and manipulation come only *after* data provisions. The latter need thought patterns, but do they also need a thinking subject and its conscious thought formation?[16] In any case, we should say, the issue of embodiment returns here. Bodies are signs for consciousness. A consciousness is represented or symbolized by the concept of subjectivity and its relation to an outer (often material) world indicated as objectivity. Does the question of data, which profile human life, bring us back to this nearly old-fashioned subject–object scheme?

2.3.8 The Cyber-Story

What are 'data profiling human life'? Are they components of real life, or just elements of a virtual reality, or a process one could call the 'datafication' of human life? Will someone ever know? Or is cognition in this context only a matter of imagination? Once we lose the subject–object concept, we do not know anymore. The questions are real; they

---

[16] See the components related to our knowledge formation in David Eggers, *The Circle – A Novel*, Vintage Books, New York, 2013.

belong to today's reality, and yet belong to a past imagination called 'cyber-reality'. In the days that candles provided the necessary light, the word 'electricity' or 'electric' was magic, as the famous US poet Walt Whitman's 1855 line 'I sing the body electric ...' expresses. His words foreshadow the body on our streets, which cannot be thought of without embodiments of the electric nowadays becoming electronic. Whitman's contemporary, Orson Fowler, had already described electricity in 1844 as the 'grand agent or instrumentality of life in all its forms, all varieties of human, animal, and vegetable life included ... the master workman, or grand executive, of every animal function and mental exercise'. Consider that very same electricity as the new appearance of an old principle and technique, manifesting itself far beyond simple forms of communication. It is true on our streets when Whitman described electricity as 'the pulses of fire ceaseless to vivify all'. Background and inspiration for his revolutionary thoughts was his strong belief in the unity of body and mind, of soul and body – an inspiration shared by many of our contemporaries in all political and social ideologies. The famous study of Aspiz on Whitman mentions another contemporary who declared that electricity was 'the Jacob's Ladder' between the material world and the realm of angels. Walking our streets filled with hands holding a smart phone connects us to the notion that being on the Web, connecting to the Internet, surfing pages and files assisted by specific search engines, reconfirms *the body electric*. In the final chapter of this book, we come back to the features of the street where Whitman wrote: 'And if the body does not do fully as much as the soul? And if the body were not the soul, what is the soul?' Is it an illusion to suggest that the *body electric* is in essence what the *body interactive* or even the *body virtual* is today, although the word 'electric' may not be more than an expression of fascination regarding the newness of the world around us?[17]

It is not, and in fact the pen on paper already did the same in earlier days. A study on virtual reality of the last century argued:

> Non-linguistic tools, like erasers, do indeed insert a distance between ourselves and our context-embedded mother tongue ... using a rubber eraser does affect us in subtle, psychological ways. Teachers understand that getting a student to use an eraser marks a significant step on the road to good writing.

---

[17] Walt Whitman, *Leaves of Grass*, in: *Poetry and Prose*, The Library of America, p. 118 (1855), p. 250 (1891); Orson S. Fowler, *Love and Parentage*, New York, 1844, p. 26; Harold Aspiz, *Walt Whitman and the Body Beautiful*, University of Illinois Press, Chicago, IL, 1980, p. 143; Jan M. Broekman, *The Virtual in e-Education*, IIS Publ. Cie., New York, 2004, p. 96.

> A self-critical attitude distinguishes good writing from bad writing, and picking up an eraser means that we are beginning to evaluate our own words and thoughts. With electronic texts we speed along a superhighway in the world of information, and Boolean search logic shifts our mental life into a high gear.[18]

2.3.9 Bodies and Law

All these observations consider the intensifying sensuous experiences that do not lose their grip on the bodies walking around. Their provoking extension is no longer purely instrumental and the tools become organs of a new body with extended and sensuous possibilities. The 'likes' and 'not likes' focusing on Google, the sometimes-vicious legal battles about the rights of the search engine only underline the importance of the consequences pertaining to the new body. Today, there are fundamental differences between the cyborg of the 1990s and the actual Walkman; between the data-suits and data-gloves of the cyborg and the smart phone fingers' exploring reality; between the freedom of the virtual Self and today's freedom of the 2016 '*Pokémon Go*'-playing hand of the WorldViews blogger. The game is described as a worldwide craze, eclipsing Twitter, Tinder and other social media. Pedestrians are endangered; properties disrespected; places in danger of becoming sites of disorientation.

Via the cyborg and cyberspace phenomena one returns to the issue of *data* as related to the human mind/body. Did we understand the human body too perfunctorily when we talked about that body in terms of flesh and blood as well as its metaphors? One of the problems is the integration of data in a human life – a consequence of the abovementioned datafication. The provision of data can no longer be detected with an individual body's own senses. That distance between body or mind on the one hand and data on the other creates social problems, of which an awareness of alienation is important. Is the reception of data linked to those alienation feelings?

The coexistence of real world experiences and computer generated synthetic objects causes a superimposition of the virtual in relation to the real world. We do not know yet what the psychological conditions are and in what way we can transform that superimposition into a positive experience in which law in its traditional sense would have a place. We are hardly aware of the problems this lack of knowledge evokes. The

---

[18] M. Heim, *The Metaphysics of Virtual Reality*, Meckler Ltd, London, 1993, p. 58.

cyber-story of the recent past did not provide an answer to that question. It only tells us that a renewed appreciation of the human body can appear in metaphors, but the dimensions of those meanings reach far beyond the scope of our daily life. The human body remains the central point of reference, including in our attempts at empathy with cyberpunks.

The latter foresee, as A. Rosanne Stone wrote in her 1991 text: 'a time when they will be able to forget about the body. But it is important to remember that virtual community originates in, and must return to, the physical. No refigured virtual body, no matter how beautiful, will slow the death of a cyberpunk with Aids. Even in the age of the techno-social subject, life is lived through bodies.'[19] Does our notion of the body, as outlined in these words, reconnect us with law and legal discourse representing a discipline in which the presence of the body relates to maintaining the basic norms and values of Occidental culture?

Law's casuistry accompanies us in that direction.

That direction, or specter of directions, is complex and multilayered. We are not surprised when we encounter mothers who Twitter, are on Facebook, phone, or read e-mails during their breastfeeding. The baby is fed and that has nothing to do with the mother's behavior, she may think when critically questioned. That misjudgment leads towards various directions. The breastfeeding is not a moment of solely feeding the baby, but it is in *all* regards a *holistic* event. Attention, speech, attitude and the bearing of the baby are all marks of the mother's actual behavior, a behavior that includes the engenderment of a mother tongue. The breastfeeding, the bodily tongue and the mother's words are therefore not only linguistically close but seem basic stages in the development of a human being. Notice that the baby is learning sounds and sound patterns while developing in the mother's womb. Twitter and other WiFi related sounds are included in the language learned at *all* moments of the baby's life. The naïve-natural language transmitted during this most vital scene from mother to child is apparently neither purely naïve nor absolutely natural, but rather scenes of a continuously changing pattern that determines the very beginnings of life. The post-cyborg features on our WiFi streets do indeed reverberate in the nursery room and its breastfeeding.

---

[19] A. Rosanne Stone, 'Will the Real Body Please Stand Up? Boundary Stories about Virtual Cultures' in M. Benedikt (ed.), *Cyberspace: First Steps*, MIT Press, Cambridge, MA, 1991.

2.4 CASUISTRY DISCOURSE

Many of the above considerations illustrate that law focuses on *all* senses and components of the human mind. If that focus is unsuccessful and legal practice appears fragmented, then feelings of revolt develop – legal institutions and their citizens do not function in peace, they lose their orientation and tend to dysfunction in social and political frameworks. Speech performance is a provision in which sensuality and rationality operate together and as a whole. The particularity of law is, as legal practitioners experience every day, in the exclusive reference to and use of components of language. Words and verbal fragments, parts of sentences and even of texts belong to the *speech act materials* of the lawyer. The specificity of those fragments and parts characterizes the profession in its totality – no matter whether one focuses on a particular lawyer, a judge or any other functionary of law as an institution.

2.4.1 Materiality and Articulation

The expression 'word' functions in a metaphorical sense if one claims that 'words are the materials of the lawyer'. No word exists or functions alone; each word is embedded in a context of linguistic and cultural nature. No word on its own will ever bring a solution to a problem, no word will be understood if spoken alone, no word is ever the 'unit of language' we imagine. That simple observation is also relevant for the legal case as a predominant concept inherent to the legal profession. The case is often imagined as a word, but cases need an embracing context to function and thus, to be understood, need discourses – but all discourses are not equal, and their differences need cognitive means to be made operational.

We consider that not all discourses possess the same degree of vigilance. Some are extremely level headed and others are like an articulation of drowsiness. Not all linguistic utterances are clear and not all discourses have the materiality of what our speech activities engender laid out before us like a landscape that invites us for a walk. We seldom experience the material components of our various speech activities in all clarity – a philosophical issue of importance that is neglected in multiple philosophies of language and speech. Material components of our speaking are at a distance from our words and their intentions; the literary light thrown on legal cases only confirms this interval in this peculiar situation. The interval makes us think of a large tree at the borderline of a wood: the tree perceives its scenery/context through its foliage; a broadleaf tree thus differs from a pine as far as the possible clarity of observation is concerned. But even when leaves are dropping, clarity is not achieved. The tree remains wood and no stargazing will change that characteristic feature.

Do humans differ? We perceive the materiality of our speech in different moods, which are seldom completely at a level of total awareness. In a woolgathering mood, we view an impressive landscape through our eyelashes that includes the materials of our cases in law. Through our eyelashes we see the foliage of the soul, and in how many ways we are involved in our daily and continuous stream of utterances. In that mood, the main components of the materiality of our speech compose a fascinating landscape. The landscape of material components demonstrates what is inherently present in the referential powers of words on the basis of which meaning is created. The total composition may deliver an imaginary outline but the relation between matter and articulation remains of primary essence in understanding speech activities.

Through our eyelashes we perceive a landscape with little plants, flowers, cacti, remnants of various meals or richly filled dinner tables – all together objects our speech acts refer to, no matter whether they exist or not. We see chunks of all kinds, find notes as well as bills, cash money, tax forms, papers with conclusions and duties described that are overgrown by grass and fruits, we notice animals walking around, cars driving and trains on the horizon, we remember images of friends and people known and unknown, are suddenly aware of paintings we recognize, art objects next to rubble, books drowned by music of various categories, or sounds we hardly recognize but seem present in daily life. The landscape is omnipresent, flat and hilly, watery and dry, unordered but always impressive, attractive and abhorrent – never ours but never completely separated from us. Materiality and articulation belong together, but we lost the relevant cognition about that togetherness. Do we know what we say? Rarely, this reflection tells us. The strings of words we utter are incidentally and certainly not systematically meaningful but seem enough for our communication to appear reliable.

It is remarkable that gaps between the materiality of our speech and its articulation are equally important for understanding the case in law as for law's discourse. It does not help to give cases the property of a discourse, so that one is held to understand cases as miniature discourses. The real problem is not solved in that manner because uncertainty about the relationship between a word and its materiality remains. Can articulations overcome that particular uncertainty through their meaning-making activity? It does *not* seem to be the case, because that activity incorporates but never dissolves the uncertainty. The imagining that words are clean and properly defined particles of a language, well-ordered and loaded with explanatory energy predominates many philosophies of language – but that image is utterly wrong. Uses and misuses of the 'discourse'-concept illustrate that conclusion. A word is a wager, a tiny sheet from an exuberant dossier, a smallest particle in an ever-turning basin, an extremely reduced particle that stems from a collection of treasures called a 'thesaurus' in linguistic theory. If that were not the case, I would have to be a genius at every moment of my daily conversation and amidst all I articulate in my lifetime, to offer the proper word at the correct moment and with just the very meaning. How do I then imagine the speech situation: is that a togetherness of speakers exchanging the precise words needed to clarify a peculiar moment of life? Is a speech situation, a 'talking about' or 'saying for' a form of linguistic utterances without the need for mutual trust and respect? Those properties are absolutely not necessary when words have this precise character and can be placed in such a correct form and position.

2.4.2 Discourse and Speech

Indeed, theories of language often underestimate the significance of the speech situation. The latter is a matter of togetherness, of expectation and trust encapsulated in a process of speaking and hearing surrounded by many other social components that vary from one speech situation to another. Law and its casuistry belong to the latter speech situation and are rich in varieties of social components. The character of *action* in any speech situation is extremely rich and complex and giving that character the name 'interactivity' is already a dangerous simplification. The concept *discourse* has the same features: it is too simple and lacks any deeper understanding of a speech situation. That is most certainly the case in modern philosophical approaches pertaining to knowledge and cognition. They emphasize the importance of *change* as a feature of meaning, and not the *momentary* articulation of meaning. Each articulation is a reduction of an encompassing material reality and a fixation of utterances, which the incidental and actual mind supports. It has been expected since the 1970s that the concept of discourse could help overcome those difficulties in the heart of a philosophy of language. That expectation was lively in the field of *legal* discourse – but legal practices illustrate today that no substantial change of viewpoint and/or practice took place.

A discourse can change its content, system of references and meanings at any moment. Do we have a reliable insight into the features of a discourse? Its words are solely one aspect of the content it provides as the sum totality of speech acts performed in daily life. Already in

Ferdinand de Saussure's 1915 *Cours de Linguistique Générale* there were doubts about the possibility always straightforwardly to articulate this wealth of linguistic utterances. These led in the midst of the twentieth century to new theoretical attempts in philosophy of language, the *linguistic turn* and the movement called *structuralism*, but the real issue was not even tackled: does the material or immaterial concept of something always need a correlative language? It is clear: if that is really the case, then words are needed. But are they?

The question whether they are, or are not, needed, focuses on reality. Does reality need a language to exist? If that is the case, all that is real depends on the word. Is that a feasible thought? Remember Ludwig Wittgenstein's posthumous notes published in 1953 as *Philosophical Investigations* with the central thesis that philosophical questions arise when the logics of language are misunderstood. Today, it could be a TV quiz: do things need a language, a word – or does a word need a thing? The producer of that quiz would perhaps remark that *both* views are correct but decidedly different! That difference indicates what role language plays in reality, so that language is never just a means to fully master reality. But if language cannot achieve an understanding of reality, does, perhaps, the concept of discourse contribute better to that understanding?

2.4.3 Foucault's Discourse

In the last days of the year 1970, the French philosopher Michel Foucault pronounced his inaugural lecture at the *Collége de France* in Paris.[20] He opened that lecture with bewildering words: 'Instead of taking the floor, I would have liked to be covered by the word and led beyond each possible commencement.' The speaking or what has been spoken beyond a single speaker position receives the philosopher's attention. That is a revolutionary viewpoint and a context for the discourse concept that received much attention in modern philosophy. What is spoken finds an identity. The terms discourse, exposé or oration, indicate a series of speech clusters brought together in a specific perspective. Its spoken words, written texts or other articulations include their specific references. The most fascinating aspect is that such a discourse profiles speaking people while they speak and exercises power over them. Those powers are in the first place powers of exclusion – their analysis plays the major role in Foucault's lecture. In other words: what is said means in his

20 Michel Foucault, *L'ordre du discours*, Gallimard, Paris, 1971.

view also what is *not* said and was *not* allowed to be said. Linguistic semiotics reaches further than a material evidence on the dynamics of language. But that dynamic becomes clearly visible in the social effects of a discourse. Discourses control, select, organize, distribute or redistribute social powers, and discourse techniques unfold in social processes of exclusion. A unique contribution to the Continental philosophy of the 1980s is this lecture's emphasis on the reverse side of reference and meaning-making, which is a social process rather than a determination of linguistic insight or a new viewpoint within a philosophy of language.

Three observations pertaining to the lecture are of interest:

(1) The first concerns the speaking subject, its name and position. A subject is not a natural phenomenon but should be understood as the product of a social process: a speaker is allowed to speak because of social implications. Limitations, contradictions and truth-values are the most powerful directives a speaker encounters the moment he or she enters the discourse. Today, half a century later, we speak about '*post-truth*' as the word of the year 2016. The *Oxford Dictionary* mentions it as 'a circumstance in which emotions and personal convictions are more important than objective facts or data'. One is a speaker (a speaking subject or a subject because of a permission to perform a speech activity) because of a specific competence, a legal position or a cultural determination. Selective processes, in particular exclusions, create the subject. They name the subject 'speaker' and the speaker 'subject'. Hence the beginning phrase of the lecture: 'I would have liked to be covered by the word and led beyond each possible commencement.' Can one escape from those exclusionary mechanisms?

(2) A second concerns the birth of concepts, which function as means of describing reality. These concepts are commodities in the market of science; they appear neutral terms that are at home in a language but in each of them social powers are embedded that guide citizens and society.

(3) Finally, each discourse relates to its own community. That is in particular the case with discourses, which are the home of a scientific discipline (like law). They are based on a specified language and the artificiality of that language suggests a reliable and codified access to reality. While unfolding its meanings through words, discourses create a subject together with social appreciations and a specific community.

Foucault would add that language may be seen as a natural phenomenon, but as soon as sounds, signs and meanings enter social spaces, they are submitted to social control via norms, values and expectations: exclusionary features altogether. The discourse unfolds through the speech activity of a subject that acquires its name and position through that very same activity. Words seldom touch their own essence. They are not able to save their meanings in the selective processes of social norms, which decide what to say and what not to say. Their essence might be in plural but the singular is their appearance. Suggesting that a language is a natural phenomenon implies the negation of exclusions that go with its social embedment.

This Foucault lecture suggests that there is no human speech activity, no spoken, written, registered or in any other manner fixated word beyond the limits of social patterns, norms and values. Freedom of the word is a freedom within the boundaries of social norms and their patterns. Even the speaking subject itself is an instrument of that patterning. Discourses are the linguistic product of such socially governed areas of articulation. Their specificity is not in a language but in a social code. Only speech patterns engendered by institutions are viewed as a discourse. Various discourses explore multiple words and meanings to sustain the discipline and institution they represent. It all includes the consequence that there is no 1:1 relation between word and meaning. Making-meaning culminates in a complexity of signification which often differs among terms even when the matter at hand seems identical. One meaning in a discipline discourse thus differs from another although they concern the same reality. Foucault's lecture is after all a deep sociological analysis of power and its influence machinery that creates our self-awareness even when we speak, articulate or make meaning.

A conclusion from these considerations has pivotal importance. Foucault's focus on the discourse concept did not involve subtle linguistic analyses and discoveries but was limited to the social force fields in which a discourse unfolds. That has interesting consequences for legal discourse, as his famous lecture opened the gates to a wider acceptance of the 'law-and-language' theme in legal scholarship, theory and semiotics.

2.4.4 Law's Discourse

Only a few years later, the concept of a 'legal discourse' was introduced to the legal community.[21] Its acceptance soon became general in the

---

[21] Jan M. Broekman, 'Recht en Structuralisme' and: W. van Gerven, 'Over Recht en Systeem' in: *R & R, 4 Maandelijks Tijdschrift van de Vereeniging voor*

Occidental world: it became, via exclusionary social forces, the discourse of a discipline and its community, with a strong ritual and authority. A legal discourse was, in contrast to a legal system, defined as 'a totality of speech acts embracing particular features', which are – as explained in the above pages – institutionally anchored. It was clear from the very beginning that a legal discourse articulates and thus engenders a particular *episteme*, a specific view of law's eye, the view engaged in all 'talking about law'. Jurists agreed by means of exploring their legal practice to the principle that the discourse within which they practiced would be and remains *constructed* (that is: a non-naïve language operation) in accordance with social principles and values like security, certainty, procedural correctness and a general acceptance of translating signs and facts from everyday life into legal language.

One of the major purposes of this specific discourse is in its pretension to be total, and thus embraces a specific totalitarian view on reality: there is nothing that cannot become subjected to the law – an ultimate statement that dominates the legal practice in all regards. Even an urgent appeal from my fellow creature (an often existential moment in life) becomes transformed via the legal discourse into a *right* – and thus becomes a matter of human rights. Through the introduction of this interpretation of a *right* the language of legal discourse is able to reduce a human, social or even intimate relationship with another person into a legal relation, including obligations and accountability. The subject of language must transform itself into a subject of the legal order. It all implies that the dominating legal discourse causes a specific reduction of speech and text, which prepares for the (reduced) specificity of legal meaning.

This observation is at the borderlines between 'talking about law' as occurs in society in general, and the 'performance of legal speech acts' that characterizes a lawyer's practice. The citizen and the lawyer clash at this line in understanding fundamental approaches towards issues of humanity. A lawyer's attitude, including his or her intuition, human feelings, social values and ethical ideals, while grasping the essence of law in life, cannot withdraw from an ultimately transformational activity. Legal articulation is the goal to never forget. That articulation is laid down in the dynamics of legal discourse, which has to perform its speech activity even in texts and textual understanding in the many prescriptive

---

de Wijsbegeerte des Rechts, Vol. 2, No. 2, December 1973. See also G. C. J. J. van den Bergh and Jan M. Broekman, *Recht en Taal*, Preadvies van de Koninklijke Notariële Broederschap, Deventer 1979.

ways law dictates. A lawyer's feelings of humanity can lead him to choose a particular word, expression, sentence or text, argument or insight – but it can never lead away from a final *legal* meaning of a decisive pronouncement for which he is completely responsible. That responsibility can be transformed into accountability when tested in law: here is the anchor which law's discourse provides for its subjects. All these remarks illustrate that a legal discourse is not composed as a naïve-natural language, but it is, being the discourse of a specific discipline, an *artificial* and therefore non-naïve-natural language phenomenon. The striving of each lawyer to compose a perfect 1:1 relationship between fact and word within that discourse seems a basic requirement. Law's discourse is in this light the most general and also the most radical instrument law provides to manage its (social) practice. The legal case functions as its central goal and at the same time its central methodology.

The radical breach between occurrences on the street and what occurs within the boundaries of law's discourse, in other words between the ordinary citizen and the lawyer in Occidental civilization, is a breach of meaning and major signification processes. Law and politics are close neighbors at that moment and in this regard. The difference is perhaps solely but importantly at the level of the absolutism inherent in the relevant maintaining of meaning. To conclude that *meaning* is the key for law and order seems correct. The consequences of that upholding are indeed manifold.

This insight is confirmed in each legal case. Cases are constructed, written with specific purposes in mind, spoken with a selected authority and applied with eyes on one and only one predominant social stance named 'objectivity'. But remember Aristotle's remarks and observations on *time*: all connections within which time plays a role display a different feature. The *hic et nunc* may remain identical with itself, although the context differs continuously. The identity of the *now* goes hand in hand with the differences it displays in all regards. The difference is in the case of the *now* inherent in the identity. This appears as a genuine philosophical riddle. The tensions of that enigma are registered in the legal case, which seems blind to that complexity of the *hic et nunc*. The case wants the momentary to endure, and not to show any difference of importance with the moment in the past. The denial of change equals the denial of the flow of life itself. Each human life is directed towards any form of o/Otherness. That life-bound direction withstands the (legal) immunity to the changing otherness one meets in everyday life. But in daily life, one cannot resist the continuous change and the immanent otherness of all occurrences. If one attempts to resist, one will not be able to live on.

Meaning and sense of each possible discourse include a specific dependence on the involvement of o/Others in life. The features of my involvement in others and vice versa: their involvement in me, characterize my participation in life – there is no way out of this pattern of determinations, which is basic for the totality of life. It is clear that this structure surpasses any dialogic understanding. This is because the social is not based on relations between two independent subjects towards which one can appeal. The totality of life is more complex and a greater wealth than the sum total of individual participants. George Steiner was confronted with this issue in his modern classic on the study of translation, and wrote:

> Only a small portion of human discourse is nakedly veracious or informative in any monovalent, unqualified sense. The scheme of unambiguous propositions, of utterances as direct pointers or homologous responders to a preceding utterance, which is set out in formal grammars and in the extension of information theory to language study, is an abstraction ... Scarcely anything in human speech is what it sounds. Thus it is inaccurate and theoretically spurious to schematize language as 'information' or to identify language, be it unspoken or vocalized, with 'communication'... Human speech conceals far more than it confides; it blurs much more than it defines; it distances more than it connects. The terrain between speaker and hearer – even when the current of discourse is internalized, when 'I' speak to 'myself', this duality being itself a fiction of 'alternity' – is unstable, full of mirage and pitfalls.[22]

The relevance of those remarks becomes clear when we consider that a discourse of law reduces this totality into a mathematical sum total of individual entities. Legal practice focuses on a total that cannot exist in daily reality. Legal cases illustrate the despair that is engendered when this notion is brought into the practices of law's speech activities. Foucault has *not* analyzed the notion of discourse in its linguistic components but he did illustrate in what regards a discourse functions socially as a force field that implants and maintains norms and values, meanings and significations, which are alienated from the major features of daily life. In that regard, one could formulate somewhat enigmatically: 'the power of legal discourse is the power of discourse'.

---

[22] George Steiner, *After Babel: Aspect of Language and Translation*, Oxford University Press, 1978, 3rd edn, 1998, p. 240.

2.5 DISCOURSE AND THE NARRATIVE

A legal discourse seems exceptionally deterministic. Why speak? Why construct an ensemble of conversation so incumbent for speaker and hearer? Is legal speech at the greatest distance to everyone's daily reality? It wants to regulate, to order, to comprehend everyday life, so what is the problem? But there is one central issue not mentioned and certainly not considered until now: the words, phrases, texts and other articulation activities featuring the legal discourse are never uttered as such and independent from other discourses or speech activities, neither by the citizen on the street nor by the professional lawyer while exercising his practice. In this regard, a legal discourse differs from a physician's discourse, a chemist's or a mathematician's discourse or the speech of a psychologist or a physician, because it enters inter-human behavior in all layers, so that the term 'stalking' was not used in vain. So: what narrative engenders law's discourse?

Consider that a lawyer does not only *speak* as participant in a professional discourse. He or she also *listens* – to the client in the first place – in the performances of that discourse. But his listening is already in itself a form of translation from the natural everyday language of conversation fragments exchanged with the client to the totality of possible articulations legal language embraces. The force of stalking is concealed in this ability of translation. What is articulated has been translated. That is the basis of the legal practice, and the *case* is the first product of this transformation, which takes place beyond the conversation level. A case is never brought to a lawyer as if it were a brute fact: his listening to the story *makes* the case via the translating during his or her listening! In the latter unfold the powers of a precious and forceful 'stalking' and this process emphasizes the speaking of a lawyer into an opposite of the 'talking about law' we hear in public places.

2.5.1 The Speaking Lawyer

Is reality only adequately described with words that possess solely one meaning, and with expressions that are beyond interpretation? Would it not be wonderful to concur with this idea and to continue our walks in life solely over the 'one word – one meaning' bridge? However, such a world indulges us in an unequivocal language and obliges us to annihilate all plurality of meaning, interpretation, perspective and ambiguity, so that a scary world of uniformity and the univocal is there – which is by no means our world! But is that world the lawyer's? Indeed, accounting for our daily life implies accounting for the language we embark upon; the quality of our thought formation and actual thinking enhances our awareness of the imperfections of language and linguistic expressiveness. Are social situations and scientific states of affairs unclear or ambiguous? We also do not dispose of a more precise instrument in our language, which was once described by Anatole France as the 'perfected cries of monkeys and dogs'. And how naïve is it to believe that the perfection of that instrument would result in a more perfect society? Yet, we are longing for a word unbound! It should show a suspension of unambiguous patterns of life and thought.

Unbinding is what metaphors do. To enjoy the unbinding of one word as one precisely defined meaning is to enjoy the power of *comparison*. Metaphors compare the incomparable when they compare seemingly unrelated issues in a fruitful repetition. So: 'An "A" is a "B"': but where is the emphasis – on the 'A', on the 'B' or on the 'is'? Any defense of a metaphor is the defense of either A or B without explaining the 'is'.

Lakoff suggested in this context that the 'A' is always a *target* and the 'B' a *source*, whereas the 'is' seems socially and philosophically *problematic*.[23] In our case, an *attitude towards the client and his brain* is the 'A' or the *target* in an artificial legal language and the *stalking* expressed in a daily language is the *source*. With the comparative dimensions in this language we register indirectness. The quality of our concern about the human brain is not addressed directly but circumscribed by the perhaps surprising expression 'stalking'. Any metaphoric operation hopes to contribute to a more intense and conscious understanding of (in the words of Lakoff) the *target*. The contribution is clearly what Black considered as 'an extension of meaning', which one way or another commits the reader to intensify his or her understanding of the situation, the target.

The central issue to be considered more properly focuses on the fact that a discourse of any specific discipline is never spoken in exclusivity! In the case of legal topics, one has to appeal to the artificial language of the law *and* at the same time and context to the naïve-natural language of everyday. And *a discourse is always embedded in a larger articulation entity*, which, for instance, both Lacan and Lyotard named 'a narration'. This entity is anchored in cultural norms and values, traditions and world views in which the institutional discourse of a discipline is embedded. 'Talking about Law' engages in *both* levels of expressivity, whereas

23 Max Black, *Models and Metaphors*, Cornell University Press, Ithaca, NY, 1962. See also: I. A. Richards, *The Philosophy of Rhetoric*, Oxford University Press, Oxford, 1936, and G. Lakoff, *Women, Fire, and Dangerous Things*, Chicago University Press, London/Chicago, IL, 1989.

'saying for law' *solely* engages a specific disciplinary and institutional level of language. Two contrasting understandings and uses of what can be called a 'legal conversation' thus come together. *Target* and *source* of speech remain *changing*; they remain to be moments of the dynamics of social life that incorporate law in different ways. The speaking of the lawyer is characterized by this dynamism, which is strongly supported by his desire to fixate, stabilize and define the indefinable moments of the life of language.

One should conclude: *all power of a discourse remains mastered by the narrative that embeds the discourse*. It thus follows that all expressivity of a discourse is secondary in view of the narrative it articulates. That conclusion is in any case *about* law's discourse and by no means a matter of *origin* of a discourse as articulation form.

THE TRIAD

'Talking about law', a specific region of speech and significance, appears in this light as component of a more encompassing *triad*: (a) the talk on the street and in everyday life; (b) legal discourse, in which graduations of position are included (for instance, a lawyer not being entitled to perform the speech act a judge is expected to perform); and (c) one of the great narratives in Occidental culture.

Only this triad unveils the multiple articulations in which life embraces law – the 'speaking' as well as the 'saying'. The triad indicates the levels with which the speech acts of a legal professional engage and mirrors the multiple articulations in life.

Neither Foucault's study of the concept of discourse nor legal theory's investigations of its proper discourse studied this triadic structure. It is, however, already implied in the definition of law's discourse. Remember that a legal discourse always functions in an encompassing discourse in which it can become meaningful. Its organization manifests the creation of a specific *episteme*, which is 'a legal world view'. There is no cultural fragment without this view, since there is no view that manifests itself as the sole representation of the entire culture.

The triad of human articulation relates to regions of meaning which the speaking lawyer has in mind. One perceives borderlines between everyday talk and artificial language on the one side, and between artificial/discipline language and naïve/non-naïve expressivity of a great narrative on the other. All those borders possess *constitutive relevance* in that they determine articulation and its meaning. This is a bridge from analyses of law's discourse towards an insight into larger complexities of social nature, such as attitudes, speaker positions and fields of interactivity or political values, norms and ideals that reign over street and court.

Foucault's principle of selection, choice and exclusion are effective in both. Notice, for instance, that the citizen 'talking about law' on the street is not allowed to enter the inner circle of legal decisions but is given the right to perform speech acts of all kinds that relate to the encompassing great narrative of his cultural context.

The relevance and effect of such determinations deepen the importance of the distinction between discourse and narrative. Consider the various levels of speech, in particular the semiotics of their signification, which are explored while we 'talk about law' on the street.

Within this complexity created by the essentialities of life, *Homo sapiens* needs to create a *narrative* in all cultural settings. That narrative creates and articulates him, and thus makes him find a place where he can withstand the overwhelming mass of articulations in nature and in social life he has to cope with.

But the challenge of this insight in the life of the *Homo sapiens* is that a *narrative* is *not* the product of an individual speaker nor of an individual hearer! He might already experience this in his growing awareness of what was described in the above lines: the narrative creates and articulates him, so that he can play the role of interpreter, translator, manager or speaker. Indeed, the overwhelming awareness of being constituted as a speaking subject by the all-embracing narrative could be paralleled to the feeling of being spoken to another speaker.

2.5.2 Voices of the Narrative

Nobody speaks or talks on the street as an isolated, completely self-aware and single individual! On the contrary: each individual lives amidst narratives articulated by voices of others. What characterized 'an individual' in Occidental culture has many philosophical implications. Some of these took and still take form in basic expressions, among which the words 'I' and 'Thou' or 'You' play a most prominent role. These function constitutively in the process of self-understanding, in social relations with others and still more generally in an awareness of the other or of Otherness.

Nietzsche experienced the importance of this process, and formulated his insight:

> [T]he engenderment of language and of consciousness … go hand in hand. And add to this that not only language builds the bridge between humans, but also their glance, their animation, their gesture; the consciousness of our

> sensual impressions in our Selves, the power to fixate them and to put them beyond us at the same time, when the necessity grew to pass them on to *others* by means of signs. The sign-creating human being becomes at the same time more and more self-consciousness; a human acquired self-consciousness as a social animal, and he still does, – even more and more.[24]

Do voices of the narrative focus on the described *otherness*? Steiner posed the question when he wrote in his foundational study on translation (the link between the question at issue and the linguistic-cultural necessity of translation is clear): 'We need a word which will designate the power, the compulsion of language to posit "otherness".' That sentence comprises a declaration of principle: *there is no language or voice without 'otherness'*. The question comes up: does the narrative provide any 'otherness'?

Steiner writes:

> [P]ower, as Oscar Wilde was one of the few to recognize, is inherent in every act of form, in art, in music, in the contrarieties which our body sets up against gravity and repose. But it is pre-eminent in language. French allows *altérité*, a term derived from the Scholastic discrimination between essence and alien, between the tautological integrity of God and the shivered fragments of perceived reality. Perhaps 'alternity' will do: to define the 'other than the case', the counter-factual propositions, images, shapes of will and evasion with which we charge our mental being and by means of which we build the changing, largely fictive milieu of our somatic and our social existence.

The remark is challenging as well as encouraging. Voices of the narration will, in the first place, be *heard*. The narration teaches us that the power of an ego is in the listening instead of the speaking. The expression 'alternity' was suggested to characterize this turn, and that suggestion should be well understood:

> The decisive step from ostensive nomination and tautology … to invention and 'alternity' may also relate to the discovery of tools and to the formation of social modes which that discovery entails. But whatever their bio-sociological origin, the uses of language for 'alternity', for mis-construction, for illusion and play, are the greatest of man's tools by far. With this stick he has reached out of the cage of instinct to touch the boundaries of the universe and of time.[25]

---

[24] F. Nietzsche, *Die Fröhliche Wissenschaft* (*The Gay Science*), Werke in Drei Bänden, Wissenschaftliche Buchgesellschaft, Darmstadt, Vol. III, 1882, p. 7ff, § 354.

[25] G. Steiner, *After Babel*, *supra note 22*, p. 220ff.

The reception of voices of the narrative is a tool that should be properly understood. It is in the first place a tool that allows language and linguistic articulation to exercise primordial power. But that power is, just like all voices of the narrative, never in unison, monolingual and an individual speaker's achievement. 'Ambiguity, polysemy, opaqueness, the violation of grammatical and logical sequences, reciprocal incomprehension, the capacity to lie – these are not pathologies of language but the roots of its genius', Steiner concludes: 'Without them, the individual and the species would have withered.'[26] Voices of the narrations would thus never have been understood – but are they what we think they are?

The case of the speaking and listening lawyer is exceptionally clear. His listening is entirely directed to the possibilities of speaking a professional word. In semiotics this attitude would be characterized as a process of translation: meanings of everyday must be translated into meanings of a professional character, which after selection must fulfill another, ruling role in daily language and life. But one must add that listening cannot take place beyond the exploration of a natural, everyday language. The listening and speaking must form a unity, for instance in the ultimate legal decision. The lawyer's speaking thus creates words with various meanings on a clear path: from the first signs the client sends him to the final words of a decision that intrudes on and orders life occurrences. None of them are completely separated from legal discourse as embedded in one of the great narratives in a cultural setting. *Law's discourses are profiled discourses*, and those profiles determine their fate in politics and other regions of society.

A recent, most powerful example in international politics and cultural life is the impossibility for Western law and Sharia law to meet at any moment of their unfolding socio-political structures. The absence of relations, visible in phenomena of mutual misunderstanding and distancing, is *not* a matter of differences in the respective discourses of law, but in the tragic mutual refusal to understand any of the voices of their respective great narrations. In other words: Western law is not able to recognize appropriate otherness in the great narrative that embeds Sharia law. The inverse is observable in the same regards. Contrasting voices of a great narrative do not perhaps sound conflicting. But they can, particularly in the realm of law, form a most powerful background for conflicts among large sections of humanity and disqualify the dynamics of human rights ideas and ideals.

---

[26] G. Steiner, *supra note 22*, p. 248.

2.5.3 Post-Modernity

The example illustrates that great narrations confront the *ego* with the complexity of its own structure. Moments of that confrontation are exciting, especially where the fixated meanings (already absorbed by the ego for its self-determination) fail to fulfill their semiotic task. It unveils that *the presence of the other (and of otherness) appears a condition for constituting the self* – at all levels of semiotic importance. Those conditions seem to be anchored in a great narrative.

There are many links with the concept of post-modernity, although it is an already old-fashioned concept today. They concentrate on the concept of the *ego* as a pillar of modern Western society. All reasons to consider a number of issues of that character do not appear in any theory of law or legal discourse. Why? The answer illustrates a worrisome feature of the latter, including its semiotic approaches. It suggests that law is regarded as an element of culture and in this quality submitted to the transitions of culture – post-modernism included. So, what has post-modernism to contribute in the framework of our reflections? It is always included in the subject and will never appear as the outstanding decisive factor. This will be reinforced by the fact that post-modernism and deconstruction theories seem to belong together. A post-modern jurisprudence will be witness to how the practice of law has to consider the fundamentals of deconstruction theories in order to better understand its proper textual and narrative character. But deconstructionist authors do not provide clarity about the relations of their philosophical insights and the practices of law.

How would a legal practitioner react to a prominent deconstruction formulation that tells him, how 'from the standpoint of deconstruction, every writing embodies a failed attempt at reconciling identity and difference, unity and diversity and self and other. A writing may give the impression of having achieved the desired reconciliation, but such impression can only be the product of ideological distortion, suppression of difference or subordination of the other'?[27] What is suggested here about writing is also valid for thought formation in general. The understandability of each practitioner, in law as well as in other disciplines, is at stake. Are insights in critical sections of philosophy and culture useless for law? Is the distance between the presence of the other or the experience of otherness as a constituent of the self so far from

[27] M. Rosenfeld, 'Deconstruction and Legal Interpretation: Conflict, Indeterminacy and the Temptations of the New Legal Formalism' *Cardozo Law Review*, Vol. 12, No. 5/6, 1990, p. 1212.

legal experiences and the practices of law? The links between law and post-modernity challenge that consideration.

There is, however, more to say about law's relationship with post-modernity. J. -F. Lyotard (1924–98) underlined in his globally recognized essay on post-modernism and the concept of 'narration' that many aspects of thought formation and doubt, suspicion and distance surround scientific certainty. In the case of *legal* certainty – a pillar of more than one well-known form of society – this observation is even more powerful and relevant. He writes:

> No industry is possible without a suspicion of the Aristotelian theory of motion, no industry without a refutation of corporatism, of mercantilism, and of physiocracy. Modernity, in whatever age it appears, cannot exist without a shattering of belief and without discovery of the 'lack of reality' of reality, together with the invention of other realities … Within the tradition of the subject, which comes from Augustine and Descartes and which Kant does not really challenge, this contradiction, which some would call neurosis or masochism, develops as a conflict between the faculties of a subject, the faculty to conceive of something and the faculty to 'present' something. Knowledge exists if, first, the statement is intelligible, and second, if 'cases' can be derived from the experience which 'corresponds' to it.[28]

But, Lyotard argues, our idea of the world in its totality, our idea of simplicity, the infinitely great, the absolutely powerful cannot be exemplified – they are beyond the faculty of creating a 'case' and are, in short: *un-presentable.* One of the issues that surpasses this characterizing of post-modernity, fits to the concept of the 'narrative': *every narrative is un-presentable.* A narrative is not the creation of a narrator, nor of a listener and not at all of a reader: it exists, and the knowledge of the persons confronted with the narrative is also engendered far beyond their specific ability or capacity. That existence is a fragment of a presence; the narrator and the listener or the eventual reader solely function as a component of that presence.

Lyotard suggests that this experience is the innermost feature of post-modernity. The latter is completely estranged from *legal* experience, which desires to strengthen presence (up to the barriers of absolutism) and detection of those who play a role in the case (subjects and objects). In contrast to any legal experience, the un-presentable – for instance the idea of justice – lives in presentation itself. It 'denies itself the solace of

---

[28] J. -F. Lyotard, *La Condition postmoderne: Rapport sur le Savoir*, edited by Minuit, Paris 1979 (English edition, *The Postmodern Condition: A Report on Knowledge*, Manchester University Press, 1984, p. 79ff).

good forms, the consensus of a taste which would make it possible to share collectively the nostalgia or the unattainable; that which searches for new presentations, not in order to enjoy them but in order to impart a stronger sense of the un-presentable … Hence the fact that work and text have the characters of an *event.*'[29] Narrations embracing a discourse are in this light an event. They reject the slavery of recognizing an author or listener and their constituting force; this rejection is their power of narrations to embed discourses. How can this power ever be incorporated in the world of a legal discourse that is so dependent on translations of meanings performed by specialists in the field? The question transcends *legal* discourse and pertains with this transcendence to the specificities of narrative knowledge.

2.5.4 Embedding Narratives

Narratives have no determinable subject which functions as their constituting speaker or fixated hearer. The speaker or hearer is never in a permanent position, and the same is true for the participant in a narrative. The latter unfolds his or her life *in* the narrative, but the narrative embeds that life without causing any determination. *Presence* is vividly there, but no grip in words or logical frames seems possible for that presence, nor any semiotic understanding of the *sign* character, which the absence of speaker or hearer fulfills. Those are the features that fit to post-modern thought formation; they are a challenge for the legal discourse embedded in narratives like all discourses.

All this leads to a precision of the term 'narrative' in the first place. Lyotard is honored as the author who introduced the concept in social sciences. He often referred in his essay to narratives like 'folk tales' or 'myth' and in that context the absence of speaker and hearer, as well as presence as indeterminacy, seems most acceptable. Lacan introduced in the same context two coherent and mutually meaningful concepts: the *master signifier* and the *master discourse*. Both are somewhat different speech acts: one immediately directs towards signification processes, and the other towards speech as a language-performance. The two guide, restrain and lead linguistic communication. The power of these masters (*sic*: masters) is in the importance those signifiers give to a subject's identification with them, so that ordering of all other signifiers appears in their perspective and meaning context. Lyotard is most generally known for his introduction of the narrative as a notion of equal importance as the

[29] Lyotard, *supra note 28*, p. 81.

discourse is given. He furthermore differentiates between a 'grand narrative' and 'master-narratives' or 'fragmented master-narratives' – from singularity mystically defined to plurality experienced. There are, however, many more uses of the term 'narrative', and even a firm determination of a narrative's subject: 'The narrator must be a meta-subject in the process of formulating both the legitimacy of the discourses of the empirical sciences and that of the direct institutions of popular cultures.' Indeed, all signifiers order and reorder opinions, prejudices and the coordinates of a Self that indulges fragments of history.[30]

Is there any analysis of a narrative possible without repeating the ground lines of an embedding narration? Keep this question alive while reading Lyotard's remark: 'knowledge finds its validity not within itself, not in a subject that develops by actualizing its learning possibilities, but in a practical subject – humanity'. And his words bring us nearer and nearer to the 'talking about law' we located on the street and other public places. They underline the importance this book gives to *that way of talking as a force of embedding legal issues*: 'The principle of the movement animating the people is not the self-legitimation of knowledge, but the self-grounding of freedom or, if preferred, its self-management. The subject is concrete, or supposedly so, and its epic is the story of its emancipation from everything that prevents it from governing itself. It is assumed that the laws it makes for itself are just ... because the legislators are, constitutionally, the very citizens who are subject to the laws.'

Is the street conversation about law a signifying power? It is extremely problematic to determine the limits of 'valid positive law' as signifier on the one hand and the narrative of 'Great Ideas in Law' represented by fragments of master-narratives within the boundaries of the legal discourse on the other. It is true that 'legislators are, constitutionally, the very citizens who are subject to the laws'. But are written *laws* and *justice* always, nearly automatically, in conformity? The question leads to the central thought in this book and remains of essence for an analysis of the structures of narratives. Lyotard concludes about the above lines: 'As a result, the legislator's will – the desire that the laws be just – will always coincide with the will of the citizen, who desires the law and will therefore obey it.'[31]

---

[30] Jan M. Broekman and Larry Catà Backer, *Lawyers Making Meaning*, Springer, Heidelberg/New York/Dordrecht, 2013, p. 80.

[31] Lyotard, *supra note 28*, p. 34ff.

But a citizen's feeling that articulates thoughts 'about law' on the street and at other public places is *definitely not* the same as the justice linked to valid positive laws. This is exactly the reason why 'talking about law' was introduced in this book as different from 'saying for law': the two languages cannot be incorporated in one and the same discourse; a citizen's discourse on law is not identical to law's discourse exposing positive law. This could also be understood as a complexity of what a narrative in a society or even cultural setting aims at. Despite the many levels of languages, which are often not compatible, we can experience a narrative's social power. The narrative as a form of life and language delivers a portrait of what a culture wants to perform or eventually fails to perform. In all cases appears a narrative – no matter whether it embraces a smaller or a large scale – as a *power* to articulate reality by means of apparent world views. That power (which is in essence a power to master the process of signifying in general) dissolves speech acts amidst everyday realities of conversational nature.

But what is more important is that it dissolves them without indicating the subsequent positions of participants in the articulation activity in which narrations are determined to perform. Even the force that lawyers esteem *ex professio*, that is: the *text*, seems not to retain that dissolution. Narratives are, one could say, texts from anonymous authors. They are only articulated 'to live in' and thus make very clear how life is in itself an ongoing articulation. The anonymity is so powerful that even historians cannot solve that lack of fixated identity in terms of their natural language grammars or syntaxes. The narration is told before the concept of a text is in effect. It has no Sacred Book or Text, as nearly all civilizations have. If speakers play a role in those great narratives, which Lacan and Lyotard incidentally mention, then those speech activities are institutionally prescribed and protected – they do not conform to any type of speech act in an ordinary language characterized as naïve-natural. Greek mythology, in contrast to, for instance, Indian, Hebraic, Christian or Islamic culture, has no Sacred Book. Speakers are everywhere and at all levels: on the streets of Athens of, for instance, the fifth century BC, educators reciting myth, participants in the tragedies, dramas and comedies of that period.

Without the precise determination of speakers or listeners, the narratives embedding varieties of discourses are empowering articulation faculties of individuals, laymen and professionals alike. The master-narratives we hardly delineate in our conversations or texts are masters of a hidden articulation force. That force, or those forces, cannot be detected, described, or determined as if they were a political power or a scientific – let alone *legal – master articulation* we have to follow. It implies that an embedding of discourses is not a matter of institutions or of preferred institutional behaviors that can be qualified as 'good' or 'unseemly'.

A challenging example of such a misunderstanding is in the description of a master-narrative by the well-known US Institution for Public Innovation, the Harwood Institute.[32] It suggests, 'our adherence to a master-narrative dictates how we frame stories, whom we interview, the questions we ask, and ultimately the work we produce … typically reinforces our belief in the master narrative'.

Many of the above considerations come together in that short formulation. An institutional author understands the master-narrative (the great signifier). The latter presents as *a speaker* how an institution unfolds. There is a tension here: on the one hand, it contradicts the concept of a narrative to suggest that only a natural speaker can perform this retracement. On the other it makes no sense to have this done by a bearer of that feature itself: the institution and its formative power on language and language formation. Furthermore, a master-narrative is not a club or political party one can adhere to, become a member of and choose to speak its language. The narrative is rather a component of culture that can contribute to the many forms of shaping human life without the participation model of a social institution.

Not only in philosophical perspective, but also in a political as well as in a constitutional (and thus legal) view does the difference between a *master discourse* and a *master-narrative* count! The Harwood Institute suggests that the *narrative* dictates an individual behavior, whereas a master *discourse* is understood as a specific expansion of a signifier in social directions. The latter addendum does *not* mean that individuals dissipate in a social context but rather that they develop towards forms of individuality which conform to the social norms and create sociability.

This suggests by no means that the participation in a discourse as compared to a narrative is different, or that this structure of participation, which touches the concept of the subject or individual, differs in any of those two. While enveloped in a discourse, one speaks and takes speech activity initiatives, whereas in a narration one is a more passively positioned object of the story and submits to its categories created by actors of history and of linguistic constructs formatted during preceding ages. A myth or legend is not a discourse; it is a narration. One always

[32] Covering Communities, 'What is a Master Narrative?' The Harwood Institute for Public Innovation, 2007, available at: www.theharwoodinstitute.org.

belongs to both and is formatively influenced by both, but with different structures of identity and activity.

Those two: activity and identity are decisive in political perspective: identity is an equally important issue in politics as is the format of a person's (social) activity. That is summarized in one sentence. When I perform a speech act, I put myself at risk because of uncertainty about the position of the o/Other. The risk is on the wane when the o/Other in the same discourse is constituent in the same narration. The situation of the o/Other or of any forms of Otherness is often asymmetric today: 'I participate in your discourse but have only minimal experience with – or appreciation of the basic norms and values in your (master) narrative' – this particular asymmetry is, as was already exposed in the above lines, basic in relations with migrants, refugees, religious or racial groups, or in issues of constitutional law.

2.5.5 The 'I' and 'Thou' in Two Narratives

The problem of asymmetry is inherent to a deeply anchored variety of narratives and with those ties a centuries-old philosophical problem: what was called *alternity* or the problem of o/Otherness. Otherness is a constituent of the self; it is also a desire to take distance within the self; otherness seems a continuous confrontation with the impossibility to engender a self without recognizing it as an overwhelming force named 'alternity'.

The latter notion is anchored in at least two master-narratives that play a role in the post-modern world of the Occident. They embrace different legal thought patterns founded upon different interpretations of the 'I – Thou – It' relationship as well as the consequences for the foundations of differing systems of law. The first is embedded in the Judeo-Christian master-narrative (Torah and Bible) and the second in the Islam master-narrative (Koran). The two types of Holy texts indicate differences within Western culture of our days, often indicated as specifically 'multicultural'.

(A) Holy Torah and Holy Bible

Two preceding remarks are about the first narrative context: (1) Attention should be given to the philosophical context of the thought patterns, which embrace major problems inherent to the enduring 'I and Thou' motive. That theme seems to be the central focus of the master-narrative and even the world of electronic communication with all its unpredictable implications focuses on that issue. (2) It interests that the history of West European philosophy pertaining to the 'I and Thou' motive brings predominantly *German* language studies to the fore. Those two features indicate structural components of the first-mentioned *master-narrative*, which dominates Occidental culture.

Buber and Rosenzweig belonged to a cultural transition that completed a superbly productive period in German philosophy with Hegel, Schelling and Hölderlin.[33] Their ideas and texts were close to religious and philosophical insights as well as motives in the works of the German philosophers for whom the concepts of 'I' and 'Thou' represented a leading motive. They were aware of the fact that earlier philosophical achievements in German thought patterns already emphasized their major concern. For instance H. Jacobi formulated in 1775 the unity of *I* and *Thou* as a fundamental viewpoint: 'I open eyes and ears, or I extend my hand and feel in that moment how inseparable they are: I and Thou, Thou and I.' Ludwig Feuerbach's *Principles of a Philosophy of the Future* (1843) mentioned how philosophical ideas were wrong when they strove to understand an *I* without a sensed *Thou* (§41). And they opened the gates for new conceptions of reality and of social life, forming a sound prelude to existentialism (Jaspers, Heidegger, Marcel, Sartre), phenomenology (Husserl) and philosophical anthropology (Scheler, Pleßner, Gehlen). What was a spiritual reality also became a political reality: Buber's opinion was more than once sought in international conflicts, which were a hinge of Western culture in the first decades of the twentieth century.

New experiences and new forms of dialogic life also reshaped borderlines between real and virtual communication. While reshaping the structure of dialogue, they created a sharp contrast between their new thinking on the one hand and education as limited to data transfer, to information and learning on the other. Those thoughts are closely related to education as a discourse and discipline that can accomplish the inherent attitudes of dialogic thought patterns. Education should create dimensions of *respect* between participants in educative relationships. This principle reaches beyond the balancing of interests of single individuals. It is also beyond the reach and understanding of a strictly formalized legal discourse: respect is neither in the perfect equilibrium of interests, nor in the outbalancing of subject-positions in society. Education in dialogic perspective has to achieve more than just training in whatever sort of individual give-and-take status or balance of individual rights to form the common good in society. It interests in this perspective that virtual scenes in education are no longer compatible with such

---

33 Martin Buber 1878–1965; Franz Rosenzweig 1886–1929.

thought patterns. There is no reliable connection between the world of electronic images and communications on the one hand and the life-world based in a concept of the common good that results from the arithmetic of individual interests.

Respect fulfills the life of individuals and is clearly not the result of negotiation, but rather a condition to participate in education as aiming at an individual's *becoming.* Goals and standards of that becoming are not pragmatically engendered by authorities or institutions, but by an enhanced self-understanding pertaining to one's own role in life. Emphasis is therefore on education as a particular environment, often shaped in a technological as well as a social sense of the word. It therefore requires *interactivity* between all participants in that environment *as a source for respect.*

Foundational texts on dialogue were not the result of renewed interest in social sciences or psychology.[34] Buber knew Freud and had read many of his writings. A dialogue appears a cornerstone of social life, a nucleus of personality development. Did Freud sufficiently notice? Again: what importance should we give to this specific constellation? The answer can be short: if no reading of a word is without reference to education, then only the most favorable milieu for reading is in an educational institution. But this observation is rooted in social and psychological, not in any legal understanding.

Two important dimensions are highlighted here: *time* is in the *immediacy* that makes encounters possible and lends them their value. *Reality* is in acknowledging that all spiritual and material existence is grounded in actively *encountering*. Time and reality constitute a double face – a face to be recognized by all of us, a process deeply influenced by 'being together' as an educative exigency. One side of that face is determined by what we already experienced in life, our history, the many paths we already walked. The other side is the mark of *our confrontation with the other* – his or her being that gives us the possibility of experiencing the wholeness and complete reality of our life.

An encounter is never an act on its own. Each fragment of spiritual befalling is a form of meeting, its dynamics are found in *Exodus* and *Encounter*. Reality is in two parts, one half and another half, one could say. A part is mine, and a part is yours – that is the fascination of *I* and *Thou*. It was already the basic conviction of Immanuel Kant, who

---

[34] J. Fleischmann, 'Le problème de Martin Buber' *Revue Philosophique de la France et de L'Étranger*, Vol. 149, 1959, p. 351, emphasizes that Buber's philosophical attitude showed more clearly in religious studies than in sociology or psychology.

explained in his 1795 essay *Zum Ewigen Frieden* (*On Perpetual Peace*) how hospitality is a necessary condition for being a person worth the high esteem of others. Only he who reaches out, can take in. Hospitality is one of the two forces that meet, beyond any artificially acquired passivity, receptivity, social conditioning or psychological reinforcement.

I and *Thou* are an experienced path, a vivid presence, presence like a vertical, a hazardous undertaking to bridge the *I* and the *non-I*, to play the game of identity and non-identity. The world as it is, and humans as they are, seem twofold: one and one. They are only one in so far they are not one, but this *and* of one and one. However, do not forget that this approach results from the use of *words* whereby even the experience of one's own identity of the 'I' is marked by a linguistic articulation.

Western thought understands this as an act of *representation*. It means that words mirror reality in a one-to-one relationship. The dialogue approach emphasizes, however, that words lay foundations, constitute relations and are not a reality *in se* but rather create reality. That contrast also characterizes an educational relationship. If an educator represents traditions, as he mostly does in the Western tradition, he represents secured values and norms and a stable set of knowledge. His knowledge precedes the knowledge of all students and forms the basis for all educational relationships. Transference of that knowledge gives him a solid social position, including the respect of his students and society at large. Doubts about his position and indeterminacy pertaining to his knowledge would immediately diminish such an educational relation. But real transference does not pertain to secured knowledge from which a social position is deduced. An important point of departure is envisaged here. Any teacher is together with his student in a situation of search and discovery. They exploit a totally different attitude. Teacher and student must be open to all possibilities that communication offers – the information knowledge of the Internet with the indeterminacy of e-devices and computers included. Any *I–Thou* relation includes immediacy between partners, and finds it base in a common interest, yes, psychological openness of all participants towards the unknown dimensions of meaning and knowledge. What is spoken needs the other.[35] Computers participate in the constitution of the otherness of all participants in manners never seen or experienced before!

---

[35] This overshadows the Western desire to *possess* knowledge about being and reality before utterances can be performed. That desire suppresses how the other presents reality as it is.

This leads to another aspect of the *dialogue*. It is necessary to understand that this analysis and its far-reaching consequences are apparently *structural*. In other words, the *dialogue* indicates *positions* between participants of conversation and discourse. This leads to subtle distinctions, to a form of mapping of utterances, which are directly related to words in conversation or even written in texts. A starting point is not a substance, but a relation. There is the *I*, but the *I* is nothing, that is: not-a-thing. The *I* is always either from an *I–Thou* or an *I–It* relationship. These two are two *worlds*. An *I* is existing in both. That coincidence does not imply any ground for the emphasis Western thought gives to the *I* as a privileged subject. Three remarks, which characterize the Judeo-Christian narrative, are at issue.

(1) The 'I'–'Thou' motive reveals a clear profile of its master-narrative, and the motive could lead us with that insight towards a deeper semiotic understanding of its actual context. The motive forcefully represents its narrative thought-profile. The two words would be incomprehensible without their embedding in a larger context of articulation. Spoken solitarily would neither the 'I' nor the 'You' make sense. They need not only each other, but also Buber's 'and', which clearly refers to Freud's 'Es', but the three together need a discourse articulated in whatever native tongue.
(2) This is not a purely linguistic conclusion but a far-reaching philosophical conclusion. The three words are important *signs* of the narration in which related elements and situation function as reference. They envisage a master-narrative with a character that is idealistic and archaic, political and religious, descriptive and prescriptive at the same time. And, above all, it appears to be a master-narrative in which *texts* play a dominant role. Some of those texts are even called, and treated as, *Sacred Texts* and require an attitude of devotion when read, quoted or meditated on.
(3) The profile of the master-narrative that influences the 'I'–'Thou'–'It' discussion is detectable in all details of the Hebrew Sacred Text, in particular the first fragments of the *Torah*, in the book *Bereishis/Genesis*, as well as in the Holy Bible. These fragments do not fascinate just because of their unfolding of the Creation and thus the mode of Being of everything on Earth and in the Cosmos.

What is most important in our context: they position in that text *God as the first Speaker* and understand that positioning as a key to the Creation of Cosmos, World and the Human. *It is this specific pattern that dominates the signifying power of the master-narrative*: the 'Beginning of Everything' narrated, is the narration of a Speaking and the positioning of the Speaker, as the third verse of the *Genesis* Book describes. After a sketch of the situation of 'Being' before: 'The earth was without form, and void; and darkness was on the face of the deep' follows *an ultimate occurrence* described as: 'Then God *said* ...' This follows *nine* times, until the conclusion is there: 'Thus the heavens and the earth, and all the host of them, were finished.' The creation of man follows, and with the latter the 'You' that evoked conversation.[36] Each Divine Speaking is followed by an index of reality in the form of a Divine confirmation of the Speaking.

(B) Holy Quran

The abovementioned texts of the Holy Torah and Holy Bible belong to two often intertwined but sometimes contrasting master-narratives, which both expose the 'I'–'Thou'–'It' motive, that is: the unfolding of speech, in a specific manner. Such an unfolding is *in se* an attempt to articulate *alternity*, because that is understood as the ultimate power to *constitute a Self.* In this articulation is the essence of two neighbored master-narratives. Fragments of an answer to the question how narratives are effective can be unveiled in the description of this 'master motive', which is inherent to the narratives described.

A comparison with other, eventually non-Occidental master-narratives, includes studies far beyond the scope of this book and, above all, of Western law and legal discourse. However, one exception must be mentioned. The preceding paragraph suggested that the settling of *alternity* was essential in the engenderment of the Self. So there is a specific problem when discourses cannot cope with the challenge of intertwining. It will in general be described as: 'I participate in your discourse but have minimal experience with – or appreciation of norms and values in your (master) narrative.' The difference of one legal system living together with another in one multicultural system, each being anchored in its own master-narrative, indicates the correctness of the title of this book: all conversations about law are signifiers of importance.

One can easily observe the dynamics of such an asymmetry in cases of fundamentally different viewpoints in master-narratives that influence, for instance, Western legal discourse. The legal system belonging to a master-narrative has often a meaningful *sign function.* A comparison

---

[36] See *The Torah: with Rashi's Commentary etc. Bereishis/Genesis*, edited by Rabbi Y. I. Z. Herczeg, 3rd edn, Mesorah Publ. Ltd, New York, 1997, and *The Holy Bible*, New King James edition, Thomas Nelson, Inc., Nashville, 1990.

between master-narratives and their legal thought patterns can unveil foundations of asymmetry. This becomes immediately clear when we compare the first fragments of the three Sacred Texts anchored in their master-narratives.

One reads, for instance, the first pages of the Holy Torah and the Holy Bible in comparison with first pages of the Holy Quran.[37] They all pertain to the 'I–Thou–It' module. The first-mentioned texts direct their signifying energy to a cosmically first Speaker. His word precedes the reality of all Creation and the 'Thou' which is thereby created in that world. *Speech* is the key to the issue of *alternity* and the latter the key to the human *Self*. The 'I'–'Thou'–'It', in daily language: 'conversation', appears most important in the two master-narratives sustained by their respective Sacred texts. Law mirrors this module with the position of the judge as speaker.

But the master-narrative with the Holy Quran as its Sacred text differs considerably from the two other, abovementioned narratives.

That is the case although both earlier mentioned Sacred texts are considered to be the precursors of the Holy Quran. That consideration refers also to the 'I–Thou–It' module as it functions in the Sharia legal system, and thus is embedded in a religious context. Western law focuses on human freedom and dignity, Sharia law on the human being going on a prescribed path, a path to the Source paved by traditions and the necessity to follow that Path as a true believer, as the name 'Sharia' indicates. The meaning of 'legal subject' in Western law, in Civil Law as well as Common Law, is a subject determined by meanings of Western legal discourse. The meaning of a subject of law in the Sharia context is religiously determined and reinforced by Sharia law as its completing component. The strong ties with casuistry as a legal method to develop an instrument that prevents conflicts could provide a profile: family issues are, for instance, a matter of Sharia but economic or international law issues predominantly matter in Western law. The question whether life in contrasting legal views, particularly on the 'I–Thou–It' module, remains possible, remains crucial.

The question arises whether social life is possible in conflicting master-narratives. The Second Surah in the Holy Quran reads: '(6). As to those who reject Faith, it is the same to them whether thou warn them or do not warn them; they will not believe.' In this master-narrative the conflict between those who accept and those who reject faith is the

---

[37] Garry Wills: 'My Koran Problem' *The New York Review of Books*, March 24, 2016, p. 16.

essence of the engenderment of a self. As was said, in the Holy Quran text itself (in Surah 3) are the two precursors mentioned: '(7). Allah hath set a seal on their hearts and on their hearing, and on their eyes is a veil; great is the penalty they (incur).'[38] In a multicultural society of the Occidental culture the subject-positioning within the boundaries of law is *not* a matter of free choice.

The distinction that counts is the distinction between Believers and Non-believers – a distinction that surpasses any difference between 'Thou' and 'I'. In Surah 25 one reads: '(52). Therefore listen not to the Unbelievers, but strive against them with the utmost strenuousness, with the (Qur'an). (53). It is He Who has let free the two bodies of flowing water: One palatable and sweet, and the other salt and bitter; yet has He made a barrier between them, a partition that is forbidden to be passed. (54). It is He Who has created man from water: then has He established relationships of lineage and marriage: for thy Lord has power (over all things).'

The contrast of meanings – in particular between the freedom of Human and Divine speech *versus* the necessity of speech in Faith – remains decisive when the signifying force of the narrative's text is concerned. Notice in what regards a conversation about law on the street has a signifying function. Concordance and discordance in master-narratives will echo in the words of such talking. A conversation will always deliver variations of the 'I–Thou–It' module, and will make them concrete in the context of different forms of social life and culture in general. Law colors differently in the context of speech, dialogue, conversation or dispute about identifying with faith, belonging and understanding – altogether components of the 'I–Thou–It' module. That difference is most challenging and articulated in 'talking about law' at whatever location it occurs.

REFERENCES

Aristotle, *The Physics, LOEB* Harvard University Press. Translated by Wicksteed and Cornford, Vol. IV, Book IV, xi.

Aspiz, Harold, *Walt Whitman and the Body Beautiful*, University of Illinois Press, Chicago, IL, 1980.

Barthes, R., *L'aventure sémiologique*, Editions du Seuil, Paris 1985.

[38] *The Holy Qur'an*, English translation by Abdullah Yusuf Ali, available at: http://www.wright-house.com/religions/islam/Quran.html.

Bergh, G. C. J. J. van den and J. M. Broekman, *Recht en Taal.* Preadvies van de Koninklijke Notariële Broederschap, Deventer, 1979.
Black, Max, *Models and Metaphors*, Cornell University Press, Ithaca, NY, 1962.
Broden, Thomas F., 'A. J. Greimas: les anneés de formation' *TEXTO! Textes and Cultures*, Vol. XX, No. 2, 2015.
Broekman, Jan M., 'Recht en Structuralisme' in *R & R, Maandelijks Tijdschrift van de Vereeniging voor de Wijsbegeerte des Rechts*, Vol. 2, No. 2, 1973.
Broekman, Jan M., *Intertwinements of Law and Medicine*, Leuven University Press, 1996.
Broekman, Jan M., *The Virtual in e-Education*, IIS Publ. Cie., New York, 2004.
Broekman, Jan M., 'Trading Signs: Semiotic Practices in Law and Medicine' *International Journal for the Semiotics of Law*, Vol. 20, No. 3, 2007, 223–36.
Broekman, Jan M. and Larry Catà Backer, *Lawyers Making Meaning*, Springer, Heidelberg/New York/Dordrecht, 2013.
Castoriades, C., *L'institution imaginaire de la société*, Du Seuil, Paris, 1975 (translated by K. Blamey, MIT Press, Cambridge, MA, 1975).
Covering Communities, 'What is a Master Narrative?' The Harwood Institute for Public Innovation, 2007, available at: www.thehardwoodinstitute.org.
De Haan, Jacob I., *Rechtskundige Significa en hare Toepassing op de Begrippen 'Aansprakelijk, Verantwoordelijk, Toerekeningsvatbaar'*, Versluys, Amsterdam, 1916.
Eggers, David, *The Circle – A Novel*, Vintage Books, New York, 2013.
Feuerbach, L., *Grundsätze der Philosophie der Zukunft*, 1843 (English edition, *Principles of the Philosophy of the Future*, M. Vogel, Tr. Hackett Publ. Cie. 1986).
Fleerackers, F., *Affective Legal Analysis: On the Conveyance of Legal Awareness*, Duncker and Humblot, Berlin, 2000.
Fleischmann, J., 'Le problème de Martin Buber' *Revue Philosophique de la France et de L'Étranger*, Vol. 149, 1959, 345–54.
Foucault, Michel, *L'ordre du discours*, Gallimard, Paris, 1971.
Fowler, Orson S., *Love and Parentage*, New York, 1844.
Gadamer, H. -G., *Wahrheit und Methode*, J. C. B. Mohr/Paul Siebeck, Tübingen, 1960.
Goodrich, Peter, '*Jani Anglorum.* Signs, Symptoms, Slips and Interpretation in Law', in C. Douzinas, P. Goodrich and Y. Hachamovitch (eds), *Politics, Postmodernity and Critical Legal Studies*, Routledge, London/New York, 1994.
Heim, M., *The Metaphysics of Virtual Reality*, Meckler Ltd, London, 1993.
Jonsen, Albert R. and S. Toulmin, *The Abuse of Casuistry*, California University Press, Berkeley/Los Angeles/London, 1988.
Kant, I., *Zum Ewigen Frieden*, 1795 (English edition, *Perpetual Peace: A Philosophical Sketch,* M. Campbell Smith, Tr. Swan Sonnenschein & Co., 1903).
Kristeva, Julia, *SEMEIOTIKè: Recherches pour une sémanalyse*, Du Seuil, Paris, 1969.
Lakoff, G., *Women, Fire, and Dangerous Things*, Chicago University Press, London/Chicago, IL, 1989.

Lyotard, J. -F., *La Condition postmoderne: Rapport sur le Savoir*, edited by Minuit, Paris, 1979 (English edition, *The Postmodern Condition: A Report on Knowledge*, Manchester University Press, 1984).
MacCormick, N. and O. Weinberger, *An Institutional Theory of Law*, Springer, Dordrecht, 1986.
Nietzsche, F., *Die Fröhliche Wissenschaft*, Werke in Drei Bänden, Wissenschaftliche Buchgesellschaft, Darmstadt, Vol. III, 1882, p. 7ff.
Posner, R., *How Judges Think*, Harvard University Press, Cambridge, MA, 2008.
Rakoff, Jed S., 'Neuroscience and the Law' *The New York Review of Books*, Vol. LXIII, No. 8, May 12, 2016, 30–33.
Richards, I. A., *The Philosophy of Rhetoric*, Oxford University Press, Oxford, 1936.
Rosenfeld, M., 'Deconstruction and Legal Interpretation: Conflict, Indeterminacy and the Temptations of the New Legal Formalism' *Cardozo Law Review*, Vol. 12, No. 5/6, 1990, 1211–69.
Searle, John, *Speech Acts: An Essay in the Philosophy of Language*, Cambridge University Press, Cambridge, 1969.
Steiner, George, *After Babel: Aspect of Language and Translation*, Oxford University Press, Oxford, 1978, 3rd edn, 1998.
Stone, A. Rosanne, 'Will the Real Body Please Stand Up? Boundary Stories about Virtual Cultures' in M. Benedikt (ed.), *Cyberspace: First Steps*, MIT Press, Cambridge, MA, 1991.
The Holy Bible, New King James edn, Thomas Nelson, Inc., Nashville, 1990.
The Holy Qur'an, English translation by Abdullah Yusuf Ali, available at: http://www.wright-house.com/religions/islam/Quran.html.
The Torah: with Rashi's Commentary etc. Bereishis/Genesis, edited by Rabbi Y. I. Z. Herczeg, 3rd edn, Mesorah Publ. Ltd, New York, 1997.
Unger, R. M., *The Self Awakened*, Harvard University Press, Cambridge, MA, 2009.
Weber, Max, *Wirtschaft und Gesellschaft*, Mohr, Tübingen, 1914.
Whitman, Walt, *Leaves of Grass*, in *Poetry and Prose*, The Library of America, (edited by J. Kaplan, New York, 1855 /1891), pp. 27–146.
Wills, Garry, 'My Koran Problem' *The New York Review of Books*, March 24, 2016.

3. Compliance and the radical

3.1 LAW, A DISCORDANT DISCOURSE

3.1.1 Introduction

Our talking about law on the street or in other public places, in our family circle or our workplace, is inspired by a world view constituted by rules, fixated and obligatory habits, and by documented or even codified texts. The subject of that conversation: 'the law', also turns everything into a highly *emotional* conversation. On the street, we talk about responses to the legal power of binding, obliging, fixating or ruling. These should bring order and peace, solve or suppress conflicts and enable us to act on a stable basis of law and order. Can that be? The subject of our talk is not the legal system but our feeling about that system. Those emotions are often decisive when legal meanings have to function, and in particular when their functions are connected with restrictions or encapsulations.

A double underlining appears necessary: on the one hand we underline the power of the legal system in the context of rational thought patterns (the first chapter of this book) and on the other that the study of signs and signification, called legal semiotics, is not prepared to take dimensions of emotion as a relevant signifying force (the second chapter). Is that important? That seems indeed to be the case.

The Ancient Greeks knew how to appreciate emotional dimensions of talking about law and the related political forms of democracy for more than a century. The perfection of their democracy in the fifth century BC unfolded parallel with the Dionysian festivals, their dramas and tragedies. We still admire those texts and their political embedding.[1] They are

[1] Sir Arthur Pickard-Cambridge, *The Dramatic Festivals of Athens* (2nd edition, edited by J. Could and D. M. Lewis), Oxford University Press, Oxford, 1988; Chester G. Starr, *The Birth of Athenian Democracy*, Oxford University Press, Oxford, 1990; H. W. Parke, *Festivals of the Athenians*, Cornell University Press, New York/London, 1977; M. H. Hansen, *The Athenian Democracy in the Age of Demosthenes*, Basil Blackwell, Oxford/Cambridge, MA, 1991;

empirically/factually unknown, but appeal to emotions as if they were contemporary experiences.

It is important in this regard that a non-institutional conversation about law seems today of no interest for legal semiotics or for a legal theory, or is, in the words of Eco, a matter of psychology, in particular:

> [O]f empathy (*Einfühlung*) traced by human hands or found in the natural environment. We may consider all the cases of empathy as mere *stimulations* that should be studied by the physiology of the nervous system. In a semiotic framework it does not make sense to assert or deny that these 'expressive' properties of signals are based on the 'universal' structure of the human mind or that they can vary according to many biological or cultural variables.

Eco acknowledges access to emotion as empathy as a *programmed stimulation*, because 'in so far as the expression relies [on] more or less coded units and the reaction of the addressee cannot be completely foreseen, one must consider programmed stimulation as the invention of a complex text'. He would therefore place *emotion-driven conversations* in his study pertaining to the theory of sign production at the level of 'analyzable and replicable behavioral "discourse"', which:

> [M]ay generate a vague discourse on the content plane. Among such programmed stimuli one might list: (i) all the programmed synesthesiae in poetry, music, painting, etc.; all so-called 'expressive' signs, such as those theorized by artists like Kandinsky, i.e. visual configurations that are conventionally supposed to 'convey' a given feeling directly ... and that have also been studied by the theorists of *Einfühlung* or empathy ...[2]

This refined categorization illustrates a denial of the fact that an inclusion of emotionality in the process of sign production is necessary and effective at the level of semiotic questions about the genesis of signs.

An opposite viewpoint is articulated in this book and in this chapter. That view unveils a shortcoming, not only of legal semiotics but of a majority of contemporary approaches to law and legal discourse. Rational

---

M. M. Austin and P. Vidal-Naquet, *Economic and Social History of Ancient Greece*, California University Press, Berkeley, LA, 1977; R. K. Sinclair, *Democracy and Participation in Athens*, Cambridge University Press, Cambridge, 1988; J. -P. Vernant, *Les origines de la pensée grecque*, Paris, 1962 (English edition, *The Origins of Greek Thought*, Cornell University Press, Ithaca, NY, 1982).

2 Umberto Eco, *A Theory of Semiotics*, Indiana University Press/Midland, Bloomington, IN, 1979, pp. 203ff, 242. On 'synesthesiae' see: Sarah Marusek (ed.), *Synesthetic Legalities: Sensory Dimensions of Law and Jurisprudence*, Routledge, London, 2016.

components of law seem to evaporate once the wealth of emotions and their overwhelming form of meaning-creation come to the fore. 'Talking about law' occurs in an emotional mood and seldom leads to purely rational conversations. That level of articulation touches, however, an *affective* legal analysis, of which Fleerackers in 2000 distinguished three levels in legal theory that are relevant to our thesis and to an eventual extension of the semiotic project in law and legal discourse. He first mentions that affective legal analysis 'is a counterpart of rationalizing legal analysis', furthermore that this approach 'reaffirms their affective impact on the legal subject, and consequently the significance of law's affective dimensions, i.e. the way law affects its subjects', and finally that this analysis 'serves as a means to analyze contemporary legal discourse's interpretation of legal awareness and its conveyance'.[3]

One does indeed hardly notice, even in ardent debates on the street, how emotions are constantly drawn out from us at all levels of encounter and mutual understanding. But they are most forcefully shaped and activated when social and political means for a better life are at issue. Those are in need of a constantly improved internalizing of the many ways to respond to others. So, as was said Chapter 2: *alternity* has a key function in the developing of a Self! This aspect functions in a more profile manner at an emotional level than in purely logical and rational contexts, and thus enriches our understanding of, and support for, law in our lives. It also completes the semiotic dimensions of law in a society and their specific techniques from signs to significations. The many ways we have cultivated are never solely emotional, as customs and rituals illustrate in each perspective of a cultural setting. That is what we can learn in a first instance when we observe the many talks about law in daily life.

Here comes *their semiotic profile* again to the fore: semiotics is *not* a matter of rational considerations being one-by-one steps on the path towards meaning, but rather an all-embracing dynamic process of concretely *walking* that path. The emotions we experience in the life of others and in our self are *signs* we should not neglect – certainly not when confronted with the law and its obliging discourse. But they tell us a story, the story of the wealth of a human life when it is truly *going* a path, a *dynamic* data and thus a multileveled *process* in which we play a major role.

---

[3] Frank Fleerackers, *Affective Legal Analysis: On the Resolution of Conflict*, Duncker and Humblot, Berlin, 2000, p. 44ff.

> When we talk in public or in private about law, one has to consider that this level of talking is of equal importance for law and legal discourse as a general cultural issue as is the professional talking of lawyers or judges.

Two levels are again at stake: there is the level of everyday life conversations and the level of the professional discourse parallel to a talking about law by the layman and by the professional. Both levels do, however, approach a social reality, which is *dynamic* and *a developing process* in essence. Any *talking about law* they engender will create a labyrinthine totality of paths, but they are paths nevertheless and have to be paved in any phase of life. A talk about law is emotional, indeed, but at the same time a step on the path towards signification. Those articulations intertwine with legal rationality, although the latter remains a riddle on the path to deepened knowledge of law as a science – or a specific applied social science. As such, law carries the riddle of human life in its innermost thoughts and practices. The 'path' from sign to signification is its energy trajectory that wants to be identified with everyday life. The latter is an emotion of importance: law is not for science or any rational enjoyment, but for life as a phenomenon that needs order. What represents that order: *alternity* and its emotional component, or *rationality* and its many accompanying feelings?

(A) The path

The path is external as well as internal, deeply layered in complex meanings – it is in itself a multicultural metaphor that stimulates the mind and behavioral faculties at the same time. The path: an ongoing confrontation with dualities and a fight against total fixation of poles of expressiveness within those dualities. The path: a challenge to become 'being': never laid out before us, always to be mounted, never completely passive but also never completely active. The path: always entangled in controversies: the question 'which way to go' seems universal and enduring. The path: requiring compliance, envisaging discordance everywhere. The path. As if lighting the path to go is paving the path itself. Old questions concerning the sources of our knowledge come to the fore, but all of them are misjudged positions the walker on the path cherished. How often they are in his eyes a sign of evolvement towards signification – but in law as well as in semiotics that evolvement is misunderstood. Our thought formations create the trail we walk into a path; there is no walking without a path-creation, there is no expressivity without a language.

A semiotic analysis of law, studying the path from sign to signification, never moves from A to B or to the rest of the alphabet. While analyzing, it does not analyze 'what there is' but it recognizes the complexity (which is a form of togetherness) of 'all there is'. The swimmer drinks the water in which he swims, but he does not experience the drinking as such. The walker walks in the mud, where no path is to be mounted: his thoughts move brightly in the air. Walking the path is always an adventure in context, and thus happens amidst others; it is never a solo performance. Water, mud, or air is all language – like law.

A conclusion goes with all those experiences and their articulation. It suggests: *discordance is everywhere*. It inspires our mind and brain, it influences our actions and our inactivity as well; discordance colors law and legal discourse because humans live in a *fragmented world*. The latter is a personal sensation as well as a cultural treasure. Both reflect in our emotions, but form an unsolvable riddle for our rationality. Talking about law directs citizens towards law's discordance as well as to law's position in this fragmented world. This is a far-reaching conclusion while walking the path of knowledge and analysis: the stance of everyday life is rare in the field of philosophy. It is unattended by the legal practitioner, who cannot even speak about that form of life without translating it into his artificial and professional language. So, confront him or her with the question law and legal semiotics neglects: 'How are you living your life on a daily basis?' Both question and answer are of vital importance in understanding the many ways our talking about law is a signifying power.

3.1.2 Linguistic Levels

Discordance is everywhere. That slogan could not be more effective. Discordance is the climate for our soul, our creativity, our habits and daily experiences. The quest for order is based on discordance, as is our desire for ruling forces. Frictions, collision courses and controversies of opinion, deviations and disputes, quarrels and disharmony, disputes and clashes of all sorts determine the climate of our spiritual life. No talk has a different background – even when conversations evolve in harmony and peace, or are meant to confirm unanimity. The discordance is defiant and appears rooted in all words we bring to the fore. Their majority of words in our daily language have a wide range of meaning and sense, so that different and even contradictory options are included. Only recourses to the context suggest what meaning to embrace.

The same problems characterize all discourses and not in the least the legal discourse. Its words mean more than their meanings laid down in the law books, and defy any striving for a unilateral understanding.

Talking about law continues, however, beyond defined terminologies and influences law in a constitutive sense mostly via the detour of politics. A failure of a 'one-to-one' relationship between reality and language is strongly experienced in law. Law's positivism can be conceived in legal theory, even in philosophy, but never in the flow of daily life emotions. As mentioned in previous chapters, that 'one-to-one' relation cannot unfold for linguistic and philosophical reasons. In the case of law, concept and discourse cover at least three very different planes: (1) law in constatation; (2) law in life; and (3) law as a discourse offering solutions to problems. The three embrace more than three different linguistic levels, which cannot meet in one concept, expression or idea. In short: *law's discourse is by definition enveloped in discordances* – a thesis which was never precisely researched in legal semiotics or any other theory of law. That thesis is also *against* opinions in daily life: law, once empowered, brings what it is meant to be in itself: unification, harmony, justice and peace. Can a discordant discourse meet expectations that are evidently rooted in, and representing, deeply anchored misunderstandings in everyday life conversations?

An insight into at least two determining motivations could provide access to a possible answer.

(1) First, there is the multileveled character of language in general and its inability to present fixated generally accepted meanings. If that were not the case, the title of this section, 'Linguistic Levels' would be misleading. The fact of language's leveled structure awakens the often completely unreasonable desire for 'one-to-one' relations between meaning and expression. They strongly further that feeling in law and legal discourse.

(2) Second, there is the naïvely formulated and often disregarded fact that particularly in the case of laws and in particular State laws, not solely humans (citizens) speak, but also institutions. All embrace their functioning under private law, under public law or under mixed legal patterns within a specific legal system, such as Civil Law or Common Law. Citizens on the street do talk with representatives of local, State, corporate and other institutional bodies which function as discussion partners – often a source of discordance.

Ad (1): The *multileveled character of language* and its incapacity to present fixated meanings, which are accepted at various levels of society, is an important *linguistic* feature. It is often as important as issues of grammar or syntax of a natural language. This character, one concludes, is in its linguistically relevant form never studied in legal semiotics. We restrict our argumentation to emphasizing that suggestion. It is, for instance, important when the production of signs in law is at stake. Roberta Kevelson's suggestion that law should be studied as 'a system of signs' was extremely valuable but did *not* consider the multileveled character in which signs emerge, or the possibility that signs display multiple levels of meaning and sense in themselves. Her famous book, which became a challenge to law as well as to semiotics, was based on Ch. S. Peirce's world view. His name is the first word in her Preface. The book's ultimate goal is convincingly formulated as 'providing a framework for linking diverse systems of inquiry into new unified relations'. The relations envisaged must, as Kevelson suggests, be understood against the theoretical background of what she refers to as the 'dynamic, "motion-picture" universe that is continually becoming, that is infinitely developing and changing in response to genuinely novel elements that emerge as existents'. In that case, 'the basic concepts of rights, resources, and reality take on new dimensions of meaning in correspondence with n-dimensional, infinite value judgments or truth-like beliefs which one holds'.[4] In other words: the many paths towards a temporary stop (a meaning) are moments of a process and not of a totality of fixated entities. A stop on the path is in the context of Peirce's philosophy not a standstill but rather a specific meaning, which is a basis for action and – above all – interaction in the world of human experience.

A specific observation underlines her understanding of the discordant basis of legal discourse: 'just as there is not one ideal legal system, but rather a legal system as actually a network of competing and conflicting legal subsystems, so there is not one type of legal discourse but conflicting modes of legal reasoning which interact in any given period of time and are coeval in any given society'. Peirce's methodology and discourse are 'an open-ended mode of reasoning capable of further inquiry and indicating that although one and only one decision may be made in each case other options do exist and through this manner of possible reasoning may be explored. Herein is the key to analyses of the structure of reversed decisions and of contradiction between rules of law.'[5]

This insight conveys an important factor at issue. The observation of a network of competing and conflicting legal (sub)systems goes hand in

---

[4] Roberta Kevelson, *The Law as a System of Signs*, Plenum Press, New York/London, 1988.

[5] Kevelson, *supra note 4*, pp. 11–13.

hand with conflicting modes of legal reasoning. Discourses do not automatically solve discordances while they are in the articulation mode. Law's discourse is no exception in that regard. Its language remains leveled and thus vulnerable, especially at the level of meaning(s). Legal solutions are initiated and accepted at levels of discordance. Law is never in unison and law's conflict solutions are never without discordances in opinion and effect. Politicians know by experience how law works in that regard. *Legal meanings are most vulnerable at the level of obedience and compliance; to express them* (an idea, an opinion or a desired position) *in language does not provide security of any kind.*

Ad (2): Not only do humans (citizens) speak *with* and *in* us, but also institutions and corporations. As a consequence, we should notice that many voices resound in a Self and many speakers join the speaking institutions in that Self because they are trying to find a partner in their conversation. Speech acts are never a single individual act, which is performed with just one voice; they are always an activity of a voice selected from an entire chorus! Philosophers seldom consider this multiplication of the features of a speech act in law and legal practice. John Searle's ideas fail to consider this dimension and are influencing legal reasoning only by means of their dual character, mirrored in the 'speaker–hearer' relation.[6] This simple observation directs us towards an improved insight in the complexity of speech activity, the leveled character of language and the socio-political components of legal conversation. The signifying activity of talking about law is rooted in the complexity of speech in general and of legal speech in particular.

That activity is the place to consider compliance, participation, solidarity and obedience as attitudes required by law and discussed in the majority of talks about law. They are essential in contemporary democracy's citizen participation, divided between daily language and the language of the legal profession and in essence already discordant. Both are not based on 'free' speech but on a limited choice out of limited linguistic material for composing speech acts. Participants in conversation explore those limitations as well as (often more forcefully) institutions. This was why the concept of 'stalking' was introduced in the preceding chapter.

The expression 'stalking' illustrated how powerfully institutions are important and forceful speakers.

[6] John Searle, *Speech Acts: An Essay in the Philosophy of Language*, Cambridge University Press, Cambridge, 1969.

In law and legal discourse their speech activity is anchored in three levels of legal articulation: cases, texts and acts. Each speaker *in* legal discourse as well as each speaker *about* law displays expressions that are, apart from personal sources, mastered by institutional levels. They are often in effect as if they were not just levels but words and special meanings, which social forces (especially institutions) prescribe. There is no need to underline in this context that 'legally correct' behavior includes compliance with legal rules. But what is true for behavior is also true for speech. The philosophical presuppositions in the case of speech are important, and determine the relation of legal speech and institutions. Legal speech inside legal discourse is defined by rule references, including cases that function as rule prescription, texts that provide rules, or types of verbal behavior that confirm law's rules. Speech about law from outside legal discourse and doctrine has to submit itself to the same predetermined patterns.

These patterns are anchored in institutions, which in their turn try to be compatible with the main outlines of the master-narrative in the culture concerned. Searle's single-word related understanding of verbal utterances, which he refers to as 'speech acts', brings him to facts created by institutions.[7] In that light is the creation of institutional facts featured by linguistic utterances, which are characterized as performative speech acts. His example is simple and often also mentioned in other words:

> If you are the chairman, then saying in appropriate circumstances 'The meeting is adjourned' will make it the case that the meeting is adjourned. Saying, in appropriate circumstances, 'I appoint you chairman' will make it the case that you are chairman. The same words made by the wrong person or in the wrong circumstances will have no such effect. Because the constitutive rule enables the function to be imposed on a speech act, then just performing that speech act in appropriate circumstances can constitute the imposition of that function, and thus will constitute a new institutional fact.[8]

As a conclusion, Searle suggests that a performative utterance can always create a new institutional fact. The above pages in this chapter suggest two critical considerations about this view: First, Searle's suggestion is based on a philosophy of language in which linguistic utterances and words in particular are autonomous and non-contextual acts. Second, the

---

[7] Jan M. Broekman, *Meaning, Narrativity, and the Real*, Springer, Switzerland, 2016, pp. 93ff, 106ff.

[8] John Searle, *The Construction of Social Reality*, Allen Lane, London, 1995, p. 54ff.

language of institutions is *not* a contextual social structure. Both restrictions are in force when the creation of institutional facts is related to words in a language. The status-function of any expression of those facts is *not*, however, the consequence of a single-word based language.

The link between language and institution is of essence, Searle also concluded. He writes: 'The solution to our puzzle is to see that language is precisely designed to be a self-identifying category of institutional facts.' He also recognizes that language has cultural roots by definition. But language remains for him the use of words as single elements – institutions are in that light a body that masters the use of words according to its proper principles and interests. The discussion about institutions as speakers is in this light shrinking to considerations pertaining to the use of words in institutional settings. Searle's example proves how correct this point of criticism is. He quotes the Muslim habit of divorcing through the three-times-use of the words 'I-divorce-you'. He concludes that in such a case 'a new status-function has been imposed upon an existing sentence form'.

Ask a lawyer. Is a divorce, as used and understood in private law within the context of a Civil Law system, just a word that creates the legal fact called 'divorce'? Law is far more, and more deeply, rooted in cultural components than in the utterance of a word and the institutional consequences of that utterance. Searle and other philosophers of language suggest that the sentence does not change but just creates a new institutional fact. But do words (a sentence is just a combination of words in the light of analytical philosophers) change their status while creating new institutional facts; is that creation of facts completely dependent upon the use of words, and also the speaking of an institution? It would include that social reality in its entirety depends solely upon words. But is a dictionary the key to the construction of social life? What about the multiplicity of languages and their leveled character? While considering the linguistic levels of language and law, one enters the field of the many 'law-language' connections again.

The latter observation is not without importance. Language *precedes* analysis and consensus, two concepts of language and mind that are continuously in danger of denying the constitutive power of the social. Language proficiency is a prime condition for action – hence the importance of the major brain processes pertaining to language, which are becoming profiled through modern research. Language capacity is not solely a means or just an instrument for human communication, language is the *milieu* in which the capacity unfolds to speak and make oneself clear. A *social structure* comes via this milieu into existence, which is much more than a sole conversion of speech acts. Speakers and hearers, senders and receivers depend on contents and structures of that *milieu*.

3.1.3 Socio-Legal Levels

Language is our most important mental construct, Husserl explained and Derrida, Foucault, Lacan, Piaget reformulated. Language sets man apart from other organisms, and functions as the basic tool of thought and reason – even in processes where humans transcend their biological limits. Consider how a view behind appearances is not an *optical* but a *linguistic* option: perception becoming language! Remember Nietzsche's mistrust of language suggests that any form of pragmatism was always a validation or a subversion of cogent standards. Peirce knew the tension between objective and subjective dimensions of pragmatism, whereby the latter precluded deconstruction efforts, which were for him in his days idiosyncratic and negativistic.

Legal practitioners often show that overwhelming attitude they also call *pragmatic*. A challenging question is whether semiotics ever meets such a pragmatic legal mindset and what exactly the semiotics of legal pragmatism should mean in this context. One remembers how human history might be a matter of graphs, trails and inscriptions, of acts and deeds that leave marks behind as if they were inscriptions in the stones of the ages. The Latin expression '*pragmaticus*' refers to the '*jurisconsult*', the advisor in legal issues who grounds his advice in experience with and knowledge of the facts and their history. His pragmatic knowledge does justice to those facts and in doing so creates an equilibrium that can be appreciated as 'just', or even 'right'. It thus becomes clear that a pragmatic attitude embraces more than an incidental appropriateness of applying norms to facts, or principles to forms of disequilibrium and conflict. Semiotics claims the renewal of attitudes that makes the multicultural prevail. In doing so, it engenders *a view beyond the surface* of our perception. Those views are always a view at reality behind the scenes of appearances: a truly semiotic move and a privileged code in the deconstruction mood. The latter is only useful if *structures* are recognizable in non-apparent layers of reality – even in the often-mysterious depth of virtual realities. It imports that those are perhaps solely accessible by means of linguistic articulations and (re)constructions. The field seems open for socio-legal insights of this character.

Today, we appreciate those efforts rather as a key to have the human mind reach beyond the apparent, and underlining the wealth of possibilities to deal with reality. This is today's cultural and spiritual background for lawyers who just want to practice law. How do they manage the many meanings of their expression: 'to practice law', we already formulated in the preceding chapter? Yes, they *manage* those meanings, because these are not given beyond their choice and their power of inventing or using words, signs, symbols and special meanings. Consider how legal practice incorporates a specific body of knowledge, in Civil Law named *dogma* and in Common Law *doctrine*. The two are not identical but aim at the same core issue: *making law fit with multiple contexts of society* by means of mastering their professional language without neglecting the all-embracing natural language.[9]

The 'fit' is essential here, since the process of making law fit is hitherto only understood as a matter of human acts so that lawyers are not prepared even to consider a 'fit' created by computers. That issue is important, because the question 'What is law' does not have as a focus point what lawyers *think*, but what they *do*! And what they do cannot be characterized by theoretical considerations, especially because outsiders do not dispose of any theoretical framework to judge legal activity. Such a judgment can, as they say, only unfold from within and thus often remains an issue internal to law and legal discourse. In other words: what practitioners do does not relate to abstract criteria maintained by others.

The Romans already had an adage for that attitude, when they stated that *law is what jurists say that law is*. In other words: professionals tell non-professionals that they are not able to determine the qualities of law because they are positioned outside the profession and its discourse. The background difficulty pertains to the fundamental question (again!) how professional language is able to use natural language for the sake of its clarification and therefore also for communication with the world outside the profession. In other words: the issue is in the operational value the professional can give to a natural language. We already noticed how legal practitioners tend to say that concept and interpretation of legal '*practice*' is theoretical in itself. The word 'theoretical' means precisely this 'outside the discourse'. But in what regions is one outside a discourse? What is the task of semiotics in this context? The question again leads to a master-narrative influencing a professional discourse.

Obedience and compliance are an outcome of the thought patterns of legal practice laid out over society as subtle and fine linen. The study of the 'law and semiotics' relationship illustrates the central position of legal practice in law and society. Practice has an epistemological importance that dominates all legal meanings, signs and symbols and differs from

---

[9] Jan M. Broekman and Larry Catà Backer, *Lawyers Making Meaning*, Springer, Dordrecht, 2013, p. 99ff.

'doing law' or 'practicing law' in terms of non-lawyers. Not the application, but *an 'applying essential meaning-components of legal character' while 'creating them' leads to the final result that law 'fits'*. That is in essence a linguistic occurrence. Both types of components are relevant in a semiotic view, and therefore one could say that not the 'fit' itself but the 'leading to the fit', a process, is a core issue in the 'law and semiotics' relation!

If law as a discourse is dominated by actions and thought patterns of its practitioners, how then should semiotics be understood? Does semiotics have to focus practices of law because these practices express all dimensions of doctrinal nature, which constitute the legal discourse in its entirety?

A first possible answer is to *oppose* this semiotic analysis and to categorize that idea in the generally accepted form of a 'theory-praxis contrast' – which is a typical European cultural context and Civil Law approach.

Secondly is, apart from opposing, the possibility to *mirror* semiotic and legal practices and treat legal semiotics like literature or religion. Hermeneutics as well as narrative theories of law, and a strong 'law and literature' movement would perhaps justify that approach.

A third answer would treat semiotics as a *non-legal* discipline – a discipline that has no influence on legal discourse and the practice of law.

Those three approaches do not solve the question how to mold the law and semiotics relation. We keep those approaches and attitudes in mind when perceiving other dimensions in the 'law and semiotics' complexity: the concept of '*application*', the concept of '*analysis*', and Deleuze and Guattari's expression *assemblage* as a borderline concept that leads to the concept of '*engineering*' meaning. The latter appears as a constant operation in the unfolding of human thought. Deleuze's example contributes to our deeper insight and challenges our habits of engineering those insights. He refers to the generally accepted difference between nomads and sedentary peoples. He claims that the first did not precede the latter: nomadic life is essentially a movement, an engenderment, a dynamics that challenges all forms of life. Fleerackers underlined that 'the nomad is nomadic solely in the engendering, in interaction'.[10]

---

[10] G. Deleuze and F. Guatteri, *Milles Plateaux*, Paris, 1980 (English edition edited by B. Massumi, *A Thousand Plateaus*, University of Minnesota Press, Minneapolis, MN/London, 1987) p. 362; F. Fleerackers, *Rechtsdenken. Vade Mecum*, Larcier, Brussels, 2016, p. 35; F. Fleerackers, 'Conflict Resolution and Social Complexity' *XXVI World Congress of Philosophy of Law*, Editora Forum, 2013, pp. 690–96.

The lawyer's concept of application represents, as a social form, a *limited* reach of knowledge and interest – semiotics being the application of signs and symbols, and law the application of rules, norms and laws. The narrow scale of knowledge operating here has its philosophical implications. The thought model named 'application' is generally operating *atomistic* patterns. That is clearly visible where legal practices perceive language as a composite of linguistic elements and where semiotics perceives meaning as a composite of individual signs or related semantic units. Jackson described the consequences of that pattern.[11] His major motive is that the relation between semiotics and legal theory shows dimensions, which bring a positivist, a naturalist and a realist interpretation of reality together. Semiotic applications to law are *positivist* in so far as the semiotic object is taken as a fixed datum, a definable and empirical object. They are *naturalist* in so far as the existence of universal systems of meaning need to be embraced for that particular application, and *realist* because the semiotic analysis reads the message that is codified in the object. The inherent epistemology of semiotics thus combines the three major philosophical approaches, whereby the positivistic perspective is the most proximate to law.

It is not without relevance that this theoretical construct is based upon an interpretation of the relations between semiotics and law as both belonging to the dynamics of application as a linguistic act that manifests empathy and compliance. The procedure itself, however, is based on atomistic presumptions: meanings are composed of single elements such as signs and symbols, which are there before they enter specific discourses such as the law. But understanding the law–semiotics relation requires knowledge *beyond* those atomistic presumptions.

A widespread idea about the law and semiotics relation is that the semiotic apparatus applied to law and legal discourse leads to a more appropriate and reliable *analysis* of law. This idea of a dominating analysis of law and an appropriate view on its linguistic consequences is the background of many legal semiotic essays. To study the signs and symbols, as well as their operative forces in legal discourse, more than the often doctrinal explanations of lawyers, makes clear how and what legal discourse does and wants to achieve in law's institution and in general society.

But a first and epistemologically foremost important implication is that this attitude neglects the fine line between law and non-law and risks to

---

[11] B. Jackson, *Law, Fact and Narrative Coherence*, Deborah Charles Publishers, Liverpool, 1988.

be judged irrelevant by law practitioners. One can read in Kevelson's publications how she tries to avoid that risk through paying attention to the dialectics between the legal system as a discursive total on the one hand, and historical as well as doctrinal fragments that play a constitutive role in understanding law in terms of lawyers on the other. She underlines:

> A semiotics perspective on law … is not to be confused with some recent structuralist approaches to law, which sometimes are confused with what is called here legal semiotics. Although, from a historical point of view, the emergence of structuralism and semiotics in this country coincided in the early 1960s totally different philosophical assumptions underlie each of these approaches despite certain surface similarities. Furthermore, although there are important correlations between a semiotic approach to legal interpretation and the popular Continental movement in hermeneutics, the relationship between the latter and a Peirce-grounded semiotics and its methods of interpretation and inquiry is not so much superficial as reflective of a divergence between the objectives of these two distinct modes of sign interpretation.[12]

Many issues as exposed in the above lines would be appreciated differently in the light of contemporary technical developments and knowledge, as is clear in the case of today's semiotics.[13] And they are also appreciated differently because of the strong tendency of *approximation* and *convergence* between Civil Law and Common Law, as Civil Law's construction of EU law illustrates. This is an issue in recent legal history that emerged after the first attempts to formulate legal semiotics, which develops into dimensions of *global* law. It suggests that Common Law and semiotics are closely related through the dynamics of (legal) pragmatism. And even where Kevelson tries to establish semiotic considerations (about the essence of a sign, or a functional interpretation of a complex meaning) right in the heart of legal reasoning or of a portrait of law's mainstreams like legal realism, the idea of pragmatics prevails. Analyses by means of understanding the flow of meanings in law bind legal theory and legal practice, because on that level of understanding 'the lawyer, no less than the legal philosopher, would be engaged in the same acts of law – where act is both on the level of ideas and their development in thought and in the courts with respect to practical legal

---

12 R. Kevelson, *supra note 4*, p. 274ff.
13 Jan M. Broekman, *supra note 7*, p. 251ff.

procedure …'.[14] Practicability remains the often theoretically misunderstood or underestimated force of law. Praxis is managed and translated in terms of theory, but remains in essence practice in the heart of social relationships, which are already, long before they receive attention by the legal analyst, denominated by law's 'legal' interest!

Does semiotic analysis lead to a 'one law, one world' view, the law being developed into a 'globally mixed legal system'? Linguistic approaches, often roots for semiotic analyses of legal discourse, do indeed need emphasis on a general denomination, on principles, common coherences or on disambiguated terminologies. This relates to the fact that the concept of 'law' itself changed meaning in a global perspective. There are no uniform legal systems anymore, and 'mixed' legal systems do prevail, mixed in the first place between Civil and Common Law features, and international treaties suggest that their contacts are independent forms of law. Semiotic interest in them often underlines the importance of artificial intelligence, computer skills and virtual visions on issues we normally tackle by means of natural language. The question arises whether semiotics leads in a concealed manner to a striving for unknown combinations of natural and artificial languages, whereby the status of legal language is again the subject of critical reflection.

Assemblage is Deleuze and Guattari's surprising terminology – surprising because one would not expect such a challenging translation of lawyers' activities. The same is the case with *engineering*. But is it possible to gain any further insight in the specificity of law through semiotics as its medium? It is indeed; however, under the condition that law is redefined and legal speech acts perceived in the light of semiotics in a new key. A variety of viewpoints make us understand law. Extremes of that range of various viewpoints are (a) a complete autonomous and self-referential determination what law is and how law should be practiced, and (b) the understanding of law as one of the many discourses of and about society, with an importance varying from one social structure to another. The concept of 'assemblage' that characterizes lawyers' practices approximates the latter. Deleuze indicates that contemporary law should be perceived as 'Oedipal law', which we are obliged to have behind us in post-modern ages – despite the fact that we find ourselves often back in such an Oedipal situation: law does not provide us with lawyers who are exclusively producers of new forms of life. They do not exhibit any desire for new ways of life that fit all possibilities inherent to life, and do not fully educate us in those new

---

14 R. Kevelson, *supra note 4*, p. 276.

dimensions of a non-Oedipal social situation. In order to do so, law should not remain restrictive but become expansive. Unger criticized in this context 'the cult of State law' (which forms the background for the desire of many citizens and lawyers alike), which causes us to remain in the Oedipal type of law:

> The association of the quest for latent moral order with the cult of the State and its law had its progressive aspect in its corroding effect upon the belief in a natural, pre-political system of social life. As the great lever of transformation, the State links social change with social will. The price of this appeal to the State, however, is high. It has been steadily increasing: We recognize only part of the cost of pietism about power. ... To avoid paying this price, it is not enough to cool the fervor of our statolatry by dissolving the bond between the cult of the State and its law and the search for latent moral order. We must go further and rid ourselves of the residue of the idea of latent order itself. In its place we should put a vision of the great constructive forces ... legal analysis as institutional imagination should serve. One such force is practical experimentalism embraced to heighten our powers: of insight into our circumstances, and of emancipation from drudgery, infirmity, and insecurity. At the heart of practical progress lies the relation between cooperation and innovation. ... The other great constructive force is the demand for personal freedom and self-assertion. ... Moreover, we must live in a way recognizing the truth that there is more in us, individually as persons or collectively as mankind, than there is in the institutional and discursive worlds we make and inhabit.[15]

The catchword for this appeal is in Deleuze's quest for perceiving law as *emergent*, and to embrace *semiotics* to teach us the dimensions of that emergence, as was mentioned before in the context of his differentiation of two types of people: nomadic and sedentary. All implications of this attitude are very different from semiotics as an instrument for a more perfect analysis of law on its own! Once we accept, for instance, the Civil Law metaphor to perceive law as a body that expresses law's coherence, consistency and continuity, then we are also able to understand how emergent law is constituted by information, in particular electronically engendered and transmitted information (with, as we outlined before, the cyber-story as its most recent past and smart phones on the street as their actual practice). That type of information changes linguistic categories, a change that also influences the qualities of semiotics.

---

[15] R. M. Unger, *What Should Legal Analysis Become?* Verso, London/New York, 1996, p. 183ff.

An example is how we understand a human skin nowadays as an organ that expresses its 'being an inside' as well as 'being an outside'. 'Law is emergent' means primarily that law is constituted by information, not from a non-law region outside any standardized legal discourse, but from a within-region that is exterior to doctrinal rule-following. This breaks down any organic philosophical approach. Thinking along the lines of an organism in the case of law maintains painstakingly precisely drawn lines between law and non-law. Legal practitioners consider their legal activity in that context as 'art' more than as 'science' because they are trained to walk such thin lines and manipulate them accordingly. But the power of information might strongly influence our imagination of what law is and can be in a future society, combining the virtual and the real reality the way a human skin combines its inside and outside while putting that delineation in perspective. It thus justifies the idea that understanding semiotics in relation with law depends heavily on our understanding of law!

If there exists indeed a position called *emergent law*, one should conclude, then this type of law is not yet in use by the average lawyer. Only a radical reformulation of what law is supposed to be today can clarify this formula: *law is emergent law because law is there*! It is there without detectable origin, without unambiguous source, without a first law-word ever written, without a first law or legal experience instigated. Law like language – should one say: 'there exists no law before law'?

3.1.4 Jurisprudential Levels

The 'law-language' relation is in effect on all levels of jurisprudence. The most important component of this relation is indicated by the 'two languages thesis', which delineates the continuous changes of natural and professional language in a lawyer's function. This is a matter of translation, or even of transformation, of meanings in which the signifying process plays a dominant role. The activity of the translator never suffices in the field of jurisprudence and its practices. He or she can refer to the untranslatability of certain linguistic expressions, the difficulties of intervening in the directness and uniqueness of expressions or the complexity of the legal vocabulary. But whatever argument is proposed, all are semiotic phenomena that are part of the dynamics of meaning-creation, and far beyond an individual subject's power.

This observation is extremely profiled in cases of legal *texts*, which must in the first place be understood as a preferred level of legal meaning-making. A change of attitude in the philosophical interpretation of language in law occurs at the moment in which such a translation – or transformation activity – reaches the level of texts. This leveled character of legal texts elucidates the predominance of language. Four psycho-socio-linguistic relevant processes play a role in the emergence of that character. They do so in a remarkable proximity to Foucault's insights on the structure of a discourse. First, there is a nearly psychoanalytic power at work in repression or suppression processes that characterize any semiotic research. Signs and complex significations that constitute a legal text are always survivors of repression: others had to disappear in order to let special meanings come to the fore. Second, there is the absolute necessity of syntaxes at work: focus is on the connections among expressions, which form a specific legal language topology as the basis of a text. An adjudication of places and spaces in that topology can become a decisive factor in a legal judgment. Third, authority, and particularly the power of authority in decision processes, is probably the major sociological feature of a legal text. That power is the result of an enduring selection within, fourth, a general shortage of meaning possibilities. Not everything can mean everything. Selections have to be made, shortage reigns and conciseness is prominently in demand. This causes the often-alto aberrant desire to precisely define the sometimes indefinable in terms of law and legal discourse. The four features illustrate the complexity of law's authority. But they also suggest an unexpected and surprising conclusion: legal speech acts and legal texts as special carriers of legal meanings result equally from those four processes – so text, so spoken word, and vice versa.

For instance the speech act 'I herewith declare …' is the winner of a contest which the four features constitute. It means that speech acts are only 'free' within the framework of the contest, and so is any obedience to legal rules and their authority. All change because of the diversity of results of the contest. And it is the power of that contest, Foucault would also have said, that causes jurisprudence in its most classical sense to be leveled, discordant and often contradictory. Most of those contradictions are appeased by means of completing laws or other jurisprudential measures. Law thus takes care of its own – it takes care to continuously awaken the impression of harmony, coherence and reliability despite its discordant character.

MacCormick studied already in 1984 the concept of 'normative coherence' as a concept that is essential for law and legal discourse. He treated legal rules as normative values and the meaning of coherence should represent the ideal of law being a harmonious social institution. We underline with emphasis that this harmony is the key to his final conclusion. 'I have assumed that "coherence" can usefully be distinguished from consistency', MacCormick writes:

> I interpret consistency as being satisfied by non-contradiction. A set of propositions is mutually consistent if each can without contradiction be asserted in conjunction with every other and with their conjunction … coherence is the property of a set of propositions which, taken together, 'makes sense' in its entirety … I conclude that the coherence of norms is a matter of their 'making sense' by being rationally related as a set, instrumentally or intrinsically, *either* to the realization of some common value or values; *or* to the fulfillment of some common principle or principles … [and] that in their totality they express a satisfactory form of life, and one in which it would be possible for human beings, as human beings are, to live.[16]

In short, we learn that *harmony* is the ultimate value and basic pattern of law, and that the requirement of *coherence* illustrates the layered or leveled character of law. If, however, 'harmony' is wrapped up in 'discordance', does modern law as a consequence speak in words that are winners from the above-described contest?

With his widely read 1986 publication, shortly after MacCormick's remarks, Ronald Dworkin formulated in his *Law's Empire* a central and often reconsidered thesis pertaining to *integrity* in law and legal application.

> Law as integrity denies that statements of law are either the backward-looking factual reports of conventionalism or the forward-looking instrumental programs of legal pragmatism. It insists that legal claims are interpretive judgments and therefore combine backward- and forward-looking elements; they interpret contemporary legal practice seen as an unfolding political narrative. So law as integrity rejects as unhelpful the ancient question whether judges find or invent law; we understand legal reasoning, it suggests, only by seeing the sense in which they do both and neither.

Is the position described as 'both and neither' associated with 'integrity'? Dworkin answers:

> According to law as integrity, propositions of law are true if they figure in or follow from the principles of justice, fairness, and procedural due process that provide the best constructive interpretation of the community's legal practice. … Law as integrity is therefore more relentlessly interpretive than either conventionalism or pragmatism. … It is both the product of and the inspiration for comprehensive interpretation of legal practice.[17]

---

[16] Neil MacCormick, 'Coherence in Legal Justification' in W. Krawietz, H. Schelsky, G. Winkler, and A. Schramm (eds), *Theorie der Normen: Festgabe für Ota Weinberger zum 65 Geburtstag*, Duncker & Humblot, Berlin, 1984, p. 38ff.

[17] Ronald Dworkin, *Law's Empire*, Fontana Press, London, 1986, p. 225ff.

The toolbox of interpretation is not, however, investigated with this appeal to coherence in law and legal practice, let alone in understanding what law is at the various levels of its linguistic utterances or on the basis of its close ties with language.

The fact that such a consideration can come up at all proves how radically our jurisprudence is tied to law as a changing discourse. Law's time schedules are, for instance, closely linked to *Great Events*, which are experienced first and then narrated in master discourses. They are either a World War, or a Great Economic Crisis, or Culture Shocks between Religions (Sharia law) and Political Systems (the Berlin Wall and the Downfall of Communist Regimes) and sometimes Changing Business Models (from Multinationals to Global Corporations). All examples illustrate in what regard law fights for the fixation of such settings – a fixation, which regards in the first place the power to create a standstill of rule applications, of key expressions, of new legal concepts, which, for instance, pertain to human rights, to Equality of Man and Woman, to Migrant Problems or related large scale social issues. Is the citizen, a legal subject in terms of Civil Law, protected and assisted in life with such jurisprudential mega-patterns, or on the contrary with a word of compliance by an individual lawyer?

3.1.5 Levels of Obedience

Levels of obedience and of compliance are subjected to legal decisions and definitions. What must be considered as 'following legal rules' is a matter of legal decision-making and of lawyers' engineering. There is no 'natural language' definition of that behavior – it is all tied to meanings that are a matter of law's power. Authority is not a property of persons, of institutions, or of natural language defining. To limit authority in such a manner would be a naïve-ontological interpretation of the word's meaning. The deep structure of our entire speech activity is in the reference to a social equilibrium. Aristotle already remarked that authority dissipates where this equilibrium dissolves. Modern multiplicity of social meanings unveils in how many ways authority is an essential component of a speech act. Dispersion and difference dominate in the materials from which our life-world is made. Authority is in this light a difficult to accept value judgment. Philosophical reflections experience difficulties when they want to loosen the ties between authority and power. A parallel is in the relations among authority and freedom. Freedom is decidedly not the opposite to authority. The two are tied by difference, a concept that is equally important for speech activity, authority and mastership as well as freedom – although their variant contents go with different cultural settings and master-narratives. No wonder that totalitarian as well as democratic political regimes suggest a close connection with the concept of freedom. Politics and law interpret freedom as an individual property or asset, and organize social reality accordingly. Sovereignty of the individual, its freedom and position in the history of mankind, as well as its enduring support of human rights are indispensable components of obedience to legal rules, compliance with the law and respect for human dignity. The 'received view' in legal theory underlines for that reason the triadic structure of freedom, autonomy and authority. The three form the basis for legal rule-following. Acting as a legal subject is for any philosophy of Civil Law the ultimate profile of man in society.

Here action is linguistically embedded. The levels of action in which a subject of law unfolds its articulations are limited. They are the levels of linguistic articulation (all transformative powers included), the levels of socially embedded speaker–hearer position, the levels of multicultural nature and the levels of freedom to deploy specific views and underlying opinions (from active citizenship and radical social interpretations to group behaviors in politics and political debates). All those levels of compliance with law are a matter of meaning-creation.

This is why legal semiotics is so important. It creates insight into the meaning-making and meaning-management of the legal discipline, which has consequences for legal discourse itself as well as for society in its totality. Lawyers are the preferred experts of legal meanings: if they cannot manage a meaning or a set of meanings, then they *create* meanings; if they cannot create meanings, then they *manage* meanings – meanings are always reconsidered, renewed, reissued, replaced, reactivated or revaluated – remember Deleuze's expression 'assemblage'!

Lawyers accept the idea that they *manage meanings*. Their management is a form of engineering society through meanings. As was explained several times before: the *language of everyday* delivers to a lawyer the meanings of life in a directness that does not exist in law, and the *language of law* delivers to them meanings to operate in a jargon that does not exist in daily life. Legal and State institutions wish to have the citizen's interests translated in legal language so that the latter dominates their lives. An irony is how lawyers and institutions compel us to 'forget' the scope and dominating force of those translation efforts, which are vital for State and Citizen alike.

Multiple dimensions of 'engineering' are at stake. They form a counterbalance against concepts such as 'application' or even 'analysis' in the law and semiotics relationship. One should bear in mind that *legal hermeneutics* is indeed accepted by a well-considered focus on the two, but is missing a semiotic context. Twentieth century hermeneutics in philosophy and in legal theory did *not* pay explicit attention to legal semiotics – they did not even mention the word. No wonder that 'application' and 'analysis' were taken by lawyers as the pillars of their activity while operating with meanings, which they called their (that is: law's) 'practice'.

To mention the concept of *engineering* in the context of law and the legal sciences is not aberrant. 'The Acropolis and the Parthenon in Greece, the Roman aqueducts, the Hanging Gardens of Babylon, the Pharos of Alexandria, the pyramids in Egypt, Teotihuacán and the cities and pyramids of the Mayan, Inca and Aztec Empires, the Great Wall of China, among many others, stand as a testament to the ingenuity and skill of ancient engineers', a Wikipedia page tells us.[18] And – one can add – so does the Justinian Code, an, in essence, Roman Code conceived in a Greek speaking country, the Bologna studies of that very same Code, the Napoleonic Code or modern treaties around the world. They are mega-constructions of legal texts aiming at an ever effective and just order of a society. But micro-constructions for daily life situations bear the same characteristics, and are produced in equally conceived discourses. However, one needs to overcome the limits of application or analysis and value the semiotic dimensions of law as an engineered discourse to understand its engineering dynamics.

Of particular interest is the concept of re-engineering. Originally used for business processes, it is nowadays enjoying a wider interest. Two elaborations of *re*-engineering law and legal discourse are in the *re* of *re*peated, and also as the *re* of *re*constructed. It is clear that both differ fundamentally, and also have a different epistemological status. The most surprising and renewing use is in the second concept: the re-engineering as a dynamic reconstruction. A major problem is that re-engineering legal discourse means in the first place tackling the structures of law's institutional hierarchy. Why are we trained to refer to *higher* cases, *higher* courts, or *higher* judges? 'What is up, must go down' could be a slogan for re-engineering, which would rather inverse hierarchical levels.

Re-engineering might become a far more important mode of operation to acquire knowledge of all sorts of processes, among them the question of our references to *higher* levels of authority. They illustrate the effects of jurisprudence as a leveled phenomenon. One could ask: 'Do higher levels of authority, expressed in cases or court decisions, fit the concept

---

[18] See www.wikipedia.org/wiki/Engineering#Ancient-era, accessed 13 April 2017.

of emergent law?' They do not, is the answer – and that challenges the semiotics and law relationships. If one accepts that lawyers manage meanings through semiotic operations, then the meanings themselves are to be understood as signs, symbols and other semiotic entities.

De Saussure and other linguists have taught us that the meaning of a sign does not completely determine the semiotic operations. To shuffle signs and symbols has not a meaning in and of itself, we experienced. One should discuss this with lawyers or judges high and low in legal hierarchy. They understand that there is not *one and only one* theory of consciousness. Relating law with semiotics is not a matter of treating legal understanding and articulation as an exclusive issue of broadened awareness. Meaning and understanding that emerge in legal discourse are *emergent* properties of its complex patterns of activity. Emergent patterns have the same role in non-biological, in particular social, systems as they do in biological systems such as the brain. They are objects of re-engineering as a major epistemological operation. Semiotics would propose legal theoreticians to accept re-engineering in order to join 'talking about law' and pay attention to its emergent patterns.

That viewpoint is disavowed where one extends the meaning of the concept 'discourse' of law and semiotics, and re-engineers the concept according to non-individualistic and eventually non-consciousness determined criteria. A specificity of each discourse is that it is never constructed from single fixated linguistic or semantic elements one can apply from one discourse to another. That is often translated as 'discordance'. But meaning as a constitutive element of a discourse is by definition fluid and in a process of continuous change, since discourses must be understood as a semantic milieus, which create varying meanings at varying levels with varying signifiers.

Two views on what it means to obey law are important here – they confirm the leveled character of jurisprudence. The opinion that an understanding of – and a compliance with – law is the privilege of legal practitioners only, parallels the idea that legal knowledge is the outcome of *application* of legal rules in a society. The power of that thought pattern is so dominant that the tendency is registered to accept or even share that opinion even in legal semiotics. This limits the contribution of semiotics to legal discourse, and causes a failing insight in the complexity of creating meanings in law.

This leads furthermore to insights into how semiotics intertwines matters of identity and togetherness even beyond knowledge of language, words or linguistic components. We know each other *before* words or linguistic performances blossom functionally in a social relationship.

Verbal expressiveness serves as a means to secure the emergence of social patterns in general.

3.2 A MENTAL STATE

Such emerging social patterns are everywhere. We live them while we listen and speak to others. Our movements seem concordant and fit into their order. Exceptions are difficult to accept. Our mentality could crash. A specific discourse seems designed to cope with them, a discourse called 'legal'. It often intertwines with psychological, psychiatric or medical discourses – one wonders how congruent they are.[19] Apart from neighboring discourses, conversation about legal issues takes place in various places, within various frames of mentality and according to various codes. We thus reread the major thesis of this book: *any conversation on the street about legal topics is relevant for legal semiotics*, and in that regard an important phase in understanding law paving a path from sign to significance.

In order to experience the weight of these observations, one has to listen. Listen carefully in parks and plazas, in public traffic, in café and restaurant, at home and in the workplace. Others will tell you; their conversation is most vital when you do not talk and they are not aware of the fact that you listen. Produce silence within language, register activities of others: they tell you. At unexpected moments and more frequently than you can guess, law is the subject of their talk.

What issues are mentioned while talking about law? The question sounds very normal, but cannot be answered. What words are used on the street? The question also cannot be answered. Of course, words can be underlined, questions and meanings indicated, but these are neither solved nor answered: one does not *use* words, not even on the street, and issues are not completely determined by a use of words. Philosophers like Wittgenstein or Searle suggested that a linguistic articulation takes place by means of the *use* of words. This view still dominates legal philosophy. The 'law-language' relationship tells us, however, a different story. Uttering words is a means of unfolding life. When we speak and articulate words, we *live*, and life unfolds in that same articulation. Life unfolds in every conversation, but the latter is most certainly *not* an exchange of preformatted or fixated expressions or codified meanings. This might be one of the reasons why semiotics of law did not pay much

[19] Jan M. Broekman, *Intertwinements of Law and Medicine*, Leuven University Press, 1996.

attention to our talking about law beyond legal settings. Conversations apart from legal settings are never an exchange of fixated elements. Listening to others is never a pure reception or registration of linguistic entities sent to me or any other listener.

Moreover: there are several accompanying factors which characterize a linguistic articulation with an equally determinative power. A speaker (in legal settings as well as in unspecified public spaces) is never alone. Nor is he or she folded in dual relationships – even if such a duality is recognized as a basic element of a more encompassing 'I–You–It' module.[20] Any speaker needs a multiplicity of constituting elements to create a speech situation. Not only gravity, or air, light, water and other substances are needed, but also other participants to just utter one word on the field of human meaning and signification. This multiplicity is a condition for creating compliance – one cannot comply with anything on its very own. But multiplicity is also not without problems. Western Europe became in an exemplary manner challenged to acknowledge the multicultural as an important feature of society. That brings a new orientation to the fore in attitude formation and it challenges us to develop compliance amidst unknown standards of behavior and above all the need to reach beyond the modality of conflict and harmony. As a consequence, listening to, questioning or analyzing one's talking about law is a complex task to fulfill.

3.2.1 Mentality and Conversation

Conversations, debates and discussions in which legal topics play a role on streets and in other public places are in those talks indicated by their legal terminology. One should notice that these terms have a place and meaning in regions outside law and legal discourse as an institution – regions which we indicated as belonging to a 'natural language' or 'mother tongue'. It means that people talk, for instance, about taxes, police activity, traffic rules, food, health, finances, debts or contracts in legal terms without being able to oversee all components of the exploration of those expressions. Their talking about law as a separate phenomenon confirms that 'law' exists in our midst, but it does not confirm the existence of law's precise activities, nor does it mean that every citizen in a democracy accepts them. The linguistics of talking

[20] As outlined in the last paragraph of Chapter 2.

about law have not only semiotic, but also emotional and mental dimensions. Their mixture is a complicated issue in every form of society.

That becomes very clear when one pays attention to the variety of perspectives in the many, and quite simple, acts of talking about law. There is never an issue that does not in one way or another express a sentiment, a feeling or an emotion. People can become angry when they talk about the legal implications of suspected actions initiated by a bank, when they reconsider public payments, when different actions like traffic controls or restrictions in health care provisions are concerned. Public talk about law is seldom an all-over positive expression of consent, enjoyment or adherence. On the contrary, the talk often tries to mediate opposing viewpoints or cries out in that perspective to see political measures become effective – and sometimes the talk wants to cause changes in the thought patterns and behaviors of lawyers and judges. It implies that a citizen's talk about law in family circles or in public spaces expresses an emotion versus positive law rather than a direct participation or compliance. In a specific semiotic term, one observes a more general set of meanings in effect which does not restrict to purely technical meanings of law and legal discourse.

Talking about law on the street has primarily to do with 'how things are', that is: with 'the world' around us. Law stands for that concern called 'the world' or for many that is also 'reality'. People talk about law and legal discourse because law keeps in their eyes control over any world situation. Law connects Presidents and People. At least: that is a feeling which people express in their conversation – and which Presidents all too often tend to neglect or to place solely in the context of legal-political language. But this is not all there is to perceive: the bounds between the 'talking about law' and the 'world as it is' are in the majority of cases an utterance of anger and anxiety, sometimes a paranoia expressed in slogans and on banners.

Via law and legal discourse a symbol has been created, a sign on all banners and often also in any signifying conversation on the street: *the State*. The State is a metaphor for the world as perceived and experienced in the talking, and in the 'State'-concept all technical expressions of the law are included. Talking about law is ultimately talking about the State. Its innermost mentality, however, guides all participants in their search for laws that are adapted to their anxiety and ardent wishes, the format of their thought formation and the scale of their social activities. The search is – here the title of this chapter has a double meaning – for a 'mental' 'State'. It concerns a law liberated from chains to the State; in the words of a well-known slogan: a *law without State*, or: the 'people side of the law', although that concerns much more than only 'a side', that is: all there is in society and its many levels of reality! The slogan is often heard on the street and in other public places where talks and debates unfold. It must be underlined that those words do *not* immediately refer to anarchism. On the contrary: the words call for a law and a legal system that has other (eventually: better) features because it is not the product of State power and/or does not recognize the State as the highest legal authority so that citizens can better be heard and regions acknowledged.

The role of non-State actors in the law-making process was already noticed in the European Middle Ages. Outside the State various law-making forces were active; they influenced the inside of a legal system. The State concept we know stems from approximately the seventeenth century in Central Europe. Cities, lordships, customs, ecclesiastic norms and even market authorities exercised important powers of law-making or justification of norms and laws. It appears that merchants in the Middle Ages developed a more or less autonomous legal system covering a large variety of markets and behavioral rules of merchant behavior in many countries. The modern desire for law without State seems a desire to return to the European Middle Ages; the State concept as law-maker engendered around the middle of the seventeenth century and is critically debated at the beginning of the twenty-first century. We also observe that together with this relatively short period of State dominance, the international and multilingual merchant law is nowadays transferred into legal provisions among corporations on global markets, as the 2016 discussions pro and contra the Comprehensive Economic and Trade Agreement (CETA) and the Trans-Atlantic Trade and Investment Partnership (TTIP) Treaty prove. These economic and trade agreements have, apart from trade, consequences also for active citizenship, environmental issues, labor law and public services – all in the grip of the contractual interpretation of life in the partner States and their countries.

Indeed, *law without State* is also a slogan. Its words have been considered by Hobbes, Montesquieu, Marx and many other thinkers about law, society and State, about authority and compliance, about the genesis of written laws and spontaneous legal rules. But today, these words are texts one can read on the street, are painted on walls and are clearly readable on banners that after the demonstration will return to the garbage can. Is that a sign that law cannot exist beyond the State? It is doubtful because its words are already in the minds of people before the slogan is in effect.

Teubner quoted two decades ago what the Austrian legal philosopher Eugen Ehrlich formulated already in 1936 when he stated: 'the center of gravity of legal development … from time immemorial has not lain in the activity of the State, but in society itself, and must be sought there at the present time'. Teubner confirms Ehrlich's words and insights in view of the development of a global law. He does not, however, make the point for a reinforced interest in the regions and the talks about law citizens have on the street, which were also not envisaged by Ehrlich: 'I believe that it will turn out to be right, both empirically and normatively, for the newly emerging global law. Empirically, he is right, because the political-military-moral complex will lack the power to control the multiple centrifugal tendencies of a civil world society. And normatively he is right, because for democracy, it will in any case be better if politics is as far as possible shaped by its local context.'[21] But do not forget: a global legal system can be entirely in a State's grip and interest, and not within reach of citizens. A regional legal system as a recognized source of law can indeed be of direct interest for a citizenship, and even global issues can unfold within the control and reach of citizens.

However, the 'law without State' theorem has a very important implication: its focus on what (for instance in Hegel's philosophy) was called '*recognition*' as an act of acknowledgement as well as an act of knowledge creation.

The two meanings come close together when the *other* or some *otherness* is at stake. Formulated in the language of the street: being a citizen includes a position of authority and sovereignty: 'we the people' – words that are often misused and misplaced, but nevertheless of great importance. People's awareness accentuated in talking about law tells us how a State-enforced identity of *reason* and the *rational* is rejected, since the latter (rationality as a State-mastered concept) does not allow one to freely articulate the first. *Reason* is in talks on the street often meant as a power to think anti-institutionally without destroying the foundations of language and its expressivity. In other words: the self-organization of the citizen is at stake in the expression 'law without State', whereas freedom and equality are its key words. Notice that the validity of valid positive law is *not destroyed* in the context of the meanings implied in the slogan, but the sources of that validity are rather *replaced.* This emphasizes beyond doubt the importance and semiotic relevance of the *recognition* concept. When the people on the street insist on exercising their sovereignty conceded to them by the constitution, they do not in their talking about law listen to the government that underlines its respect for

[21] G. Teubner, 'Global Bukowina: Legal Pluralism in the World Society' in Günther Teubner (ed.), *Global Law Without a State*, Dartmouth, Aldershot, 1997, p. 3ff.

the formal limits that oblige citizens by constitution and its legal system. A mutual position is not realistic here. This becomes very clear when governments use, for instance, their police forces to concretize those formal limits. Streets and other public places experience how such forms of power are unfit to create mutuality and thus misuse authority.

That type of experience is embedded in broad and layered meanings; the semiotic constellation at hand is a sign in itself for the unpreparedness to accept directives and rules with which a State seeks to influence or even prescribe citizen's behaviors. Krawietz underlined the strong bond between the slogan 'law without State' on the one hand and the 'self-organization of free and equal citizens' on the other. He remarked that 'this trend raises the question whether and to what extent the law and a judicial sentence – both understood as structural forms and normative paradigms for the genuine legal process of argumentation, substantiation and deciding – do require public or private acceptance or recognition at all'.[22]

Whoever tends to answer this question in the positive should be prepared for a confrontation with the argument that a State is not *by nature* (or in other words: only by cultural determination) a source of authority to issue laws and legal measures that limit free citizens. Can we ever find or create *other* sources? Are rules or laws *by nature* limited to specific sources, among which the State had become the most important in the Occident's Middle Ages? Or do we have to look for other views while finding a solution to those questions, and consider another anthropological level that reminds us how far all *inter-subjectivity* needs a form of *social order*? In other words: can the explained 'I–Thou–It' module ever become realized *beyond* any form of social life that precedes the theorem?

Krawietz does not pose the question directly, but refers (in a way that characterizes legal philosophy and theories of law up to these days) to the position and activity of a judge. He states:

> Many an anxious judge asks himself nowadays – in view of the increasingly critical assessment of numerous laws by the public – whether he, too, can, may or even must do something towards increasing, if possible, the acceptance of those sentences, at least, which he himself has to pass in the course of making judicial decisions in the context of the validity of this statute law.

---

[22] Werner Krawietz, 'On How to Accept a Legal Norm or Legal Order and Different Rules of Recognition' in F. Fleerackers, E. van Leeuwen, and B. van Roermund (eds), *Law, Life and the Images of Man: Modes of Thought in Modern Legal Theory*, Dunker and Humblot, Berlin, 1996, p. 524ff.

> From the normative point of view this question does not make sense, though, unless it is not only the validity of the *general* legal norm fixed by law and institutionalized that requires recognition but also the validity of the *individual* legal norm pronounced by a judicial sentence.[23]

The latter is mostly a point of exploration to begin with in the 'talking about law'-field we envisage. But a deeper philosophical reflection concerns the structure of the term 'recognition'. In that regard, the above formula must be repeated: 'all *inter-subjectivity* needs a form of *social order*'. 'Recognition' is the basis for each self-organization of free and equal citizens, as the 'I–Thou–It' module illustrates, and the same term provides a semiotic access to more specific forms of social order, among which is 'talking about law' in public places beyond courts and law offices. However, deepening an insight into the fact that 'free and equal citizens' can only organize themselves in contrast to any State-related organizing, needs to be pursued. The puzzling difficulty is that neither the 'I–Thou–It' motive nor the insight that *inter-subjectivity* needs *sociability* is a fixated form of (social) life. They cannot be treated as separate linguistic entities or as coins in the busy traffic of mutual understanding.

Modern society itself is a proof of the dynamic and continuously meaning-changing character of these life forms, especially if one considers the ongoing fragmentation in twentieth and twenty-first century Occidental life, in which terms like 'organization', 'freedom' or 'equality' are never fixated but always an element of political merchandise or social utopias. Not only do traditional life forms change considerably during the follow up of generations, but also completely new and unforeseen forms unfold. We mentioned how IT techniques, e-communications and expansions of the human body by means of smart phones constituted such new ways to conduct a social life. The need for recognition, its major character traits included, changes with the speed of its changing meanings. Recognition is no longer a mutual occurrence considering an 'I' and a 'You', but a specific social process in its own right, based on a variety of 'I's and 'You's. That concerns the pattern of *knowledge* as well as the pattern of *acceptance* and *recognition*: the two meanings of the word form dimensions of a process – they become more and more separated, whereby each of them influences social life in a different manner. That makes life more complex, and understanding life a more difficult task to accomplish.

Any self-organization of citizens is influenced by the same powers; their task and goals become increasingly harder to achieve. Maintaining

---

23 Krawietz, *supra note* 22, p. 526.

such life forms asks levels of insight and education which hitherto did not exist in the field of recognition in times when the latter was simply a matter of mutual understanding! This notion has far-reaching consequences: our philosophical insights on the legal foundations of social life also became more complex, and their identity changed considerably. Take the concept of 'freedom' as an example within the context of self-organization of free citizens. Our twenty-first century idea of freedom is by no means identical to 'freedom' in Hobbes' *Leviathan* (1651) or Kant's *Critique of Practical Reason* (1788). Philosophy should be aware of the fundamental changes its vocabulary has undergone during the ages we think to be guided by those authors/philosophers. Look solely at one continuously debated aspect of freedom: the distinction between a 'freedom to ...' and a 'freedom from ...'. Electronics expand and have expanded the 'freedom to ...' towards unimaginable dimensions, including extraterrestrial considerations, whereas 'freedom from ...' would form a catalogue of new achievements, including medicine, physics, psychology or social sciences and ... the law![24]

The conclusion challenges: freedom is not the same anymore as it was before and thoughts concerning 'free and equal citizens' must continuously determine and defend the meaning of freedom and equality they provide and presume at the moment of their formulation and application. That is by no means a purely theoretical remark, but is experienced on the street by every citizen with a smart phone at hand. The extension of notions and values such as freedom or equality are hardly imaginable because they became so generally accepted in such a short period of time. Computers and smart phones took their place in life within a few decades, and they are not alone in indicating important changes. They 'bring to daily life some of the qualities of another artifact of the digital ear: the video game in which the player sustains an anxious state of vigilance against sudden unpredictable intrusions that must be dealt with instantly at the risk of virtual death', Edward Mendelson concluded. His hint towards the broadening of meaning indicates the impact of deep changes in citizen experience: 'This too has its benefits: drivers who

[24] The cultural depths of the digital age frighten – for instance, in the ways recent IS (Islamic State) propaganda films copy Hollywood horror films we do not object to our children watching, with perfect skills, materials and story-building. Their horrifying interpretations mirror Occidental values and exploit the multilayered character of what we call 'reality' in film and TV. Notice the distance of those digital techniques and mentality to the demand for correct data as a basis for the construction and judging of legal cases and law's ruling mechanisms.

grew up playing video games are reportedly quicker than others to respond to sudden danger, more capable of staying alive.'[25]

Can law and legal discourse perform under those unique conditions of change? Do not forget how law's acceptance and defense of changes in meaning and relevance are always threatened by the general but radical requirement to safeguard legal certainty. How can a modern citizen accept to remain an addressee of law, when law changes meanings of its fundamental concepts in parallel with the flow of life, which is illustrated every day in such a convincing manner as is the case with our digital world? Emphasis on *recognition* is of importance again.

3.2.2 Conflict and Harmony

Tensions between the concepts of conflict and harmony are present in all dialogues on 'law without State'. Their question remains vividly present. Is acceptance (or acceptability) of law necessary for legal claims to become valid? It implies: law does not make citizens' claims valid, but citizens make legal claims valid! Feelings and emotions of citizens are framed in the classical equilibrium between conflict and harmony. Do not make a mistake: 'law without State' is *not* a declaration of war on the State, it does *not* imply a distancing from the State in general but rather a re-positioning of law and its authority. Moreover, the meanings and contents of the concepts in this formulation are *not* fixated but change with the flow of time and culture. Krawietz posed the question, whether 'the acceptability of the law is *necessary at all* in order to justify the claim of the law to be recognized as valid. Do citizens and partners in law embark on a critical search for the better reasons in each case?'

Could their strivings focus another form of law, which is not 'State-dependent law'? In other words: there is a deep reflection needed pertaining to the share of an individual or individualized addressee in the process of law-making and legal practice. Not the State, but its citizens decide here! That condition is, however, based on the important premise that law's emergence is influenced by all partners in the social process named 'law'. If that process is beyond our influence, as is often the case in the natural sciences, then we can only perceive and obey the law as it occurs or is. Hence: 'Do law and judicial sentence really require recognition – of whatever kind – by the affected addressee? Or is it not, after all, the case that the legal order is a coercive order consisting of

[25] E. Mendelson, 'In the Depths of the Digital Age' *The New York Review of Books*, June 23, 2016, Vol. LXIII, No. 11, p. 34ff.

directives and norms, addressed to human conduct and vested with the means of legal power which, on the whole, citizens only comply with because they owe legal obedience to it and because they can be forced to compliance or because sanctions are applied against them in case they don't obey the valid law?'[26] When we take one step backward, we can see that the discussion is apparently on the question whether *law is a social or a natural phenomenon.* That is probably the basic consideration in the case of non-State law. Talks on the street concerning law and specified legal issues cherish a clear answer. It signifies the opinion: law is in our hands!

That does not, however, in this discussion solve the implied uncertainty about the addressee of modern law. Recognition, which is always considered in concealed manners, needs precision pertaining to the character of the addressee. Do our observations about law and its practices focus on a citizen in social contexts (the participant of a mother tongue, a natural language) or on a lawyer in legal contexts (the participant of an artificial, a legal language *and* of a natural language, in which to communicate with the client)? In other words: *who* needs a justification of law's validity? Is it the lawyer who can only perform his duties on the basis of this validity, or the citizen who cannot be 'free' and 'equal' and live his or her life without that validity in function? There is no clear answer that embraces *both* addressees at the same time, and there is no answer that is not the result of a thought pattern, which dominates this entire discussion: *the duality of 'conflict' and 'harmony'*. This duality is also at the background of the 'law without State' discussion. Can there be a law in effect that is not backed by any form of State power, by any form of authority? Insights into the validity of law concern 'harmony' as the dominating value that colors law in any cultural setting. But that 'harmony' has 'conflict' as its opposite meaning-creating power.

Is a legal discourse the appropriate means to regulate social life on the basis of those opposite values? An answer to this question may surprise because of its complexity: first, the opposition between conflict and harmony is by no means multicultural or globally accepted – there are cultures in which one cannot imagine anything when the question arises. Secondly: the two terms are value judgments which can vary in a specific social structure as well as in the course of the history of a cultural segment. The terms never played a dominant role in Occidental culture and each of them was meaningful in a different manner in different times

---

[26] Krawietz, *supra note 22*, p. 523.

and under varying conditions. Thirdly, one has to consider that the two do not form any polarity in value judgments, but each term depends on the specific activity pattern of an individual or a group. That pattern appears to be larger than a philosophy of fixated values which the terms 'conflict' and 'harmony' indicate. We conclude that both indicate a *process* under the veil of a *choice.*

Compliance with the law is in that context intensified and not broken down. It rather finds its articulation in volitional acts of decision-making. Any conversation on the street proves the correctness of this observation. But streets are never filled with languages that contain prescriptive or imperative values alone. Von Wright puts the latter in perspective and calls them 'interjections' – a syntactical category. 'To value is more like exclaiming than like prescribing. To say this is not to deny that evaluative and prescriptive discourse are logically related. They are even closely related. We even do not suggest that the study of interjections is the best, or even a good, introduction to the study of value.'[27] But nevertheless: 'interjection' is an important term, which suggests a process character that does not fit to the style of logical considerations but rather to discourse and conversation. Compliance as interjection rejects a static understanding and emphasizes that reconfirmation in different forms at all differing moments of life is needed.

This focuses particularly on *citizens* and their multifaceted roles during their talking about law in non-institutional settings. *Compliance with law is in essence a form of juridification.* But there are contrasting powers in that feature, which concern a legal subject. Compliance was originally understood as a means to overcome conflicting tendencies in and around citizens striving for harmony. But how could a free and equal citizen talk and imagine a 'law without State' on the street while it experiences disharmony all around? The question illustrates that the 'citizen'-concept has many meanings and functions in different positions within the process of a general juridification of modern society. The latter leads sometimes to transnational and sometimes even to global legal structures in which a citizen is supposed to fulfill its role. Do legal thought formation and legal power indeed create harmony in social life?

Developments in EU law during the first decade of the twenty-first century illustrate that incongruence and tensions, conflict and harmony characterize law in more than one respect – as was suggested already when legal discourse was in the preceding pages named 'discordant'.

---

[27] Georg H. von Wright, *Norm and Action*, Routledge and Kegan Paul, London, 1963, pp. 7, 96ff.

The years after the 1992 Maastricht Treaty (TEU), especially the period of the so-called 'Third Generation Agreements', brought not only Europe's unification but also attention to nationalism and regionalism, which were qualified as an effect of the increasing distance between global and local dimensions of life, that is in essence: the distance between natural and artificial language.[28]

A consequence pertaining to the legally affected dimensions of the citizen is of great importance. Local, national, international and even global law (even while a topic of talk on the street) is an issue of a *fractured Self.* It thus appears to be of interest to interrogate the participants on the street whether such a *Self* is, despite fractions and splits, an adequate description of being a legal subject in this context.[29] Their talks are in need of being qualified as talks between *differently affected* Selves. Two lines of thought are twisted in that question.

(1) The first is that fractures of a *Self* appear to be caused when the subject is enforced to engage in the internalization of norms and values that are not reconcilable.
(2) The legal-philosophical issue is whether such a fractured Self, embedded in multicultural contexts of very different scope, can remain to be considered as a whole and unimpaired identity for legal thought patterns, for instance as an undamaged point of reference in questions of civil liability.

All this is important because the main thought patterns in law and politics focus on the individual as a person and – formulated in legal language – consequently as a legal subject.

Such contrasting tendencies can, for instance, be registered in legal documents of the European Union. On the one hand, texts of EU Treaties, Agreements, Declarations and the Commission do not cast any shadow of doubt about the referential function of an intact and unhampered *Self* in law, legal language and legal thought patterns. On the other hand, particularly texts of the *Committee of the Regions* do not display such an attitude, and develop a view on a citizen's *Self* as an issue of social and cultural developments, which are most often discordant. They view institutional and administrative commitments of a *Self* in that light

---

[28] Jan M. Broekman, *A Philosophy of European Union Law*, Peeters, Leuven/Paris, 1999, pp. 225ff, 371ff.

[29] On the concept of a fractured or split Self in philosophy, see Broekman, *supra note 7*, Part I.

and relate to increasing or diminishing feelings and practices of nationalism among citizens. The fractured Self mirrors the widening gap between democracy as the result of supra-national economic integration and democracy in the way it became interpreted at the level of a nation State and its law-making. There is no doubt that the role and positioning, the self-understanding and political maturation of the citizen are a key issue to determine the importance of this gap. Multiculturalism is not the gap itself, but just one of its actual forms.

The role and function of citizens in political philosophy has often been connected with the post-modern term *difference.* This is not only the case where the behavior of citizens appears as directly caused by their proper intentions, but also where it stems from more encompassing structures in which citizens have to live, such as their system of law or administration. This is one of the deep layers of meaning in the contrast between the two types of legal and administrative texts with their conceptions of democracy. That contrast is clear between, for instance, the texts of the *EU Treaties* and those of the *Commission of the Regions* (COR). They show different philosophical aspects regarding the spirit and intention of the administration and law, and different views are basic for their implicit understanding of an emergent *Self* in social patterns.

Max Weber mentioned already in the first decades of the twentieth century the importance of *difference* as a quintessential force in the emerging ideology of citizens. Their behavior was, in his theory, determined by a specific image of a legitimized (and thus juridificated) social order. We paraphrase Weber in emphasizing that *to think difference is first of all to think the validity of one's own legal order.* We are not surprised that this dimension is the most important feature of talking about law on the street and leads immediately to the 'law without State' motive. It is evident that diverse groups of citizens embrace specific images of the legitimacy and validity of their legal order and have different images of the legal order of others, which they appreciate in a different manner: that diversity results from their wider experience of being different. Weber highlights this experience by means of surprisingly contemporary words.[30] He describes the emergence of commonness in relation with a situation wherein commonness of fate among persons

---

[30] Max Weber, *Wirtschaft und Gesellschaft*, 1922 (edited by Johannes Winckelmann, Kiepenheuer and Witsch, Köln/Berlin, 1964), pp. 21ff, 303ff: '*irgendwelche gemeinsame Schicksale der rassenmäßig Gleichartigen mit irgendeiner Gegensätzlichkeit der Gleichgearteten gegen auffällig Andersgearteten*' (*On Law in Economy and Society*, edited by E. Shils and M. Rheinstein, Harvard University Press, Cambridge, MA, 1954).

of the same race is connected with contrasts, which they experience against others who are characterized by strikingly different features.

Two elements of his description are relevant for our appreciation of today's social reality: the contrast displays *binding forces* together with *strikingly different* features. Weber's concept of social identity underlines the importance of race because already in his view – a decade before the Nazi assumption of power in Germany – racial features created for him a *perceptibility of difference*, and the latter is a perception that even more intensively governs daily life in multicultural societies of the Western hemisphere today.

Identity, self, self-governance and minimal legal provisions were the elements with which a society with practiced multiculturalism was built. This colors the social landscape in the European Union where multicultural forms continuously increase. The problems, which Weber first envisaged, are nowadays an element of daily life experience. Among them are a changing self-awareness and self-understanding, a continuous confrontation with images that do not belong to the patterns of traditional education, emerging identity problems and ideological clashes. All were in Weber's view the influence of changes one reads in the many faces of our world of everyday.

How multiform dimensions of life can change from bewildering and sometimes frightening forms into an almost natural social climate is of great interest to perceive. If this change parallels more or less natural emotions and articulations, then extremist forms of nationalism seem to remain absent. The question is awakened, what force is at work to balance and to adjust individuals/citizens in this multiple life-format. Legal expressiveness seems here the most important element of all. Juridification of citizenship dominates everywhere. Citizenship and unification need an identical layer of semiotic nature. Treaties, Jurisprudence and Administrations focus on citizenship within the boundaries of legal meanings where citizens become understood as bearers of rights and duties.

Their balance *unites* citizens despite their obvious religious, cultural or ideological differences. Their unity is to a certain degree the result of conflict and harmony being forceful components of an in-depth process of juridification.

3.2.3 Non-Ethical Conflict Dimensions

The expression 'non-ethical conflict dimension' is of the same type as the expression 'law without State' and both actually have their concrete stature in the concept of 'active citizenship'. This may surprise because the call to activity directed to the citizen in West European legal practices and social sciences has mostly been interpreted in terms of social ethics. The decision to act has been put in the hands of an individual, who must decide about his or her own activities. A call to enforce those activities was understood as the completion of an ethical standpoint without interfering with the close relations between State and citizen. This is, however, a shortsighted interpretation and perhaps even a social-scientific failure. Of course it implies the challenge to be an active citizen, and also an ethical viewpoint on patterns of active behavior and thoughts. But name and action pertaining to the citizen are not identical to that pattern of activity itself. Whether that pattern and its concrete activities are objects of ethical evaluation is a question that differs from the institutional qualification of active citizenship. We thus take 'active citizenship' as an explicitly non-ethical social dimensionality, an institutional qualification that serves in the first place the continuity of laws and legal practices. A call for, and the formulation of, 'active citizenship' belonged to the last decade of the twentieth and the first years of the recent century.

The expression, used before in law and social sciences, received its importance only in a context, which is exemplary in the unfolding of EU law. It is born out of internal conflicts that were active during the engenderment of a legal system. The expression confirmed, furthermore, the strong need for a clear nomination of the actor who would reinforce the practices of the rule of law independent from ethical instructions of its social environment. The word 'active citizen' is in that light the articulation of a juridification apex. It is very remarkable indeed that the 'active citizen' profile is in accordance with any legal semiotic analysis the exact counter-image of the judge. An active citizen in a culture dominated by law should *not* be tied to understand or experience reality through the pattern of *cases*. Its power of judging and opinion-formation should *not* fight personal views, presuppositions or political stances and its perception of reality should furthermore *not* be influenced by the temptations of a one-to-one relation between mind and reality. The general concept of 'active citizen' unites the creation of rights and the consumption of rights. This is most challenging, legal philosophers would remark, because one can hardly imagine the unification of those socio-legal components as a process and not as a footing of static data. Do not law and politics tend to ontologize and emphasize solely the static components of their understanding of reality? The question is at issue wherever legal institutions engender.

EU law has, for instance, provided an impressive example of all those considerations with its Article 198 A–C of the Maastricht Treaty, officially published 1995, which established the *Committee of the Regions*. These texts create, in fact, a distance between the *Committee* on the one hand and the axial *EU Commission* on the other. TEU Article 198 §A states that the Committee's members 'pursue their function in complete independency in the interest of the Union', and §C underlines that 'it can advise on its own initiative when it judges this relevant'. So where it considers that specific regional interests are involved (which are of immediate concern to the citizen), the Committee may issue an opinion on the matter. It means in essence that a discussion about *what are* and *what are not legal matters* became initiated in the heart of a legal system and was *not* left to citizen talks about law on the street. It is in this context very interesting that the Committee's practice of issuing opinions has brought more 'non-strictly legal matters' to the fore than any juridical instance could ever have done, the EU Commission included. An important semiotic change took place during that process, which was a change of meaning in the direction of a 'law without State' within the heart of legal institutions. The change caused 'non-strictly legal matters' (Art. 198 §C) to become *forwarded as 'interests in non-juridificated issues'*. The latter are legally presented as 'questions of regional interest', but regard in essence issues of 'active citizenship'. The latter acquired a central place in the legal system *without necessarily being strictly juridical.*

This observation presents an important example for a non-ethical, institutional positioning of the legal subject. In other words: the legal subject is able to reach positions which do not bring the subject, the citizen, into the realms of strictly legal patterns of activity. On the contrary: talks about law on the street display features that indeed focus on law without State, and thus do not renounce law, but only the State as a single law-making institution. An active citizenship thus strives to perform what the Committee enables it to do.

The EU Commission possesses a representational character and masters on its legal groundings the required legal and administrative procedures in the nation States of the Union. The States are in the Maastricht Treaty characterized as 'the High Contracting Parties'; but they are parties which do not further any active citizenship in EU social life. The discordance between EU practices of the *Commission* and the *Committee of the Regions* is an example of how a plurality of cultures is only in the imagination of a law-based governance viewed as a specific unity, which is itself grounded in State law. No wonder that soon the question would attract full attention: 'is such a unity as was created by a legally formatted governance *a demos?*' Once cultures are understood as entities, they are considered as if they were elements of a semi-geometric pattern and components of a complex contract. That view expresses a stable interface of law, legal regulations, institutions and administrations – all in parallel with the dominant premises of legal discourse. Yet all aspects of life, multicultural features included, are supposed to be recognized within that topology, including citizenship.

Semiotic implications of the well-known 'Maastricht Urteil' of the German Constitutional Court, the 1993 *Brunner v The European Union Treaty* case, were never researched. They pertain to two expressions: *demos* (*Volk*) and *citizen.* This supports our insight about the links between State, region and citizen within – as well as beyond – the boundaries of a legal system. The German judgment was about the question whether the EU treaties would be, or would be accepted as, 'through their ratification a historically first constitution'. It is important that this regards an *ontological* issue of *constitutional* law. In other words: this is an '*is*' question and not a consideration of law's need to '*declare as being*': both through ratification, which will be understood as a 'historically first' constitution.

All this unfolds arguments in the line of the German jurisprudential tradition outlined in earlier pages of this book. The Historical School at the end of the nineteenth century mentioned and deepened the concept of the *demos*, the '*Volk*' as the organic and natural, ethnic and cultural basis for a nation State. The latter was in those thoughts the ultimate and legitimate expression of the voice of the '*Volk*'. States belong to nations as nations belong to States. That interpretation of *demos* as the natural foundation for State and democracy (with a democratic administration as well as citizen activity) originates in a State-centered, nation-bound and often nationalistic interpretation of law. The court's ideas express what binds people spiritually, socially and politically, and constitute the traditional German jurisprudence on an organic, natural and ethno-cultural basis.

The German Constitutional Court did not perceive such a basis in the emerging European Union (it was called the '"No demos"-thesis') so there was no argument for any compliance. It thus provoked a reinforcement of nationalistic attitudes of citizens.[31] '*Active citizens*' were doomed to be *no 'Volk'*, and that was founded, apart from this specific constitutional judgment, on an important semiotic observation: *only after a legal determination of the citizen comes an ethical qualification of any citizen's behavior.* The decision in the *Brunner* case thus included

[31] *Brunner v The European Union Treaty*, *Common Market Law Reports*, Vol. 69(2), 11.01.1994. See also Broekman, *supra note 28*, pp. 145ff, 262ff.

whether there was, or was not, any *desire* to establish a European '*Volk*' – and consequently accept the existence of such a State. It included that there was no attention nor any political striving for a *supplementary democratic support* as mentioned in the TEU §40 or any *additional factor* in that context, which §43 foresaw. The *Brunner* case denied any possibility of a 'law without State' via a legal decision implicating the semiotics of 'the *Volk*' and a 'citizenship'. This concerned the paradigmatic character of the 'law without State' expression: the latter suggests that an informal, societal law could be distinguished and thus realized in contrast to the formal State law. That contrast is, however, a non-ethical conflict dimension, which has a considerable importance in view of the 'mental State' of citizens.

We do not introduce these lines pertaining to the 1993 German/EU case because of any purely historical interest. It illustrates, however, that the theme appears to be omnipresent and also characterized the German migration policies in the second decade of the twenty-first century. The slogan '*Wir Schaffen Das*' was an appeal to the *Volk* to overcome international problems with migrants and refugees, their legal problems in the first place. In actual political situations of the very same decade, with a 2017 US Presidency and with EU States' elections turning to the far right, or with the Brexit movement in the United Kingdom, equal issues are at stake. Any search for a common denominator to determine the life status of citizens will forward *regions* (in the US even region-bound corporations) as the decisive institution to fulfill functions like (but never identical with) States. The perfection of that performance will put in perspective the weight of the *demos* issue with its anchors in a State concept.[32] Its semiotic fascination is that whoever determines the *demos* justifies the State-bound law: that is an organicistic thought. Two remarks are due in this context.

A first remark is about the *linguistic expressivity of the citizen.*

Active citizenship has always been limited for many speakers within the EU through the limitation of their language. Although recognized a priori, the uses of language – pertaining to articulation in mother tongues in the first place – has always been a rights aspect. The equality of speakers of any language was underlined in the very same texts that outlined the path or contexts for the many forms of institutional representation. A list of languages was declared to count as 'official

---

32 Jan M. Broekman, 'The Multicultural Self' in M. Atienza, E. Pattaro, M. Schulte, B. Toporin, and D. Wyduckel (eds), *Theorie des Rechts und der Gesellschaft: Festschrift für Werner Krawietz zum 70 Geburtstag*, Duncker and Humblot, Berlin, 2003, p. 146.

languages' and millions of dollars/euros have since been spent to translate into those languages. But those were never the native tongues of *all* of Europe's citizens. Ten million persons speaking Catalan (in Catalonia, France and Italy), many Basques as well as Welsh speak a language which is not legally acknowledged and yet belongs to their everyday life articulations. The gap between native tongue (not always identical to dialect) and legally official language is a discordant factor in the behavior pattern of the active citizen. The gap is never understood as a challenge to defend and to represent the rights and interests of the citizen. The European Parliament never overtly declared that it speaks about the *official* language when it refers to components of its legal discourse that deal with citizenship.

Georg Steiner once gave this issue a historically and sociologically interesting dimension, which has a direct impact on the quality of an active citizenship. 'During lengthy periods of history', he wrote, 'men and women had to be bilingual, communicating in their own idiom – which can range all the way from patois and dialect to linguistic autonomy. Largely lost to us, but undoubtedly ubiquitous, was the role of every type and nuance of multilingualism in the daily business, communal texture, evolutions of sensibility of ordinary human experience across the globe. It may well be that an authentically monoglot consciousness is historically and culturally the exception.'[33] Is the dislocation of the mother tongue in the European Union a sign of 'a monoglot consciousness' disappearing?

That would be correct if the expression '*one's own language*' was not ambiguous although it is a cornerstone of legal expressiveness on citizenship. An important component of that ambiguity is in a meaning of the word 'own', which fits to legal language as the articulation of thought patterns of possession or ownership. Experiences, emotions, states of mind and events have to become understood in the form of rights and legal relations dominated by such an ownership – and so does the citizen concept. Semiotics of law unveils to what important degree an epistemological condition is at work here: *if the transformation into possessiveness cannot be performed there is no rights-position either.* One's *own* language has thus to be perceived as one's *property*. The mother tongue is a *good*, an object possessed by its speaker in a language apparently based on commoditization. To speak is to use words; the use is linguistic expressiveness. Any legal articulation confirms this is a

[33] Georg Steiner, *Errata: An Examined Life*, Weidenfeld and Nicholson, London, 1997, p. 79ff.

double sense: through what is said in the law, and through the innermost concealed premises of language in the saying. A speaker is in this context a subject in possession of his or her language. Legal subjects (in the terminology of the Civil Law system) are only able to possess goods and other issues in a legally correct manner, that is: embedded in an *official language*.[34] The word 'own' creates the ambiguity we explained – it restricts ownership of the citizen to the premises of an official language, which is the accepted language on the basis of possession and contract. That was the structure of argument in the above-outlined *Brunner* case. Indeed: the right to express oneself in one's own language is not the same as in one's mother tongue. The German court wanted to establish a reference to what binds people and find a correct legal expression for that togetherness. It suggested 'that the decision-making process of the organs exercising sovereign powers and the various political objectives pursued can be generally perceived and understood, and therefore that the citizen entitled to vote can communicate in his own language with the sovereign authority to which he is subject'.[35]

A second remark is on *comparative law*.

Speaker-functionaries of legal discourse seem to be more or less *monoglot* speakers – but they are *not*. The comparison of certain fields of law forms an example. Legal activities may find a place beyond differences of mother tongue. They regard law as a stable discourse with well-defined concepts at a safe distance from the diversity of mother tongues. But such comparisons pertain to linguistic activities that include all presuppositions, premises and concealed meanings, which law's expressiveness hides in speech as well as in writing, publishing or debating. Such meaning-complexes are all tied to concepts such as 'possessiveness', 'ownership', 'properties', 'contracts', 'individualities', 'fixated meaning-entities' and the like. Jurists embrace their dominant

---

[34] The consequences of this observation in the relations between e-technology, e-communication and legal language have not been studied, although a certain relevance is suggested. Hillary Mantis writes in the US Journal: *National Jurist*, 2016, Nov. 7: '*Web design and technical support for law firms*: Law firms are businesses that need to market themselves. So, for every smart-looking firm website that's designed to attract new clients, there is a person behind it designing the site. Who would know better how to best describe a firm than a lawyer? Especially one who is good with technology and familiar with how law firms work. That also goes for supporting all of the computer programs and technology that modern day law firms all use. Not to mention training all of the lawyers in the firm on how to use the technology. There are many possibilities to combine technology skills with your law degree.'

[35] *Brunner v The European Union Treaty*, *supra note 31*, § 41, p. 87.

artificial language interwoven with their natural mother tongue, even when they do not actually read or speak that tongue. That structure makes them in principle *polyglot* citizens and functionaries, whereby the priority of language is dependent on whether they communicate in the artificial or in the natural language, or are obliged to adhere to a mixture of both. Law's comparative task is embedded in this complex linguistic role-structure. That pertains to the level of expression; the level of comparison is highly influenced by the difficulty *not* to compare laws and legal structures as *events* but to perform the comparison as if law's discourses as well as the facts and structures of law are *fixated entities*. In order to *compare*, jurists have to *arrest* the dynamic character of all legal occurrences. If one would find cases like the *Brunner* case and mutually compare them, all components like '*Volk*', 'spirit', 'language' or 'tradition' would be treated as stable data and facts.

To compare cases or systems of law includes always the premises of valid law, among which the fixation of item, speech or text is perhaps the most important. But also law in its totality cannot be presented in any comparative law, as becomes clear from the many legal-technical items that are subjected to comparative law studies. Constitutions of an actual State are the central point of interest and of authority. Within a constitutional framework legal rules are solely accepted as belonging to valid law under the condition that they were issued by governments and other State organs. Even the traditional difference between 'private and public law' depends upon that condition. The same should be observed for a legal practice as such and the complexity of its realm of expressiveness should not conceal the straightforward dependency from a single State constitution of the branch of law named 'comparative'.

The consequences are multiple. Speech acts of lawyers in the context of their professional language are *monoglot*. Their links to a mother tongue (or any other natural, non-professional language that could lead to an explanation of their artificialities) are complex, and more unreliable than any translation could offer. To unveil the relations between the various language positions in a comparative law process has seldom been at issue of semiotic research. That activity always suggests that components of legal discourse are comparable as if they were fixated entities. Comparisons in the inner process of the extremely rich articulation of legal viewpoints did not take place. The complexity of the polyglot character of a comparative lawyer was not a point of interest. If one analyzes the determinations at issue in the *Brunner* case, this is challenging. The same is true for an eventual search for comparative cases in Western legal systems or systems of other cultures. Not only the polyglot position but also their multicultural character is neglected in comparative law. This observation leads to a far-reaching conclusion: *a monoglot position is not appropriate for understanding law*, even if law is understood in its relation only to one mother tongue combined with one professional tongue.

This illustrates the complexity of law before any involvement in ethical questions. Also non-ethical, often institutional conflict dimensions are determined by legal thought patterns and decisions of lawyers. All are dominated by the 'law-language' relationship, which exercises an effect on all layers of meaning. The latter is an important semiotic conclusion. Language is everywhere, and so is law – often the two are in parallel, often they are intertwined, and often they are conflicting, but one is never without the other. Dimensions characterized as non-ethical unfold in close proximity to the '*law without State*' formula. The expression does not suggest a fierce anarchism but rather underlines the historical character of the nowadays very strong ties between law and State. Those links originated in the course of the seventeenth century in the Occident and endure strong criticism in the beginnings of the twenty-first century. That criticism provides new energy for an *active citizenship* and more legal and administrative power for the regions, as the EU *Committee of the Regions* illustrated. Two clear examples of this changing appreciation of the links between law and State are visible in the heart of the EU legal system. The first is an ever-growing distance between thought patterns of the *Committee* on the one hand and the central juridical instance, the *EU Commission*, on the other. The second is in a renewed reading of the *Brunner* case, which is a judgment of the German Constitutional Court. It suggests that deciding whether a *demos* (*Volk*) is the source of law must be a final judgment: 'no *demos*, no law' is the semiotic crux of that case.

3.3 INTERACTION AND THE RADICAL

Absolutisms in terminology and reasoning seem unavoidable. All of them outline major patterns of behavior, which are forms of meaning and of social activity. It is interesting and disquieting to discover that the constitutive power of the subject diminishes when the power of communal and non-subjective (these are not objective!) forces grow. As if in such cases, which are doubtlessly discussed on the street, absolutisms unfold before our eyes! Indeed, fields of a subject's actions narrow at the moment social and often anonymous explorations increase. Absolutisms sneak into life patterns. Anxieties generalize, appeals to make them disappear fail, and absolutisms become key words in daily language. Thought patterns crumble. Stalking becomes institutional and marks interactivity. Images replace the tasks of words and speech: any random image is suddenly 'worth a hundred words'. 'Interactivity' is a complex concept that conceals more than one risk factor; absolutism is one of the most prominent among them – that is confirmed as soon as we consult our smart phone images or watch our preferred TV series.

Absolutism flourishes when a general awareness of social change and awareness of the process character of everything become qualified in public opinion as a thread. Absolutism can restrict itself to political practices if knowledge is stable and justifiably fixated. Many Emperors, Kings and Presidents made that visible in cultures of our past as well as in our modernity; it unfolded independent from their pattern of culture. Absolutism grounded their opinions. Their activities were interpreted as sources and justifications of a legal system, which the general citizenship simply had to accept as a consequence of living in a State. Modern times force us to reconsider absolutism under those conditions. But are we still living in the regime of Kings and Emperors? Questions about the how and why of absolutism in our times are of more interest than they ever were before. They dominate politics, economics and social sciences, and are important in view of citizenship and its foundations. Furthermore, absolutism could develop towards a denying of the immanent qualities of citizenship – how can that be, and what are its roots? An answer to the latter question surprises: those roots are in absolutism itself!

Thomas Kuhn unfolded in his widely recognized 1966 publication on the structures of scientific development a theoretical framework that reached far beyond any of the established sciences.[36] His conclusions were important for knowledge itself. He suggested that there is no absolute and fixated knowledge possible, that knowledge is not embedded in any type of linear progress, that knowledge always finds itself in a milieu of incommensurable paradigms so that the claim of finding the definitive truth by means of scientific research appeared to be a false ideology – all its absolutisms included. This insight was globally accepted, and it seemed to have silenced any form of absolutism in science or philosophy. There are, however, since Kuhn's ideas unfolded, two important observations at issue: (a) tensions between absolutism and relativism did *not* disappear in philosophy or in debates on the foundations of science since Kuhn's publication, and (b) what was silenced in the sciences was *not* silenced in political practices – just as little as was the case (reluctantly formulated) in law and legal discourse.

---

[36] Thomas Kuhn, *The Structure of Scientific Revolutions*, Chicago University Press, 1962.

Is there a common denominator in the remarks (a) and (b)? It is astonishing that philosophy has not contributed much to a deeper understanding of the absolute and its applications in thought patterns or social life. The concept of the absolute initiated in the midst of the Occidental eighteenth century as *a special signifying procedure* of understanding how reality can be *One* and also viewed as a source of *Variety*. That contrast is not solved by ideas about togetherness or any variation of holistic thinking. Kant, Schelling, Hegel, Jacobi and Spinoza positioned themselves in opposition to this riddle of absoluteness in thinking the absolute. Spinoza's *pantheism* appeared for a long time Western philosophy's most acceptable solution, which also embraced the great value of appropriately *signifying* as a valuable task for philosophy. There is, however, one exception in a minor motive that could guide us. Kant suggested in his *Critique of Practical Reason* (1788) that the search for the absolute is the search for something unconditioned, namely of a *free and uncaused activity.*[37] An activity cannot, however, be an activity in a world without other human beings. The idea of an uncaused activity is therefore not without the experience of otherness, and thus of interactivity. That is the minor motive, which can inspire one to conclude that forms of inter-subjectivity are a premise, even in Kant's description of the absolute! That premise (interaction as the spiritual climate for the absolute) is hardly explored in Western philosophy; it was certainly not researched in the times when Spinoza's pantheism was prominent. A fascinating conclusion seems to be allowed: the concept of absolute and of absolutism is closely connected to forms of inter-subjectivity. *Interaction* and qualities of the *radical* are intertwined with all possible modes of interactivity, each form and formula of the absolute is engendered in modes of togetherness. Not a philosophical anthropology, but political and legal sciences and their respective practices explore that issue.

3.3.1 Absolutism in Law

Rules designed and proposals fixated, cases named and party viewpoints as dogma are all transited into forms of togetherness that will become forms of interactivity. *Law's absolutisms in legal practice as well as in legal science are modes of interactivity.* The conclusion must also be drawn when other dimensions of life are at stake: it appears that absolutism must always be encountered as a mode of interactivity – even when we qualify these modes as 'un-ethical'. And, what is most

[37] Immanuel Kant, *Critique of Practical Reason*, 1788, Preface.

fascinating in view of interactivity related to the concept of absolutism: all originate from changes of meaning accompanied by multiplicity and dynamics features of the master-narratives that engendered them. Tensions between absolutism and relativism are at issue when those properties are transposed into the networks of interactivity, so that interaction is the major determining meaning in social life. All forms of absolutism attempt to master this transposition by means of enforcing one-to-one meanings in all regards, thereby not even considering, let alone debating, the character and quality of those one-to-one features. *Legal semiotics* is the preferred method to unveil these mechanisms, which are often considered as dangerous social powers. One could say that a semiotic approach is *the* power to unveil and analyze the absolute dimensions of law. All are originating in the power to master meanings – both in engendering and in applying meanings to all occurrences in the fields of interactivity. Lawyers do not only *make* meanings, one is enforced to conclude, but they also master the *politics* of meaning. Especially the latter display very strong ties with radical choices and absolutist significations 'in the interest of all'.

'Interaction/interactivity' is a theme that profiles legal semiotics in particular. *Interaction* conceals a *static* character, despite its suggestion of dynamism. Its inherent *sender–receiver* scheme presents the idea of interaction being based on a duality and qualifies it as 'action between (*inter*) actors'. But each action in life focuses on otherness. It is therefore never a duplication story but rather the unfolding of a new vision and an instanced interpretation of life! Each link to another person and/or situation is a challenge to change attitude and position. That awareness is folded in the concept of *interactivity*. Does the latter meaning fit law and legal thinking? The question is a central issue in semiotic analyses. The process of '*being in a State of interactivity*' changes the quality and substance of all that is meant by 'interaction', so that the two expressions (interaction and interactivity) are *not* interchangeable.

However, emphasis on *interactivity* guides semiotic approaches in contrast to *interaction*. Interactivity pertains to all fragments of social reality, not in the least because most of our social life is in the first place folded in *modes of activity*: first of all the establishment of relations with sub-/objects, and further pertaining to the perceiver(s) of it all. Changes and variations in the process of activity can take place in one and the same activity mode. This view leads away from traditional communication models, which have been so fundamental and natural in law and social sciences. But what shape must be given to human communication, lawyers would argue when confronted with semiotics, if one has to accept that creating meaning is a multifaceted process which is built upon the acceptance of indeterminacy and the refutation of invariant stories or definitive codes?

Such considerations emphasize the *dynamics* of signs and sign formation, and elucidate that social relations are a *process* and never a *static* issue engendered by autonomous actors. 'Activity' is a keyword that transcends all varieties which take the 'sender–receiver' model for granted. Post-modern psychotherapy wants to make fixated, frozen, monologue or monoglot attitudes visible. It illustrates that their influences on personality and society begin to color our social awareness. This is a forceful attempt to change the speaker–hearer model in communicative practices. This model dominated Occidental philosophy for centuries, and suggested that we understand social life as the mirroring of *ego* and *alter* by means of their particular focus on representation. We are now very near to practicing communication as a form of participating in a *fluency* in which even a sign flows away from its signifier.

But no 'activity' is based on fixed positions in public space that create the social world through departing from the *ego* – either as *ego* or as *alter*! We tend to understand the public space as a space of the *politeia* (the 'body politic' so prominently formulated in the writings of Thomas Hobbes) in which positions are understood as changing. The public space (where the talking about law can take place) seemed the only condition under which citizens, subjects and social actors could transcend themselves and their monologue position while striving for a new and legally empowered status: *citizenship* – modern law's preferred concept, as semiotic analyses could point out. That pattern depicts hitherto unknown worlds and world-concepts. Communication does not relate human individuals in a one-to-one manner but stems from a world image in which individuals occupy a place and construct a diversity of realities according to their various positions, expectations and values. But absolutisms of all kinds are always around the corner.

The heart of the matter is that the image of public life as related to a common good is based on an immensely diversified 'public'. Nevertheless: there remains this important tension between the idea of 'interactivity' and possible legal practices, which – as the Napoleonic Code showed – require subjects of law to hold a position in public life that determines them physically and spiritually. As a consequence, applied semiotics suggests a forceful consideration in the form of a vital question that touches each form of absolutism in law and legal discourse: is law indeed able to leave 'interaction' behind and to perform its actions with legal subjects who are by definition in a continuous 'state of interactivity'?

The question leads us to philosophical considerations. Ludwig Wittgenstein's 1958 *Philosophical Investigations* publicized his 'private language argument', saying that a language remaining within the limits of a personal consciousness – and thus excluding other minds by means of continuously mirroring its proper position – cannot exist. Those considerations focus on sensations and impressions, memory and meaning, expression and reference, rule and sign. They sustain Charles Sanders Peirce's observation that *signs never fit exclusively one individual.* His observation that *everything can become a sign* consequently does not focus on a single consciousness and its proper position in social space, but already implies a different social philosophy!

Hence, in the words of Peirce, there *are* no signs; in other words: nothing *is* a sign, nothing *is* exclusively a sign, nothing *is* in essence a sign, a fixed sign, or in any other '*is*'-regard, but everything *can become* a sign! Even more so: nothing is a sign because if something would be one, and would be defined or definable by one, its existence would be purely esthetic! Only *dynamic* or *process* sign functions do function in the course of life. He thus emphasizes the human situation as *being in process*, and introduces the semiotic subject not as a fixed *means* to perceive reality but as one of the many *ways* of perception. *A sign is not a fixed semiotic entity but rather a meeting ground for independent entities.* Semiotics, including their applications in whatever field of communal interest (scientific theories included), entail therefore a theory about the quality, engenderment and patterning of human relations: patterns that contravene the major implications of the concept 'interactivity'. The anthropologist Geertz emphasized this relation between sign systems and their various modes of implementation, suggesting: 'If we are to have a semiotics … (or for that matter, of any sign system not axiomatically self-contained), we are going to have to engage … away from an investigation of signs in abstraction towards an investigation of them in their natural habitat …'.[38]

Such a natural habitat is a specific culture, a specific mother tongue as well as an inherited style of life. One can distinguish various *semiotic subjects* in different cultures, discourses and styles. The semiotic subject as a way of looking at the world couples semantic units with expression units: by means of this labor it becomes able to continuously abolish and restructure its social and historical concretions. The activity of the semiotic subject is first of all a *conceptual* activity. In other words,

[38] Clifford Geertz, *The Interpretation of Cultures* (1973), Basic Books, New York, 2000, p. 41f.

humans do not perceive reality with their 'eyes' but rather with their 'mind'. They no longer strive for *representing* an appearance in their social contacts but rather grasp 'an appearance to unveil among others' – indeed: in such a manner, 'everything can become a sign'. When establishing social relationships, we encounter the challenge that *activity* is the key to *understanding reality as a process* and not just a fixed idea to be applied in line with codified rules.

Social life is an event *and* an activity that unfolds in the multiple fragments of reality. It always unfolds with a different function, surface, line, circle, volume, color, sphere or mood. What is more: all have an equal chance to become entangled in acts of communication, whereby the latter can be understood as a specific activity. A communicative subject creates many forms of social contact in segments of interactivity and never in fixed positions of fixed interactions. Human individuals can be creative solely in the context of a culture and more precisely in one of a culture's many forms of interactivity. We learned from neurology that we do not exclusively see with our eyes but with our brain as well, which means that we perceive only as a complete person – which is a process in itself! In other, perhaps surprising, words: perception is a total engagement and therefore a matter of conceptualization, of mind, of vital rhythms. This stimulates insights of philosophical and above all semiotic relevance for our view on life.

Are there lessons to be learned and conclusions to be drawn for lawyers and legal thinking? Yes, indeed: 'semiotic relevance' is an expression easy to formulate but difficult to explain and even more difficult to prove. We encounter this difficulty at various levels:

(1) There is first and foremost Peirce's call to be aware of how all reality is always involved in a process of achieving *sign value*.
(2) One should mention how this relevance pertains to understanding the basic structures of human *activity*.
(3) That activity, whatever character it has, functions in the dynamics of *meaning-making* – itself an apogee of semiotics.
(4) An understanding of a strict *equivalence* of all segments or elements that compose the communication follows from there.
(5) This goes to the semiotic understanding of *meaning* in general. Meaning seems to be the result of a human activity directed towards the *order* of things rather than to any fixed and durable *essence* they should possess.

(6) Issues of human consciousness are thus to be understood beyond philosophical idealism, which says in general that human activity is always *inter*activity and thus focuses on *meaning as a matter of order*.

All these aspects could, however, be formulated with more precision, expanded and deepened, for instance, into the logic and semiotics (Peirce), visions on human growth (Lacan) and hermeneutics (Gadamer). One issue would nevertheless remain central in all those contexts: what have these philosophies and their inherent semiotic notions to do with legal thought formation and lawyer's activities as always being in danger of unfolding absolutisms and/or radicalisms of all kind?

Although not directly focusing on legal rules, norms or logic, the question touches upon many preconditions of legal meaning and expressiveness. So one should ask: what does a way of presenting reality as perceived by an artist – as a specialist in perception, perhaps more than any lawyer – have to do with legal judgment? That is a truly challenging question! We do not know how problematic the shift from *verbal* to *visual* expressiveness and the completion of *words* by *images* is for law and legal discourse, and particularly in view of radical positions and choices. Does verbal expressiveness suffice to understand reality the way legal discourse does? Or should semiotics inspire lawyers to continuously reconsider their proper articulation? Consider that law's communicative character changed under the influence of the completion of words by images, so that communication in law is no longer restricted to words or other linguistic entities. The quoted slogan that 'an image is worth a thousand words' has indeed communicative weight. The function of *visual* legal semiotics, based on the integration of word and image, challenges modern law and widens its verbal traditions. 'Finally, … reality depends on the ultimate decision of the community', Peirce once noted and he could have added that *community* also means *culture*! Although law presents itself in a variety of images in courts and other public places, there is no visual component in legal thought formation that fulfills a decisive function.

'*Absolutism in law*' appears to touch Peirce's idea that the human subject is an *order* in itself, and the self itself for itself a *sign*, forms the basis for an observation that combines literary and visual semiotics, to be finalized in a legally correct image of elaborated *citizen participation* as explored today in the legal systems that call themselves a democracy. Is it not the ultimate goal of legal rhetoric (sustained by legal semiotics) to create an emancipated opinion, combining visual and verbal elements of discourse? Take for instance the '*two* faces in *interaction*': this expression embraces the meaning of 'a face' as it is restricted to the 'sender–receiver' model and its concept of interaction. More offensively stated: two faces conceived within the boundaries of the sender–receiver model *are no faces*! They cannot be 'open' and in interactivity because they merely mirror each other. To see someone in the face: does one want to see oneself in the face of the other?

The question makes clear that any face beyond interactivity has no expressivity and is therefore irrelevant in semiotic perspective. Faces are in essence interactivity; they cannot become a *sign* outside that realm and they are just for that reason relevant for semiotics. In other words, a face is never an entity in itself but always an entity in process. That process is semiotic and precisely what Peirce described as *the process of becoming a sign*. Faces show meaning in the context of recognition. Look in the mirror and experience how interactivity gives life to that mirror image beyond how others might perceive it. The dynamics of interactivity (in itself a full actualization of interaction) concretize an enriched 'Janus' experience, which articulates itself when saying, 'I am the one I was, and will be!' As a consequence, the semiotics of interactivity is about human individuals embedded in the encompassing energy of change and transition, which we often vaguely indicate as 'culture'. Faces are culture signs and can become symbols of the specifically human character of that change.[39] It is important and philosophically difficult to grasp how this semiotics of interactivity is not the result of an individual (inter)action.

3.3.2 Grades of Absolutism

Individuality is the product of cultural change and in essence a culturally inherited articulation of an evolving position in the process of growth and development. Together with the awareness of *change* being a major determinant of interactivity grows an insight into an almost equally important component of absolutism: its *grade* character. It should not be a surprise that absolutisms (in meaning, opinion, political interaction or legal determination) are seldom absolute. Their danger is in the internal relativity, the freedom of choice within the extremely strict and unchangeable frame, the choice of means of expression or the at first sight reasonable considerations to select specific terms or concepts to apply. Those 'freedoms' are dangerous in their relativity as soon as they are forwarded in view of the realization of an absolute. The one-to-one

---

[39] Jan M. Broekman and Larry Catà Backer, *supra note 9*, p. 112ff.

relation is seldom like a sudden and unexpected explosion but is often carefully prepared and the consequence of contextual elements. That is even the case in actual threatening terror.[40] The latter is a case of radical absolutism, whereby the one-to-one meaning dynamics became fixated: one meaning *is* the entire reality.

Where law and legal discourse want to fix an individual as being in interaction, they do so by means of forwarding, for instance, concepts such as right, identity, or property. Those concepts function as signs, which transfer and communicate information about a human individual in its social setting without considering whether these positions are just tentative because of the context of the flow of dynamics traditionally called 'human history'. The *openness of the human face* unveils the flow of feelings, emotions, and expressions that is an example for the gradual.

The semiotics of interactivity is often linked to facial expressiveness. Is this the reason for the difficulties law has with the human face? When answering that question, one should keep in mind how the explanatory power of the interaction concept appears limited: a face-to-face situation is never exclusively a situation of solely two individual faces! If everything around us can become a sign that opens up to its proper signification, then each face-to-face situation is satiated by the dynamics of signifying processes (the dynamics of culture) and never reduced to two acting faces and thus to two actors. Do such limitations of the number 'two' fit to the essence of a human face? Lawyers encounter this question when they have law and legal discourse as their frame of reference and at the same time view a human face. Are they aware how ours is the age of semiotics, the method of questioning and research, of growth and transition, which focuses on interactivity because its subject is ultimately indeterminable and its activity beyond fixation?

That highlights a new sympathy for Bergson, Peirce or James: the pragmatism of each *élan vital* expresses itself in signs and symbols. It is engraved in a pragmatic *élan* of the images of a human face in which any absolutism disappears 'at face value'. Do not forget that a face is cognized in its process character while a parallel insight in the human body unfolds. Shown is a surface in growth, a skin in change, a glance in futures based on a past that etched what is mirrored and projects what is shared in the course of life's experiences. True interactivity is not in the countenances around us, since faces are essentially evolving in time and

---

[40] J. -F. Lyotard, *La condition postmoderne: rapport sur le savoir*, Paris, 1979 (*The Postmodern Condition: A Report on Knowledge*, Manchester University Press, 1984), pp. 46, 63ff.

space and thus *becoming*: becoming sign or symbol and infinitely more, perhaps a subject that recognizes itself as an 'I' – until also this 'I' withdraws from our recognition and becomes a name, a psychic entity, 'an/other'. All that requires a process that reaches beyond the path of a lawyer's experience.

Lawyers must turn their faces around and operate in a world of fixated meanings. Is this how lawyers make meaning – *with faces turned away* (the blindfold of Lady Justice)? Is the danger of absolutism implied in this turn to blindness? Consider the sentence that 'the Court may say for law': a speech act with predominantly institutional character. Does that utterance fit the features of 'an individual in grades of interactivity'? The question is a key to our central thesis: semiotics applied in the fields of legal discourse unveils that philosophical implications of interaction often oppose our ordinary life experiences. Those analyses also unveil the process of 'being in interactivity'.

It is, as a consequence, almost impossible to deliver a complete picture of all possible grades of absolutism, even if one would accept that picture to be limited to politics solely or to law and legal discourse. Being engaged in interactivity is being itself. All interactivity is embedded in a process of grading. Forms of absolutism are implied in that portrait painted with an exclusive paint called 'interaction'.

A number of items play a constitutive role when grades of absolutism in law and legal discourse have to be determined. They are often spread in a sizable number of social situations; the order in which they are mentioned is not completely decisive and there are no patterns that help to gain an insight.

First, one has to consider that grades of absolutism are never understandable without *citizenship*, without their patterns of *interaction*, among which the *meaning-making* as well as *meaning politics* are outstanding, and finally those grades are never to be grasped without understanding their ties with one or more *master-narratives*. In less differentiating words: *there are no grades of absolutism beyond our social world and its historical determinations.*

Second, grades of absolutism are not understandable without awareness of the cultural variety among meanings that are specific for a discourse at issue. In law and legal discourse the most important meanings are probably those of *concepts* (causality, reasonability, casuistry, equilibrium, etc.) and of *rules* (equity, rights, private or public directed, repetitive and non-recurring, etc.), which both lead to possible *legal measures* (taxes, fines, detentions, judgmental decisions, collective decisions arranged by lawyers and laymen, ethically relevant measures, etc.). In other words: *there are no grades of absolutism that do not refer to single or plural dichotomies, to choices and alternatives.*

Third, absolutism always displays a *local* focus. A country, a land, a setting, an institution, a discourse can be focus for its display. The local is clearly present in law. On both sides of the boundary lines of legal *discourse*, that is: within as well as outside the discourse(s) of law, there are different grades of absolutism to observe. Multiplicity is a challenge to embrace absolutisms in order to avoid a lack of clarity and to provoke uncertainty – a perspective all lawyers avoid. Those who operate *outside* the legal discourse do not share exactly the same sentiments. Citizens talking about law illustrate that a protest against any form of absolutism fits to their specific position. Their attitude in view of absolutism is an important marker. Citizens occasionally include absolutisms at the borderlines of valid law and opportune politics. Just talking about law but also performing a legal speech act are both a *limited* activity – institutional boundaries characterize the citizen and the professional. Therefore, *absolutisms vary between the professional and the citizen, but both can embrace them, and while doing so, enter the field of politics.*

All grades of absolutism influence the participants in interaction and limit their interactivity. Citizen participation in words as well as in activities is to a high degree hampered by the threat of absolutism. Talking about law on the street illustrates this clearly: during those talks, absolutisms in legal practice are criticized but absolutisms in one's own deliberations are seldom avoided. With those dynamics – only one out of many – one understands how violently absolutisms threaten commonness. This most often unfolds at the borderlines between law and politics. Law leads to legal measures in social life with meanings that originate in codified jurisprudence or in specialized studies and handbooks – only seldom are such considerations without consequences. In them the step towards politics is hardly observable. Commonness and the specific language of political purposes form a climate in which choices of meaning become one-sided and objects of fixation. Freedom of choice shrinks to minimal dimensions when political party interests prevail, ideological formulas are prescribed and reality reduced to an overall experience of the binary.

Conclusions pertaining to the absolute as a force in society and its development of a world view (with law as an outstanding factor) are difficult to formulate precisely. There is no interaction or interactivity without inherent absolutisms.

The lack of unequivocal terms and meanings in law is nested everywhere in its discourses, so that these awaken a desire for limitation, adequate application and justice as equilibrium – all are elements that appeal to absolutism in law, and enforce an even stronger appeal when the lines between law and politics are transgressed. Legal practice appears to be continuously at risk to embrace and explore all kinds of absolutism. While there are discourses with absolutisms everywhere – for instance in forms of superstition, extreme inter-human relations pertaining to wealth, health, sex, social power and the like – the practices of law try to minimize them and strive for 'justice with a human face'. One conclusion overshadows all others: the effects of law (as continuously threatened by internal powers of absolutist meaning-creation) influence the quality of interaction and thus the norms that master interactivity.

Grading absolutisms engages in a process with a unique power. Any reviewing of absolutism leads in the end to its self-destruction: to powerlessness and meaninglessness, to a total loss of differentiation, to a perception of everything that is turning into nothingness during the observation itself – ultimately turning to a world in which no word can be spoken and all interaction dies. The silence of terror is the sole indication for any ultimate absolutism: the 'absolute absolutism' is not the highest and most superb degree of grading but rather the final annihilation of absolutism. The dangerous and at the same time fascinating dynamic of each form of absolutism is therefore positioned in the self-abolishing which takes place in any encounter with *the other* or in any experience of *otherness*.

3.3.3 The Lenient and the Radical Narrative

The final pages of the preceding chapter introduced the master-narrative as proposed by Lyotard and other contemporary philosophers. The concept allowed the determination of a discourse's embedding in history as well as in actual speech activity. Discourses in their multiplicity and with their many different features varying from natural to artificial languages or from monolingual to multilingual expressiveness will always need anchors in a more encompassing narrative. The question arises, whether those anchors bind talks and speech, texts and other articulations so forcefully that they include terms of absolutism as far as their meanings and applications are concerned. Does, in the words of our theme, any 'talking about law' on the street need to explore absolutist positions because of its ties with one or more of its master-narratives?

But an important consideration places the influence of master-narratives on absolutistic views in a broader context than any differentiation between modern cultures and post-modernism. Thoughts about the master-narrative, which were presented by Lyotard, must in addition focus on Geertz's challenge we formulated above: 'to engage … away from an investigation of signs in abstraction towards an investigation of them in their natural habitat'.

That natural habitat is a historical datum of enormous importance, with more than one component involved. Think of a first and dominant question. Are all master-narratives by definition *verbal*? If they are indeed, then *non-verbal* master-narratives cannot exist. But traditions in life patterns, in art, architecture, sciences and even archeology do, however, present *non-verbal master-narratives*. For us, today, verbal and non-verbal master-narratives are mixed. Those mixtures (with a multiplicity of meaning layers) are difficult to trace, to accept or to obey and thus evoke a general need for absolutist indications in life.

But major forms of symbolism illustrate that the *non-verbal master-narratives play at least an equivalent role in our contemporary semiotic understanding of life*, so that the mixed character of such narratives prevails. Is symbolism only possible within the boundaries of verbal expressiveness? It does not seem to be the case. That theme is, interestingly enough, also at issue in archeology. The globally recognized Australian archeologist Robert Bednarik recently claimed that the origins of symbolism are momentarily debated thanks to their semiotic relevance. He distinguishes a long-range model and a short-range model in view of symbolism and language capacity of humans, and emphasizes the latter.

> According to the currently dominant short-range model, the earliest evidence we possess of human symbolism is in the forms of art and indications of language ability. No art-like productions are recognized of an age exceeding 32,000 or 35,000 years, and the earliest available language evidence is seen to be the first successful colonization of Australia, thought to have occurred perhaps 60,000 years ago. This school of thought … categorically denies the possibility of human symbolizing abilities beyond, say, 100 ka (100,000 years) ago.[41]

Symbolism and language may belong together, but they do so as different capacities in the development towards modern mankind. Goethe had already remarked in his 1810 *Farbenlehre* how 'one never considers sufficiently that a language is essentially symbolic, solely figurative and

---

[41] Robert G. Bednarik, *Beads and the Origins of Symbolism*, 2000, available at: www.semioticon.com/frontline/bednarik.htm, accessed 13 April 2017.

that its objects will never be directly expressed but only as a reflection'.[42] The important issue is their connection despite their differences. Verbal expressiveness as studied by archeology is in that context a *later* product than symbolic expressiveness; language is recognized as a form of symbolism. An intermittent remark seems justified because symbolism and formalism are closely linked: absolutisms are predominantly of linguistic nature and mostly depending on words and slogans but – once enveloped in politics – they are also symbolized, as many signs illustrate (swastika, hammer-and-sickle), which are imposed on the citizenship in order to result in compliance. One asks whether absolutism is in that very same way connected with an extended notion of human history, which belongs to the focus of an archeologist. Bednarik suggests in the already quoted text: 'that one form of symbolism, language, probably began its development some time between the appearance of *Homo erectus* (about 1.8 million years ago, at which time the species is found in eastern Africa, in the Caucasus and on Java) and his first known crossing of the open sea (perhaps 0.9 million years ago, from Bali to Lombok and then Flores)'. We underline the statement that language is one of the forms of symbolism known to the archeologist.

That leads to further formulations of interest for the quality of a master-narrative:

> Verbal language is a form of communication that involves the use of conventionalized vocal sounds in meaningful patterns. Any form of communication requires the use of symbolisms, but in order to develop beyond simple action and response patterns (which apply, in various complexities, throughout the animal world), culturally determined meanings need to be attached to the 'signs'. In other words, such meanings are not genetically passed on, but are acquired during the life trajectory of each individual; they are learned. Culture is of course not limited to humans; it is available to many other animals, albeit in considerably less complex forms. In humans culture has reached extraordinary levels of complexity, which are only possible through the use of an unusually large brain.[43]

It is clear that absolutism must be considered as a form of culture, in which dominance takes its place, has its history and developed its semiotic functions. It interests that, like law itself, this absolutism remains a component of human behavior, so that it can be given a

---

42 J. W. von Goethe, *Zur Farbenlehre*, Bd I, Tübingen, 1810 '*Man bedenkt niemals genug, daß eine Sprache eigentlich nur symbolisch, nur bildlich sei und die Gegenstände niemals unmittelbar, sondern nur im Widerscheine ausdrücke*'.

43 Robert G. Bednarik, *supra note 41.*

well-determined place in our thought patterns: 'the question is therefore not really, when did culture begin, but rather, it should be asked: when did culture (individually acquired system of "understanding") begin to become such a dominating determinant of selection that it began to rival environmental factors in determining the course of evolution, especially cognitive evolution, for hominids?'

Is the archeological conclusion that absolutism results from a craving for equilibrium with the so-called 'natural' environment? Or does it suggest the conclusion of a stimulus to master nature and to perform according to the will of a human being? In other words, and in view of a further developed insight along this current of thought, one asks: 'when did our ancestors begin to exercise sufficient control over environmental variables that a neural feedback system emerged which led to consciousness, and thus to what we regard as conscious modulation of response patterns? Such a development made the proliferation of cultural systems almost inevitable, and the increasing skill in the use of symbolisms became a necessity.'[44] Perspectives on the question of absolutism are at issue. Absolutism is a matter of interactivity, we have already noticed. It is a matter of manifold discourses and also of master-narratives, we added. And it is a matter of confronting *otherness*, as even archeology seems to confirm: human and natural challenge confrontation and encounter – both are formative powers for absolutist viewpoints, which can be evaluated as positive as well as monstrously negative.

The question whether a master-narrative has to be *verbal* has led us to unexpected regions of scientific knowledge and insight in human history. The answer is clear: (a) language is a form of symbolism and a *younger* product in terms of human evolution; (b) master-narratives can be much more encompassing in materials, duration and scope than purely verbal narratives, human history illustrates; and (c) a final and yet surprising quote from Bednarik underlines that: 'the use of such sophisticated objects as beads and pendants in the Lower Palaeolithic demonstrates, beyond reasonable doubt that its hominids possessed well-established semiotic systems of various types'.[45] The plurality and variety of semiotic systems of thought and perception illustrate the importance of the master-narrative *separated from* its materials, verbal or non-verbal, abstract or concrete. In other words: the master-narrative does not have its overwhelming power because of its verbal, non-verbal, symbolic, abstract or concrete substances but because of its *master position*. The

44 Robert. G. Bednarik, *supra note 41*.
45 Robert G. Bednarik, *supra note 41*.

question of absolutism seems to be put in perspective. Emphasis is on the master-narrative that creates, represents and masters our daily meanings through its position.

Is such a narrative necessarily verbal, or if not, what is there to say about the profile and impact of a non-verbal master-narrative? A lesson learned from the famous archeologist is that language could be understood as one of the many forms of symbolism which mankind created during its engenderment.[46]

This provides the following insight, which is (among others) extremely important for legal semiotics.

> Non-verbal master-narratives existed *before* verbal master-narratives, whereas non-verbal and verbal master-narratives engendered also in *parallel* to each other, so that mixed forms also existed; verbal master-narratives dominate in recent centuries even where non-verbal narratives are included.

An example of the latter, mixed master-narratives can be encountered in the many meanings of the pyramids in Ancient Egypt. These are globally recognized as important *signs* that functioned in an axial culture at the borderlines of Occidental culture: signs of daily life during Pharaonic dynasties. The pyramids were built from the same natural material as the earth; their measures represented maxima of the human mind. Sunrays determined directions all around, buildings were covered with reflecting limestone, solar lights and white colors inspired their names. An overall impression is that they did not solely direct human emotions towards the burial monuments they were meant to be – but also, and even primarily, towards forms of resurrection: to surmount the limitation of life. Pyramids disappeared sometimes for the duration of half a human life, or even a generation, as they were covered by desert sand. Once their renewed recognition occurred, they were honored as a sign of resurrection of man and culture. Their dominance in Egyptian culture is important long after that period of civilization. Their sign function was evident and empowered by the combination of daily life and language. The fact that all pyramids were located in a specific region on the west bank of the river Nile enforces this observation. All those elements bear

---

[46] Compare this viewpoint with the more limited representation of the language phenomenon as explored in Noam Chomsky, *What Kind of Creatures Are We?* Columbia University Press, New York, 2016, in particular pp. 1–27 and 81ff.

witness to the importance and semiotic power of non-verbal mixed with verbal master-narratives. Power and pyramids belonged together, as did sign and language, meaning and location. Pyramids are precious building stones of a culture: they are a momentum of sign and language, discourse and master-narrative, the non-verbal and the verbal.

The importance of the differentiation between verbal and non-verbal master-narratives is surprising in the framework of semiotics. Those differences illustrate how deeply *sign* and *culture* are related. Peirce's suggestion that 'a sign alone cannot be a sign' seems valid in all times and under all conditions. Are signs that exist in a non-verbal master-narrative a sign? The question is profound and suggests the usefulness of asking whether the concept of a non-verbal master-narrative is meaningful at all. Considerations of this character lead us to the limits of human culture, or to regions in time and civilization in which language apparently does not play the role it does today and pyramids cannot be erected.

We direct our attention again to archeology, and to Bednarik and his colleagues. He took the initiative to search for evolutionary first signs of human capacity to create markers. Those markers differ decidedly from what natural processes, without human intervention, create. He discovered such markers in Australia as well as in other world regions and named them *cupules* – several other archeologists immediately spoke about 'rock art'.[47] Are they the alphabet of an engendering language, we ask – and: are they truly *art*? Instead of works of art, these *cupules* could be considered as the *material substance of a non-verbal master-narrative*, and it is surprising that their forms were discovered at so many and so far-distanced locations. *Cupules* are petroglyphs created by percussion on a horizontal and sometimes also vertical surface. They are decidedly created by human hand, and effectuated by percussion-blows, whereby a non-utilitarian and often symbolic glyph dominated. Current archeological explanations refer to rites and cultural marks created with very limited means; in the words of Bednarik: to traces of specific behavior patterns.

One could interpret the experiences of archeologists and consider the *cupules* indeed as signs that functioned in non-verbal master-narratives. They mark a transcendence of the natural without any trace of linguistic character. *Cupules* are a sign of powerful and willful intervention in

---

[47] See http://www.academia.edu/4982271/Cupules_-the_oldest_surviving_rock_art. Cupules are found in groups, often several hundreds, sometimes more, in a location. They are between 1.5 and 10 cm diameter although larger examples were found. Boussaingault in France is the exception where they are found on overhead rock ceilings. Some have been re-worked by later individuals.

appearances of natural phenomena, and their high numbers indicate that their production has not been a matter of small numbers. They illustrate a profile in the mind of man living thousands of centuries ago; an attitude that masters intimacy (in the form of a human relation to nature) long before a 'self' would become conceived and articulated linguistically. The riddle of their existence is also an appeal to our contemporary emotional translations (hence the qualification 'art'): they are witness of an enduring fight between man and nature, and thus embedded in tensions between leniency and the radical in non-verbal forms of culture. Their presence in important layers of contemporary scientific knowledge can indeed be interpreted in its semiotic relevance, in short: as a master-narrative. An important consequence is that the opposition between leniency and the radical, in other words: between relativism and the absolute, appears as old as humankind. The two terms do not necessarily imply a violent and powerful individual; cultural forces determined it. Two master-narratives are *both* present in humanity's psychological features – and *both* can be brought to an extreme position. In other words: relativist relativism and absolutist absolutism belong *both* to the scale of human experience and emotional life. They are never an independent and isolated power, operating beyond cultural embedding.

Lyotard would agree. His study on *The Postmodern Condition* was lauded for analyzing how a narrative generates 'the illusion of an imaginary resolution of real contradictions' and yet remains to be appreciated as an important form of knowledge.[48] Do not forget: the opposition between verbal and non-verbal master-narratives is also changeable, together with changes of meanings pertaining to fundamental concepts such as science, information, knowledge, learning, production, consumption and the like. Will the tensions between relativism and absolutism disappear in those new names and forms of social life? And if the tensions do not disappear, do the extreme absolutisms also remain – or can they become irrelevant?

A problem with all denominations of absolutism is that they will in general remain classified within the discourse of power, the latter being a component of modern technology. Lyotard makes an interesting exception here. While focusing on the language game of technology, he excludes the most extreme and absolute form of absolutism: *terror*.

> I am excluding the case in which force operates by means of terror. This lies outside the realm of language games, because the efficacy of such force is based entirely on the threat to eliminate the opposing player, not on making a

---

[48] Lyotard, *supra note 40*, p. xix.

> better 'move' than he. Whenever efficiency (that is, obtaining the desired effect) is derived from a 'Say or do this, or else you'll never speak again', then we are in the realm of terror, and the social bond is destroyed.[49]

These words were written in 1979, but we live with them in more complex situations and global dimensions of politics, not knowing in what ways the extremity of the extreme can ever change by means of changing boundaries of master-narratives.

Two additional remarks should be mentioned. A first is that extreme positions like terrorism are even at a level of scientific activity not excluded. This insight concentrates mainly on the level of participation – a level that is seldom studied as a separate project, seldom analyzed in view of its proper dynamics and seldom in view of its understanding as a case of special interactivity. Abilities of scientists to participate can be threatened at various levels, such as economic, political, legal or semiotic levels indicate. But an extreme case is in the decision-maker's arrogance, Lyotard remarks, 'which in principle has no equivalent in the sciences and consists in the exercise of terror. It says: "Adapt your aspirations to our ends – or else".'[50]

A second remark pertains to *data*, a theme we already mentioned in the preceding chapter. In our days, a decisive issue is whether data in general belong to any field of science and scientific research – which is indeed the case with the tools providing data. Science is, beyond doubt, differential and pragmatic. Its systemic character is *un*stable and many scientific data depend on decisions scientists perform. Scientific results are created by comparison; data are valuable when argument and proof are positively evaluated. Judgments are resulting from economic factors and often opinions are finalized by ideological evaluations.

But, as was already suggested before, once data can be considered on their own, once data are independently generated by other data and consumed by still other data, then they are vulnerable for extremes like those mentioned in the context of master-narratives. Data independent from humans, circulating within their own field, controlled by other data and increasing knowledge solely by themselves is no longer an unknown situation in modern life, in contemporary sciences as well as in modern politics. The question about the nature of extremes and its strong ties with our insight into the division between verbal and non-verbal master-narratives remains relevant. All issues can become actualized in a consideration, which sounds accurate, modern and relevant but remains

---

49 Lyotard, *supra note 40*, p. 46.
50 Lyotard, *supra note 40*, p. 64.

quite unanswerable: computers hacking other computers in order to manage data with still other computers – is that an act of terrorism, or must that behavior already be classified beyond terrorism? Do we have to revisit post-modernism?

REFERENCES

Austin, M. M. and P. Vidal-Naquet, *Economic and Social History of Ancient Greece*, California University Press, Berkeley, LA, 1977.

Bednarik, Robert G., *Beads and the Origins of Symbolism*, 2000, available at: www.semioticon.com/frontline/bednarik.htm, accessed 13 April 2017.

Broekman, Jan M., *Intertwinements of Law and Medicine*, Leuven University Press, 1996.

Broekman, Jan M., *A Philosophy of European Union Law*, Peeters, Leuven/Paris, 1999.

Broekman Jan M., 'The Multicultural Self' in M. Atienza, E. Pattaro, M. Schulte, B. Toporin, and D. Wyduckel (eds), *Theorie des Rechts und der Gesellschaft: Festschrift für Werner Krawietz zum 70 Geburtstag*, Duncker and Humblot, Berlin, 2003.

Broekman, Jan M., *Meaning, Narrativity, and the Real: The Semiotics of Law in Legal Education IV*, Springer, Switzerland, 2016.

Broekman, Jan M. and Larry Catà Backer, *Lawyers Making Meaning*, Springer, Dordrecht, 2013.

Brunner v The European Union Treaty, Common Market Law Reports, Vol. 69(2), 11.01.1994.

Chomsky, Noam, *What Kind of Creatures Are We?* Columbia University Press, New York, 2016.

Deleuze, G. and F. Guatteri, *Milles Plateaux*, Paris, 1980 (English edition edited by B. Massumi, *A Thousand Plateaus*, University of Minnesota Press, Minneapolis, MN/London, 1987).

Dworkin, Ronald, *Law's Empire*, Fontana Press, London, 1986.

Eco, Umberto, *A Theory of Semiotics*, Indiana University Press/Midland, Bloomington, IN, 1979.

Fleerackers, Frank, *Affective Legal Analysis: On the Resolution of Conflict*, Duncker and Humblot, Berlin, 2000.

Fleerackers, Frank, 'Conflict Resolution and Social Complexity' *XXVI World Congress of Philosophy of Law*, Editora Forum, 2013, pp. 690–96.

Fleerackers, Frank, *Rechtsdenken: Vade Mecum*, Larcier, Brussels, 2016.

Geertz, Clifford, *The Interpretation of Cultures* (1973), Basic Books, New York, 2000.

Hansen, M. H., *The Athenian Democracy in the Age of Demosthenes*, Basil Blackwell, Oxford/Cambridge, MA, 1991.

Hobbes, Th., *Leviathan*, 1651 (Latin edition edited by Hobbes, 1668; critical edition edited by N. Malcolm (ed.), Clarendon, Oxford University Press, 2012).

Jackson, Bernard S., *Law, Fact and Narrative Coherence*, Deborah Charles Publisher, Liverpool, 1988.

Kant, I., *Kritik der praktischen Vernunft (Critique of Practical Reason)*, Riga, 1788.
Kevelson, Roberta, *The Law as a System of Signs*, Plenum Press, New York/London, 1988.
Krawietz, Werner, 'On How to Accept a Legal Norm or Legal Order and Different Rules of Recognition' in F. Fleerackers, E. van Leeuwen, and B. van Roermund (eds), *Law, Life and the Images of Man: Modes of Thought in Modern Legal Theory*, Dunker and Humblot, Berlin, 1996.
Kuhn, Thomas, *The Structure of Scientific Revolutions*, Chicago University Press, 1962.
Lyotard, J. -F., *La condition postmoderne: rapport sur le savoir*, Paris, 1979, (The Postmodern Condition: A Report on Knowledge, Manchester University Press, 1984).
MacCormick, Neil, 'Coherence in Legal Justification' in W. Krawietz, H. Schelsky, G. Winkler, and A. Schramm (eds), *Theorie der Normen: Festgabe für Ota Weinberger zum 65 Geburtstag*, Duncker and Humblot, Berlin, 1984.
Marusek, Sarah (ed.), *Synesthetic Legalities: Sensory Dimensions of Law and Jurisprudence*, Routledge, London, 2016.
Mendelson, Edward, 'In the Depths of the Digital Age' *The New York Review of Books*, June 23, 2016, Vol. LXIII, No. 11.
Parke, H. W., *Festivals of the Athenians*, Cornell University Press, New York/London, 1977.
Pickard-Cambridge, Sir Arthur, *The Dramatic Festivals of Athens* (2nd edn, edited by J. Could and D. M. Lewis) Oxford University Press, Oxford, 1988.
Searle, John, *Speech Acts: An Essay in the Philosophy of Language.* Cambridge University Press, Cambridge, 1969.
Searle, John, *The Construction of Social Reality*, Allen Lane, London, 1995.
Sinclair, R. K., *Democracy and Participation in Athens*, Cambridge University Press, Cambridge, 1988.
Starr, Chester G., *The Birth of Athenian Democracy*, Oxford University Press, Oxford, 1990.
Steiner, Georg, *Errata: An Examined Life*, Weidenfeld and Nicholson, London, 1997.
Teubner, Günther, 'Global Bukowina: Legal Pluralism in the World Society' in Günther Teubner (ed.), *Global Law Without a State*, Dartmouth, Aldershot, 1997.
Unger, Roberto M., *What Should Legal Analysis Become?* Verso, London/New York, 1996.
Vernant, J. -P., *Les origines de la pensée grecque*, Paris, 1962 (English edition, *The Origins of Greek Thought*, Cornell University Press, Ithaca, NY, 1982).
Von Goethe, J. W., *Zur Farbenlehre*, Bd I, Tübingen 1810, New York SBN: 465-03425-X.
Von Wright, Georg H., *Norm and Action*, Routledge and Kegan Paul, London, 1963.
Weber, Max, *Wirtschaft und Gesellschaft*, 1922 (edited by Johannes Winckelmann, Kiepenheuer and Witsch, Köln/Berlin, 1964) (*On Law in Economy and Society*, edited by E. Shils and M. Rheinstein, Harvard University Press, Cambridge, MA, 1954).
Wittgenstein, Ludwig, *Philosophical Investigations*, Basil Blackwell, Oxford, 1958.

4. On Hermes Avenue

Preceding chapters explored semiotic aspects of linguistic implications which characterize a 'talking about law'. But that expression – no matter how concealed or, on the contrary, how clearly indicating legal and social issues of importance – was always followed by an indication of special and unusual location: the street. The full expression was always: 'talking about law on the street' (or any other public place). As a consequence, this final chapter considers the notions at play of this *locus*, which has been known since millennia as *the street*.

Keep that expression 'street' in mind: even when you are not walking on streets, they guide you, they are in your mind, shape your thoughts and structure your perceptions. Streets, roads, routes, plazas, highways, passes, strips or runways are our markers. Are they? Often they seem a counterpart of our feet: as if they constitute an additional organ of the human body, each step actualizes feet and path, bodies and streets and remain close to your body, as if they were a part of it. Are they a symbol – a symbol of what? Streets have not always been so neatly arranged as in modern days. Stones were often just cobblestones, thrown in a seeming disorder although always limited by houses, buildings, trees and bushes, and their ground lines always linking one place with another. The latter observation unveils an important meaning of streets. Their essence is not in the disorder of cobblestones or in the fact that those stones support more and more human feet and thus create forms of commonness. The latter finds its expression in qualifying footways from path to street to lane or avenue. A 'talking about law' rather occurs as if the stones are already letters of an alphabet to be used by citizens walking their way. A grammar of their talks seems already prepared before their feet move. That commonness of feet and conversation is anchored in the coherence of all material elements which belong to the street and equally forcefully to the human body and mind. 'Talking about law' is a form of commonness and socializing bonds. It therefore does not surprise that streets have names. But what is named when streets are given names? Did those names concern stones or other pavement materials; or the intentions, which make our feet move; or habits of preferring a specific direction, so that street names signify acts of the mind? In the case of street names (not unlike legal cases) a process of enculturation unfolds. The latter is based on symbols of a community and unfolds the engenderment of meaning in the innermost dynamics of the naming.

4.1 STREETS, NAMES

Is there a difference between the names of streets and the names of cases? To answer that unorthodox but perhaps revealing question we should focus again on stones and words, because a lawyer often considers words as if they were stones. A lawyer confirms that words are important but not effective when single – they are effective only as a pile. They fit into one hand when thrown up against all forces of gravitation; they never fit to each other when broached all in one. This is how he throws words in social complexities, and honors that we all live a social life linguistically. A lawyer's practice is to throw words. The magnetism of the text changes the effects of words; laws change the coherence of a life and its potential to reorientate. Our speech is our obedience, there are powers in our words that are not ours but belong to a respectable past, a history of parts of mankind, a story of habits and vetoes, a narration of do's and don'ts – a story of names.

All those considerations qualify the importance of names in legal cases and their discourses. Words are bridges between them and sentences, or even texts, their effect. The latter are forceful: what can be read or heard must be lived and experienced. A lawyer's dynamics will not unveil the hidden forces that have shaped him or her like we all seem to be. Words fold in lives that open up for them: all are in all – the vows of a culture awaken the citizen who is 'talking about law'. Indeed, names mark thought patterns as well as the social, political and economic relevancies given to the case. It is often difficult to indicate the borderlines between the names that refer to components of the case and the names or related interests. No wonder that rigid rules try to determine those cases. Consult the websites of the 'Legal Information Institute' and others: while you read them, you are at the borderlines between everyday and professional language. All legal names suggest that they belong to a natural language – they share that suggestion with street names, but in a more concealed manner they are completely different because they possess a precisely described function and meaning of the law in its non-natural form, that is: artificial language. *The gap* between that artificiality of legal language (including the use for legal cases) and the everyday natural language of street names is concealed by the many ways law creates case names in its casuistic approach to reality. The *gap* is the problem.

While studying street names and case names in the light of the *gap* between a natural and an artificial language, an important consequence comes to the fore: *exactly that gap is a dominating theme of legal education*; it can only be revealed by a semiotic understanding of law and legal discourse.

Streets, squares and avenues change in parallel with the ever-changing meaning of words. This reveals the many dimensions of the expression 'talking about law *on the street*'. When those forms of talking occur, they are not intended to move the feet and create a happy arrival but rather to articulate feelings, emotional utterances and related forms of citizen participation. Deeply engraved values of modern communication unfold while debates on laws, on legal values and norms, take place on the street. This urges us to pay attention to the many challenges of the 'street', and in particular the 'street' as a theory-generating concept.[1]

One needs insight in crucial issues for acknowledging the 'street' as a fully fledged concept in social sciences, and for a deeper understanding of the importance of their names in semiotic and philosophical perspective. A shortlist of key notions includes: (1) *Otherness* is a most important *sign* for dealing with the 'street'; it should be read more intensely than ever before; (2) the 'street' is a sign of a deep *desire* to bond and to think the 'common' and a sign of a personal identity; its order, based on such identity, challenges the flow of events; (3) these events are anchored in institutional 'street' contexts, which provide meaning-making and management as a *political act*; (4) meanings of the 'street' come from citizen capacities to *converse* and to *educate*, so that (5) the *spatial* features of the 'street' are not architectonic or geographic but articulate communicative qualities of citizens and thus display their semiotic relevance. It is challenging to experience in how many ways all those notions connect to the *names* of streets, plazas and other locations on the basis of their differentiation of one all-determinant notion named 'Otherness'. *Streets, the aorta of modern social life, are 'named locations' because they are emotionally experienced and socially determined as a 'named otherness'.*

The Ancient Greek figure of Hermes illustrated this determination around the fifth century BC. We all walk on a Hermes Avenue! How often do we walk directionless! Of course, one can buy a house on a Hermes Avenue in various places around the world – one can buy a house

---

[1] Jan M. Broekman, 'Street as Theory' in Sarah Marusek and John Brigham, (eds), *Street Level Sovereignty: A Reader*, Rowman and Littlefield, Lanham, MD, 2017.

on Hermes Avenue for instance in California, several in Australia and several others in the United Kingdom. But are they located on Hermes' Avenue? Those houses and their streets do not form a unity, which would be necessary to experience the essentials of the street name. Pay attention to Hermes' relation with street-stones! The latter reveals a deeply anchored religious motive, since Hermes was the preferred God to keep them in hand. We already mentioned that the Greek word '*hermaion*' denoted minor piles but sometimes even pillars of stones positioned on hills in the countryside and in the city streets as marks belonging to the streets and referring to the houses. That pattern of streets combined with religious signs does not exist in any Hermes Avenue, neither in the United Kingdom nor in California. Hermes stayed in piles of stones erected in front of the houses to guide walkers and wanderers on the street. The messenger of the Gods protected travelers as well as merchants, and thus heralded what in later centuries became the Roman *pater familias.*

But a very important observation was already registered in earlier pages. Hermes' face was *not* directed to the owners of the houses along the streets – it was directed to the street: to the public and to those who were without house, without protection and often without any asset. All who were on the street, perceived the stone piles as if these piles were (a) Hermes himself, (b) a sign of otherness, and (c) a token of *commonness.* It was said: a messenger of God is a God himself: the sign is itself what it signifies.

Is Hermes a sign on its own? Can that be, can a sign be a sign on its own? Hermes doubles, intensifies, creates a plurality within himself as well as in life, and in the same time he de-doubles, singles out and thus enforces an identity of which the citizen is a witness while carrying its legally fortified citizenship. Stones are signs of a justification; Hermes' homes protect the homeless. Owners do not worship Hermes for themselves, but for others. Is this Greek inversion of worship the basis for their democracy and a socially effective altruism? To consider this question means at the same time accessing the insight that an interpretation is never the skill of one person alone – it is a spiritual force that could inspire the lawyer in his social context and in his task of interpreting occurrences in a way that makes o/Otherness prevail. Hermeneutics concern a *total* occurrence, and this totality may be one of the most powerful challenges one encounters in a lawyer's practice.

Is that a sign of its full signification for our democracy, the free use of the streets and other public places included? One cannot deny the scope and importance of this consideration. The signifying power of Hermes' stones is interesting us again. Are they symbols of the signs that are composites of hermeneutics? It remains clear in any case how far correlations between language and culture dominate our conceptualization of culture itself – and, in the end, of ourselves as a Self. The stones are neither Hermes' private property nor the result of an indifferent ramble or its opposite: a careful engineering. We found in the recent surroundings of Athens many traces of stone piles which marked paths and roads, and were visually connected with houses, baths and huts. They had a clear social function and guided walkers everywhere.

The task of stones was to keep orientation alive, to safeguard trajectories, to memorize or dream about occurrences past and present, to create an index for stratification (as the piles were not flat) and to prevent any fixation on one particular trajectory. Hermes' stones were a text, a tag, an index, a sign. Who knows, even while walking a Hermes Avenue! Consider that the stones of our streets are still burdened with equal qualifications, mostly those of essentials of modern life and their commodities. Dave Eggers described them in the very first page of his 2013 novel *The Circle* in which he observed one of his main personages walking towards her new job:

> [W]alking from the parking lot to the main hall, trying to look as if she belonged. The walkway wound around lemon and orange trees and its quiet red cobblestones were replaced, occasionally, by tiles with imploring messages of inspiration. 'Dream', one said, the word laser-cut into the red stone. 'Participate', said another. There were dozens: 'Find Community', 'Innovate', 'Imagine'. She just missed stepping on the hand of a young man in a grey jumpsuit; he was installing a new stone that said 'Breathe'.[2]

Are street names connected with their mission in this broad sense of the word? They are indeed. And that mission is even broader: street names are the cornerstones of *legal* expressiveness and in their naming thus support the multiplicity of active citizenship. Walking on *the named street* protects me legally, despite the fact that I participate in a wide innocence concerning the dimensions of enjoying my walk. Names of streets make me forget the legal bonds that signify my joyful walk – a dimension, which was neglected in Walter Benjamin's consideration of the *Passages* at the end of the nineteenth century. They are loudly speaking to me when I walk and step on tiles that are witness to my commodity-bound native tongue. The names of the street all belong to that tongue, and they thus conceal the gap between natural and legal expressiveness. I love to walk the Boulevard St. Germain or the Fifth

---

[2] Dave Eggers, *The Circle, A Novel*. Vintage Books, New York, 2014, p. 2.

Avenue, sometimes even on Hermes Avenue, without any awareness that the names of those pavements define me as an individual with rights and duties, named 'citizen', and bind me to a specific cultural hemisphere. That evidence also reigns in jurisprudence: the discourse of law remains the discourse of property and of ownership-interrelations. There is a heavy-weighted consequence to consider, which makes my walk difficult and inspires my 'talking about law' on the street corners: if I cannot transform myself into or adapt myself to dominant forms of possessiveness, I cannot perform my walk as a correct framing of a rights-position in social life. So, a fascinating aspect is that streets are opened up to experiences, in particular to self-reflection and self-understanding, which must include legal considerations – and all this is inherent in their names! *My walk on the street is an articulation of my mother tongue.* How can I perceive this articulation as my private property? Only if language is understood as a *good*, an *object* to be possessed, a *commodity* respected in social bonds.

That conclusion leads far beyond the limited number of professional speakers who are institutionally allowed to speak law, as the Dutch jurist and semiotician J. I. de Haan already highlighted during the second decade of the twentieth century. He claimed:

> The legal significian [nowadays: the legal semiotician] has to unfold its views … not in … the language of the law issued as law. Those words do not need to be spoken and they can in essence not be spoken in the language we actually use. *Law as law is not spoken, but speaks to us in the dynamics of our legal consciousness.* But as soon as law became transformed into the major force for maintaining social order, the law had to be spoken/articulated by the legislator as well as the judge. The task of the legal significian is to research the essence of the various types and categories of words and to compare the numerous meanings of words of legal language with that essence … I add that the theories of Freud about the power of the unconscious on linguistics are an important theme, in particular when he highlights his analysis of words with contrasting meanings (emphasis added).[3]

His observation focused on an *individualistic* approach of law. But expressing oneself while 'talking about law on the street' does not lead to individualistic occurrences. On the contrary: conversations can never be understood as a solitary event. Speaking is never a solipsistic act – that seems a crucial observation in the context of meaning and sign. It

---

[3] J. I. de Haan, 'Essence and Task of Legal Significs' (English translation in Jan M. Broekman and Larry Catà Backer, *Signs in Law – A Source Book*, Springer, Heidelberg/New York/Dordrecht, 2013), p. 70.

threatens the innermost anchored tendencies of lawyers to consider their speech as their proper act! But as was said various times already, Peirce stated that a sign alone is not a sign. Thus semiotics remains confronted with infinite strings or even pools of signs.[4] Their string character abolishes an understanding of reality in strictly individualistic terms – any person is a sign, Peirce noted, and any human consciousness has sign character. An individual exists only in so far as it is a part of that infinite string. A consciousness called 'legal' can, because of this string/sign character, be treated only in social terms. Can the 'street' bring this insight to practice? It could very well be. Semiotics illustrates the complexity of the labyrinth of human culture. No human culture is possible without a fundamental *sharing* of norms or values in the many ways signs are practiced. Sharing is not possible without accepting that a culture is itself an infinite network of 'interpretants' (Peirce), and not only 'interpreters' – a conclusion closely neighboring to 'streets' which are available on Google, Facebook and other IT communication systems. The 'street' is a modern achievement on the basis of a particular view of reality: signs are exchanged, everywhere meanings multiply. They also multiply electronically, as was mentioned in preceding chapters.

These components confirm a fundamental difference with the 'street'-concept as was observed in the twentieth and nineteenth centuries. 'Street' is today no longer a subject of philosophical, cultural or aesthetic reflections but a harsh reality *in se*. While *stones* have disappeared, one interrogates Hermes whether stones still have any meaning. It is a complex issue because of its multiple (often powerfully political and corporation-inspired) references: 'street' refers to cultural, aesthetic and political realities and presents itself as a reality *in se*, apart from traditional references or blocking references of any kind. The 'street' embraces social forms which hitherto did not play a significant role in politics, semiotics or social sciences: electronics and related IT-means belong to those forms. *Presidents on Twitter* – what does it imply for Occidental culture, Hermes asks us while walking his Avenue, guided by Tweets of our Heads of State?

All in all, we encounter roots of social change combined with a concept of democracy, of which the 'street' is a component. That suggestion supports Karl Popper's 1943/45 publication *The Open Society and its Enemies*. Is 'the street' just a new name for social change, or eventually for social change's preferred location, which would be a

---

[4] Jan M. Broekman, *Meaning, Narrativity, and the Real*, Springer, Switzerland, 2016, pp. 9–14.

location filled with new possibilities and options that were hitherto unknown? Is a democratic society 'open' because of disruption and innovation coming together in the attempt to evaluate the 'street' as a valid concept in semiotics and society? Popper coined the concept of an *open society* (in contrast to a closed or tribal society) which 'sets free the critical powers of man'. The 'street' could in this context be associated with an unfolding of critical powers – an association which is all too often proved to be true. It is fascinating to read Popper's words on how:

> [A]n open society may become, by degrees, what I should like to term an '*abstract society*'. It may, to a considerable extent, lose the character of a concrete or real group of men, or of a system of such real groups ... We could conceive of a society in which men practically never meet face-to-face – in which all business is conducted by individuals in isolation who communicate by typed letters or by telegrams, and who go about in closed motor cars ... Such a fictitious society might be called an abstract society. Although we do not always drive alone in closed motor cars (but meet face-to-face thousands of men walking past in the street) the result is very nearly the same as if we did – we do not establish as a rule any personal relation with our fellow-pedestrians.[5]

The 'street' *can* be an abstract concept in an abstract society, and *is* very real at the same time – both attitudes are in the mind of citizens. But more important is the conclusion that an *open* society is not an *individualistic* society, i.e. a society of individuals who live together on the basis of contract. The 'street' deeply reflects this issue: is any pursued autonomy of an individual the property of any citizen in the 'street'? 'Individual' is today indeed a very different feature and it accomplishes what traditional organic institutions in society could not achieve. 'What is truly important', Charles Taylor suggested in this context, 'is that one be able to exercise autonomy in the basic issues of life, in one's most important commitments. Now, it is very dubious whether the developed capacity for this kind of autonomy can rise simply within the family ... What it is to be an autonomous agent, to have one's own way of feeling, of acting, of expression, is an identity, a way of understanding oneself, which men are not born with.' Citizenship results from complex processes of enculturation. Hence Taylor's words: 'a way of understanding oneself, which men are not born with'. He continues: 'They have to

---

[5] Karl Popper, *The Open Society and its Enemies*, 1945, 5th edn, Routledge, London, 1966, p. 177; see also H. Bergson, *Les deux sources de la moralité et de la religion*, 1932 (English edition, *Two Sources of Morality and Religion*, University of Notre Dame Press, Notre Dame, IN, 1935, 1977).

acquire it ... Thus we live in a world in which there is such a thing as public debate about moral and political questions and other basic issues. We constantly forget how remarkable that is, how it did not have to be so, and may one day no longer be so.'[6]

The 'street' appears as a new place that is very different from the traditional family context. A first effort to meet upfront is in one of the many buzzwords of actual social and political philosophy: 'the citizen in an open society'. John Rawls tried to develop that concept as a link between a 'self' and a '(legal) subject'. Our interest in the 'street' shows new ways to understand individualism and liberalism: *individual rights are always embedded in community bonds* and thus require a new understanding of 'individuality' that has *not* lost nor conceals the fundamental necessity of *otherness.*

Those bonds are above all most important steps in the development of social dimensions, which are vital for the emergence of an actual *Self.* They can, however, be destroyed when deception, protest and negativity dominate – even on the street. Many dimensions of the welfare State did so in the course of its history. They brought indifference and apathy in institutional settings and on the streets. Politics as well as active participation of citizens became the victim. Their complete opposite are violent nationalism and extreme radicalism and those seem equally dangerous. All those positions became visible at a new location: the 'street'. On the 'street' it became clear that an understanding of justice beyond law and legal discourse would not automatically lead to a functional democracy. The latter depends upon qualities and attitudes of its citizenship, which reach far beyond a balanced functionality of law and the legal system.

An 'openness' of society can be interpreted as an important instrument to forward a responsible and active citizenship. Roots of that type of citizenship are, however, found in forms of togetherness; they were not found in the citizen's relation with the powerful national and international institutions, and not in their connections to the dominant corporations or their lobbyists driving around in the political landscape in 'closed motor cars' (Popper). Neither governmental and other cultural institutions, nor internationally oriented corporations, are able to perform what was evident in traditional family life: *education.* Initiatives of citizens to build relations with public institutions do not flourish by

---

[6] Charles Taylor, 'Atomism' in Shl. Averini and A. De-Shalit (eds), *Communitarianism and Individualism*, Oxford University Press, Oxford, 1992, p. 43ff.

nature. They are the result of education, and thus of an appropriate conversation, which can often be understood as the heart of a functioning cultural pattern. That may be an important dimension of the 'street': a new locus where education through conversation, including all forms of e-communication and data-exchange, takes place. It does so at many levels, in many languages, in powerful varieties of opinion and perhaps in the shadow of a notion of justice, which is not exclusively defined by legal specialists or democratically elected law-makers.

The 'openness' of modern society, one must conclude, embraces foundational aspects of the 'street'. An exclusively moral judgment about the latter seems misplaced. The 'street' cannot be seen as an instrument but rather as a field of meaning (a 'stratum') that enables, even invites, to create new moves of thought formation and actual thinking. Meaningful social activities find their roots in those aspects, but (as one experiences these days) also in extremisms, as recent radicalization shows. Terrorists are not educated in schools, family circles, Churches or Mosques, but on the 'street'. Today the 'street' is often viewed as an antipode of all bourgeois values, an opposite of what States, State-unions, corporations and other international organizations wish to achieve in the name of human rights and democracy. Such connotations, positive as well as negative, belong to the multiple aspects that will finally prepare us for a clear insight: the 'open' society gave the 'street' importance via the citizen and its sustained capacity of conversation and education.

'Street' and 'commonness' belong closely together. The 'street' became a social form to fight any *exclusion* of the individual. That is visible in the many modes of commonness which citizens as well as radicalizing youngsters strive to experience via the 'street'. Exclusion is the opposite of what the 'street' wants. All forms of inclusion fight the evil of a not-belonging. But during that fight, the difference between commonness and not-belonging is often lost. Its forceful social dynamic includes a mastership of meanings and signs under all circumstances. The street knows a continuous renewal of social values, changes of social order and unfolding views on a future – not to mention a diminishing of the restrictive and binding powers of institutions. 'Street'-words are embedded in discourses of social media but also in words, texts and films of terrorists and jihadists. A combination of a forceful belonging with an equally forceful desire to be freed from institutions seems to be an omnipresent power to determine the 'street' experience.

The terms 'common' and 'community' are often a decisive mark in texts and discourses that want to support modern 'street' experiences.[7] Two different dynamics are thus effective within one social structure. The 'street' fights indeed the exclusion of the individual. But it also fights the perfect fit of subject, individual and citizen in a society. 'Street' action should halt that dangerous perfection, because it threatens the freedom of the citizen. This ambiguity is one of the critical points when the acceptance of the 'street'-concept is debated. It leads to the consideration whether it is possible that *the 'street' accomplishes what the State fails to put into practice*. 'Nation State' versus 'street' as a 'common': forms of community, which are forcefully filled with ambiguities. And: does the 'street' perform a *direct democracy* where a 'State' can only deliver an *indirect* democracy with institutions and other representational activities? Ask the Athenians of the fifth century BC. Was their 'street' a sign of the spirit of a new perception, liberated from limiting powers that flourish under the heading of 'democracy'?

Watching people, architecture and merchandise while walking in the streets, and seeing how life evolves, challenges the consideration as to what images fit to what feelings. None of them can be linked to the power of a representative, or – its opposite – a direct democracy. A social ambiguity became visible on the pavements and in the shop windows of the streets. 'Belonging' remains the keyword; it can only be realized in an open society with smaller dimensions and lower levels of hierarchy. One question appears to remain essential: 'How do we belong? Who are we when we belong?' The 'open society' needs *local* communities and *smaller scales* of life in order to truly be 'open'. Do we not tinker with the concept and idea of a 'global' society? The 'street' is a *sign* of the world as a *common image*, and only as such can it be the subject of political discussion. Commonness must be concrete in all 'street' actions and remain at a distance to any romanticizing interpretation. An interim conclusion is of the greatest importance in this context: We should not discuss the 'street' as a political form but *primarily as a new and recent epistemological achievement*. The latter is a continuing process, and as such embraces what occurs beyond fixation and social planning. The street appears to be *unruly* because of its capacity for embedding differentiations and dynamics unfolding in unforeseeable manners. A *contrast* between *activism* and the *street* flourishes, because the latter's properties obviate the first.

---

[7] See for historical and political consequences, Jan M. Broekman, *supra note 1*, Ch. II, §2.

4.2 STREETS, SIGNIFIERS

Hobbes' *Magnus Homo* image accompanying the title page of his 1651 *Leviathan* brings the 'street' to the fore as the most organic feature of semiotics, law and politics. His famous *body-figure* has never been interpreted as a suggestion pertaining to *the street.* But his frontispiece shows a huge human figure (in its figurative sense a reminder of religious motives) in which all individuals as pictured in the upper half of the frontispiece are walking to the top of that figure: 'The *Multitude* ... united in one Person, is called a *common-wealth*, in Latin: *civitas*. This is the Generation of that Great Leviathan, or rather ... of that Mortall God, to which we owe under the Immortall God, our peace and defence.'(Ch. 17). They all desire to be incorporated in the all-embracing body (the State absorbs all streets) and leave churches, houses and streets behind so that the landscape is emptied and without any interactive meaning or sense. Their common wish is to become *one body* – a metaphor for those talking about law and related political issues on the 'street'. That wish would automatically lead to new forms of direct democracy – an immediacy, which was translated by Hobbes in words of the social contract. One should not forget that 'contract' was equivalent to 'freedom'. This freedom interpreted a *bond* between humans as the highest value in life and created awareness about the fact that there is no hegemony or sovereignty possible without such a *bond.* With the same words one concludes today: the 'street' is the sign of a deep desire, enforced by the experience that the nation State is not able to provide any bond among its citizens other than by legally determined articulations of life. A conclusion could be that the suggested *bond* does not suffice to understand the social impact and features of the 'street'-concept. The *street* symbolizes an unfulfilled desire, and is by no means a fully conceived and meaningful concept that can be used in law, politics and psychology as if it were a safe and valuable coin to be used in human relations.

'Regaining the commons' thus appears to be a powerful ideal of the 'street'. Its influence is of important actuality. The modern *Degrowth* movement embraces, for instance, major forms of the *commons*, those limiting or abolishing a general 'commodity-thinking' included. The movement's basic concept identifies 'the social' with a general 'bonding' as its foundation. That bonding is, however, a form of sovereignty or external power, which limits the unfolding of an actual walker's *Self.* The concept of 'the social' includes *non-bonding as a positive value.* A disregard of that value also misinterprets the *sign* function of the 'street'.

The 'street' favors the unfolding of multiple positions and attitudes of a *Self* when it walks the street.[8] Enrichment effects of those walks are not limited to the physical exercise which seems involved, but reach out towards much wider domains of brain functioning, as neurologists made clear.[9]

As has been said several times before: body, organism, togetherness, contract, freedom and rights were always understood in the fields of meaning created by the State, which in its turn was understood as a 'super-bond'. How did the latter shape our thoughts, and patterns of philosophy, science and psychology? Does the question generate an emotional desire pertaining to the view of citizens' commonness to accomplish in other manners what the State could not perform? The word *Commune* seems in this context an expression filled with frustration, because it reminds the citizen on the 'street' that clashing political realities cause social and political disasters; and the latter are loudly audible around the world.

One needs to conclude that meanings and their signs stem from a grandiose defect and a deep ambiguity: it appears *de facto* impossible *to think* the common, the social enclosure of humans and the required new forms of togetherness. Even *names* do not perform sufficiently. It is an onerous thought that neither of those concepts can be fully employed within the boundaries of a State-determined view or within the dominating fixated and *applicatio*-bound thought patterns that master reality. The discovery of that limitation goes hand in hand with the semiotic question of how far 'the street' is acceptable as a foundational meaning. No wonder that meaning-making as well as meaning-managing must be qualified as first-order political acts which are exclusively based on our theories of cognition. Indeed: *streets need names* because our epistemology is in need of them.

Do the conversations on the street signify specific issues that are of importance in our actual modernity? In other words: are streets and the talks on the street ready for semiotic consideration? 'On the street' is a very abstract location, which is often only vaguely associated with the name of the street, the plaza or the avenue. Does that suffice? A

---

[8] Giacomo D'Alisa, Federico Demaria and Giorgos Kallis, *Degrowth: A Vocabulary for a New Era.* Routledge, London, 2014, Ch. 1; Jan M. Broekman, *supra note 1*, §3.

[9] C. Hertzog, A. F. Kramer, R. S. Wilson and U. Lindenberger, 'Enrichment Effects on Adult Cognitive Development: Can the Functional Capacity of Older Adults Be Preserved and Enhanced?' *Psychological Sciences Public Interest*, Oct. Vol. 9, No. 1, 2008, 1–65.

fascinating aspect has already been formulated in the preceding pages: one *experiences* life but seldom *reflects* in a theoretical manner upon life as it unfolds on the street. In other words: it seems that practice and immediacy of everyday life do indeed fit to the street concept, but that theory, reflection and reconsideration only seldom unfold in whatever reality feature of the street reigns.[10] The question about the street-level of *theoretical reflection* goes hand in hand with the question about the *signifying force* of street and street name.

4.2.1 Are Streets Signifiers?

The word *theoria* played an important role on Athenian streets. That is an often-neglected issue in studies on the Ancient Greek and references to the Greek and their concept of democracy in modern social theory. Ancient and modern streets display, of course, technical differences but they hardly show principal differences. We are all watched on the street, perhaps not by Gods but by cameras constructed on the basis of the same Greek principles: support for individual wellbeing combined with rights and duties legally formulated by the State. Do streets always balance the two? Some want to, pretend to, might even be successful in just doing that. But none is beyond the more fundamental meaning of the word *theoria.* One must conclude in more general terms that a special, even enigmatic but nevertheless fascinating, power seems to be present in a concealed manner in the heart of one of the most important phenomena of Occidental culture.

Each individual will renounce a naïve-natural position in the course of life and give that renouncement the name: *theory*. That act embraces language, morality, society, and above all, otherness – but all components remain enclosed in an evolving, often troublesome harmony within the 'self'. How do 'theory' and 'self' meet? The question should be posed even in psychology and psychopathology. A strong argument is in this context that there is no doubt about what the 'street' illustrates.

> A human individual is *continuously in reconciliation with its Self while recognizing itself through others and otherness* and even *discovering otherness as a source of dynamics deeply inside its Self.* That process is much more than any 'internal conversation' within the self and it definitively transcends 'I-' and 'You-' positions: *it is a socializing practice.*

[10] Jan M. Broekman, *supra note 1*, Ch. III.

'The street' is the *locus* of that practice and enlarges and deepens that recognition.[11] *Theoria* is a process that accompanies the *unfolding human self.* It brings something new and uncalled-for to the front beyond what is directly present and perceivable into the realm of social, political and humane essentialities of life in the *polis*. In its deepest sense, fathomed by the Greek sense of the word, *theoria* is a *sign* to grasp the implicit meanings of our awareness and self-unfolding *with the 'street' as its milieu.* In their activity of connecting persons to persons (and in particular citizens to citizens), 'street'-meanings are not a part of fixated sign patterns, as are, for instance, 'I-' and 'You-', 'We-' and 'It-' patterns. Awareness of the 'street' has a far more holistic character and embraces less fixating and single components; street awareness can never be associated with a system of precisely defined concepts. In that precisely definable sense, '*theoria*' colors a path to citizenship in political contexts. A forceful renouncement of any naïve-natural attitude (including a renewed interest in language with its roots in regions or nations and a reformulation of cultural values) is truly a *theoric* (often mistranslated as 'theoretical') feature of the 'street'.

A citizen is in this light like the author of a successful novel: embedded in a social context, expressing values and norms, positioning in/against traditional institutions, at a distance from individual resourcefulness and geniality, continuously unfolding thought patterns. In this same light is 'street': *theory* – and *theory* is here much more than an incidental metaphor. One of the important aspects of the ties between 'street' and 'theory' is its emphasis on *participation*, a specific ability of the subject/citizen. But that participation is not a position of passivity: on the contrary, this participation is in essence a matter of creation, of *making* as lawyers are meaning-*makers*. In other words, 'street' as a direct expression for the various spatial, cultural, moral or political coordinates of participation in the sense of a 'being there', knows his walkers as makers, like the Latin expression '*Homo faber*' already

---

[11] An important theory about the semiotic dimensions and dialogue character of the locus of inner speech has been developed in connection with the idea of self-conception and the resultant actions in a recent study of Norbert Wiley, *Inner Speech and the Dialogical Self*, Temple University Press, Philadelphia/Rome/ Tokyo, 2016. It must be underlined that 'street' as well as 'theory' are not meanings as such, but only a *receptacle* for meaning in the widest sense of that word. *On* the street, one concludes, and *in* theory, everything can be or become meaningful – and that is by no means a negative conclusion.

articulated. As a consequence, 'theory' expresses the unity and almost holistic character of each individual's participation in the above sense of the word.

This is exactly what the *theoric fund* supported and wanted to effectuate in Ancient Greece – a goal, however, that is, hardly different from what contemporary philosophers, social scientists and politicians envisage today. Xenophon already mentioned how the large number of festivals in Athens, particularly in the fifth century BC, required financial provisions of all sorts, primarily State and tribal provisions. But they were also a burden to most of the citizens, not to mention the *metics* (who did not possess official citizenship although they were correctly registered). The most important of the public festivals were processions, theatrical exhibitions, gymnastic contests and games – all were celebrated with great splendor and at great expense.[12] The fund was created around 350 BC to help the Athenians to cope with all those expenses. It was established to provide enough money for poorer Athenian citizens to be able to purchase tickets for yearly festivals of public worship and theatrical productions. Public finances provided a considerable part of public festivals.

Originally, festivals did not charge for admissions. But due to the scarcity of seating capacity, fights could break out as everyone rushed to find a bench, so that it was at a certain moment decided to charge an admission fee to prevent further violence. The fee was paid to the person who was responsible for the theater and kept it in good repair and constantly ready for use, on condition of being allowed to receive the profits. But because poorer citizens could not afford to pay for admittance, Athens established a fund that covered the costs of their tickets. Each citizen was allotted the ticket cost of two *obols* on each day of the festivals. The payments would differ depending on the functioning of the State treasury (there was no money available in times of war) and how many days the festivals lasted.

Pericles passed a law to relieve the poorer classes more effectively. That law enabled them to receive the price of admission from the State, after which all those citizens who were too poor to pay for their places applied for the money in the public assembly, which was then frequently held in the theater. The theater had become its own cashier and administrator. A great appetite of the people for these sums grew by

---

[12] James J. Buchanan, *Theorika: A Study of Monetary Distributions to the Athenian Citizenry during the Fifth and Fourth Centuries BC*, Augustin, New York, 1962, p. 10ff.

additional encouragements so that they seem in later times not to have been confined to the poorer classes alone. The in-depth 1958 research of Hermann Koller into the word *theoria* illustrates that its meanings in Ancient Greece (as they did in modernity) depend upon specific regions of human interactivity. That interactivity has at least two important influences on the meaning of the word: the *desire* to participate in the many festivals of those days, and the *position* of the written or institutionally spoken word in social context.[13]

Do not forget that the dominant position of the written or spoken word was never a global cultural phenomenon. Mixed oral–written emblems serving human communication often marked a world of knowledge and culture, as many footnotes of the quoted Detienne publication richly illustrate. Questions about the autonomy of mouth, ear or eye were not always crucial for determining social positions. Koller's fascinating research unfolds, however, without taking the influence of the *theoric fund* upon the emergence of social relations among individuals and the experience of their citizenship into regard, and that has its consequences. His approach illustrates that the philology or even the etymology of a word like *theoria* does not provide an explication of the meaning in social life then and now.

Dialects, local languages, as for instance differences between Ionic and Attic articulations, complicate in addition our insights into the term. An often-cherished idea that *theoria* and the concept of *insight* are close together does not seem evident. That is important for our actual understanding of the word 'theory'. The meaning-making role of the concept *theoric fund* is not a philological issue, but its philological roots are nevertheless decisive. That is the case when we are informed that a *theoros* (meaning 'a person travelling as functionary of a Liturgy') is *not* automatically connected with any component of *insight* or another form of *seeing* respectively, *awareness*. Situations have no philological evidence. Koller underlines the institutional dimension when he suggests that the *theoros* was originally the name/indication for the person who was officially send to Delphi or other places with Liturgies, to interrogate the Oracle and bring the message home. *Theorein* are therefore never persons who go to the Festival *to see* – as a spectator or member of an audience. Only *after* Herodotus can an accent on the spectacle of drama

---

[13] Hermann Koller, 'Theoros und Theoria' in *Historia – Glotta: Zeitschrift für Alte Geschichte*, F. Steiner Verlag, Wiesbaden, 1958, pp. 273, 279ff; see also Marcel Detienne, 'L'espace de la Publicité: ses Opérateurs Intellectuels dans la Cité' *Cahiers de Philologie*, Vol. 14, Série Apparat Critique, Presses Universitaires de Lille, pp. 11, 39ff.

or tragedy be read. The *theoric fund* provided a daily allowance because of the high costs of a day at a festival, but it was never a sort of admission fee for a particular tragedy or scene. No wonder that Herodotus once reported how Anacharsis and Skyles, visitors in the true sense of the word, were impressed by the cults and festivals of the Greek, so that they wanted to have them introduced into their own country. The character of the Liturgies as a *total* and all-embracing experience is reflected in the activities of the *theoric fund*, Pericles would have confirmed. Plato's ideas about *theoroi* are well known. They should travel around in order to experience different habits and cultures and thus become wise men. They are not only wise, but also able to judge the qualities of the actually valid laws. *The link between* travel *and* theoria *is a late, but for us most important, fact since the time of Ancient Greek cultures.* Our insight into the name, meaning and function of the street has its roots in this observation.

The activities and public role of the fund and its *theoroi* brought a genuine philosophical insight about the essence of a human being into practice. Its payments (long before the concept of commodity entered social relations) were meant to profile the citizen's mind by means of a specific alienation. The latter expressed itself in actions on the street as well as in the experiences of tragedies and dramas. One should understand the multiple dimensions of this alienation. Plato explained in his *Phaidros* that a citizen's presence at the Liturgies – the citizen as a legally enabled member of the State – was a participation which had to be neither subjective nor objective, neither practical nor theoretical, neither financial nor spiritual, but a full and undivided and non-partitioned act to be described only as a being-there.[14] The structures of the mind leading to this presence at the Liturgies included the enforcement of an awakening form of alienation: the participant should become a *self*, and had for that purpose to be provoked by a most radical otherness (in the form of money), which Plato's interpreters called a '*positive ecstasy*'. The Greek provision for a deep involvement in the dramas and tragedies created in this manner a specific and strong *togetherness*, which was in essence combined with deeply experiencing forms of *otherness* in the Self.

In the lifespan of a Greek citizen a division between the period before and after his or her participation in the Liturgies was really essential. An involvement in the experience of this breach, resulting from *theoric*

[14] On the constitutive role of *division* and *partition* in understanding the human character, see Jan M. Broekman, *supra note 4*, Chs. 4 and 5.

activity, was stimulated by money and thus engendered a *self* by an alienating power. Modern citizens may walk their street and yet experience a comparable ecstasy – be it with different attitudes, views or materials. What does this observation imply for the theoretical dimensions one encounters in contemporary philosophy and social sciences? Are the street they walk, or the plaza they enjoy and perhaps the avenue they cruise not *the signifier of all possible signification* and thus: their theory? The power of theory is here the power of the receptacle of meaning, the bearer, maker and engenderment of signification. Who is not surprised about the veritable wealth of dimensions that forge theory and street? Do not forget: *theoroi* were *persons* (not an abstract thinking) walking and talking on the streets.

Exteriorization is indeed a most powerful component of a human consciousness. It is a force that forms the basis for a unique completeness and wholeness of all participation on the 'street'. The completeness does not result from a subject's continuing 'inner dialogue' as Continental philosophers of the twentieth century wanted to profile and we already mentioned in Chapter 2 while dealing with the 'I'–'Thou' theme. On the contrary: the completeness of 'street' participation expresses *that ties between 'street' and 'theoria'* are at its origin – a fact that will be fully understood once the 'street' becomes accepted in philosophy and social sciences. Participants on the 'street' behave by integrating external *and* internal powers of body and mind, as the Ancient Greek fund already wanted to achieve. Their activities aimed at opening the so-called *inner* dimensions of 'the subject's mind' – a new occurrence in psychology and philosophy and perhaps not yet fully integrated in modern politics. In other words: *in the self are forces like exteriority at work* because inner dimensions cannot be opened otherwise – they provide insight in the *self* during the unfolding of any self-awareness of the citizen and/or pedestrian.[15] The ancient *theoria* concept justifies us to redefine the 'street' as

[15] Our streets filled with quizzing and twittering are perhaps surprisingly near to Ancient Athenian practices, where a special fund supported citizens to decide the prize-winning of dramas and tragedies as a sign of their more or less direct democracy based on insight and free decision. Legal theoreticians bring to the fore that the social power of sovereignty touches on deep structures of solidarity. Any communal experience changes to the extent that sovereignty is understood as a constitutional or as a non-constitutional component of social and political life. The Athenians understood their *theoric* fund as a socially important source of support and power (Pericles) and thus as the last-mentioned (non-constitutional) form of sovereignty. See discussions between D. Grimm, Fritz W. Scharpf and Ulrich K. Preuß as well as the essay of Alain Supiot in Johan van

the place where rebellion occurs against '*totality inflicting from an outside/exteriority*' in the name of the '*totality called the holon*'. This could very well be a key to a new reinterpretation of many of the fifth century BC tragedies.

That seems a truly challenging tension, and a different, more than incidental political rebellion so often associated with the 'street'. The 'street' seems the place for a fight of the *self* against determinations that originate in forms of sovereignty and exteriority and in favor of commodity-concepts. A consequence is clear: the ultimate goal of accepting the 'street' in social theory and philosophy is an evocation of a holistic self-awareness *in foro publico*. So, what happens *outside* also happens *inside*: 'the differentiation annihilated' – a new slogan emerges for the rapper as well as psychologist related to the culture of the 'street'.

Walter Benjamin's 'phantasmagoria', linked to the Arcades, constituted an *inside*. Now we see those practices on the street as well, that is: on the *outside* – a move that absolutely abrogates the difference between the two. Should we say that the street has no longer an inside and an outside? Developments of electronic interaction commodities reinforce that observation strongly. 'The street perhaps never had', an Ancient Greek observer would suggest. Streets obliterate a disharmony between internal attitudes and external forces in the minds of citizens.

That observation is reinforced by understanding how the 'street' is in essence the understanding of a *shared* experience which became defined by a territorial notion (called 'street'). But the 'sharing' alone is not enough. It also implies new types of *self-management of the human mind in public settings*. It tells us in what ways modern pedestrians are sign-bearers of a consciousness that copes with the dominance of an alienating commodity which is continuously manifested on and around the street. Those signs are embedded in a renewed view on self-awareness and a fuller but never completed self-understanding of the subject on the street. The 'street'-concept is in that regard of immense importance for a modern subject/citizen and its milieu that always refers anew to man and society in an ever-changing relevance of modernity.

---

der Walt and Jeffrey Ellsworth (eds), *Constitutional Sovereignty and Social Solidarity in Europe*, Nomos, Baden-Baden 2015, pp. 39ff, 55ff, 193ff, 109ff. See also Jürgen Habermas, *The Crisis of the European Union*, Polity Press, John Wiley and Sons, Cambridge/Oxford/Boston, 2012, p. 53ff.

4.3 STREETS, STONES AND SPACES

How can this be? Did not Peirce tell us that a 'sign is never a sign alone'? Yes, but he did not share his insight with Hermes, who practiced the same ideas. Hermes' home in the stone piles created a semiotic phenomenon, as we explained in the above pages. A messenger of God appears to be a God himself: a sign alone is itself a sign only when it refers to other signs. We can observe that any such observation remains the result of a specific understanding of the human Self and its sociability. However, a modern citizen's desire expresses a desire beyond sign-signs. That desire pertains to *identity and freedom in social context.* Although it cannot be completely fulfilled in sign theory, it strives for a realization in social contexts. This is exemplified in almost all literature on the 'street', from its social history and political ideas up to its practices striving for a direct democracy and to anarchist ideas.

Most European literature on the French Revolution underlines the new horizons and political practices while remembering the Commune. 'What constitutes the commune is the mutual oath sworn by the inhabitants of a city, a town, or a rural area *to stand together as a body* … a commune was a pact to face the world together. It meant relying on one's own shared powers as the source of one's freedom. What was aimed for was not an entity; *it was a qualitative bond, and a way of being in the world* … It was this long lost, originary, medieval meaning of the commune that was somehow rediscovered by the federalist faction of the Paris Commune in 1871', the Invisible Committee writes in 2014. 'And it's the same meaning that reemerges periodically since that time …'.[16] The 'street' can thus be defined as *a territorially expressed whole of shared experiences.* In the *sharing* is the riddle of the *social.* The *sharing* withstands any glorification of the Commune and its underlying social structures, and awakens the desire to be 'a sign alone'. Such a desire challenges our social theories – a position that was already fortified in the Greek *theoria.* What is at issue?

No more and no less than that a one-sided understanding of 'the social' dominates all of our social sciences and their political philosophy: the idea that 'the social' always relates to a form of 'belonging'. The 'street' does not embrace this one-sidedness. Are social relations and is 'the social' possible without any well-defined belonging? The answer is: yes,

---

[16] The Invisible Committee (2014), *To Our Friends* (translated by R. Hurley), Semiotext(e), 2015, p. 199ff. See Giorgio Agamben, *La comunità che viene*, 1990 (English edition edited by, M. Hardt, *The Coming Community*, Minnesota University Press, Minneapolis, MN, 1993).

it is – and that is exactly the case where the desire of the pedestrian was characterized as the desire to be a sign alone. On the 'street', the walking citizen is socialized even when she is not belonging. The rapper, the walker and the smart phone with its tiny screen replacing the many mirrors of the Arcades illustrate how you can be abstract on the street (as Popper foresaw) and with no identity beyond a phone number, an e-mail address or a hash tag.

The generally shared phantasm of identity reflects in the *selfie* on the street: a once romantic view about the Commune developed, in our days, into an IT issue. Always and everywhere being contactable is the street's phantasm on communication, thanks to its displacement into the virtual. In other words, the pedestrian can interpret herself as a liberated *Self* only because sociability reaches *beyond* belonging.[17]

That insight opens new dimensions of the Self. The spirit of semiotics invigorates the question: when, and under what circumstances, is a meaning a sign? When does a meaning lead us to a sign that is 'a sign on its own', as Hermes' position was characterized?

The formula 'the Self as a Sign on its Own' is a post-Peircean positioning of components of the Self, which does *not* place any sovereignty in an *exteriority* of that Self. The riddle of the 'social' is that the 'I' does not accept any delimitation between interiority and exteriority of itself.[18]

The title of this section 'Streets, Stones and Spaces' thus leads us back to what we learned in this context from the streets in Ancient Greece – those of Athens in the fifth century BC. A short outline presents the

---

17 This observation challenges the hidden romanticism in philosophical positions from Benjamin to the more recent Invisible Committee.

18 Lorenzo Chiesa and Raffaello Palumbo Mosca (eds), *Figures of the o/Other: Brother, Neighbor, Stranger, Enemy*, GSH Seminar Series at the Genoa School of Humanities, 2016, write: 'Christianity preaches the love of the neighbor, yet ultimately reduces him to a repetition of the self. Modern democracy rests on fraternity, but all too often distorts it into inconsistent ideologies of identity, which pave the way for more or less explicit forms of racism. The battle for the emancipation of woman runs itself the risk of succumbing to a global dispositive of sameness dominated by Capital and its ruthless values. Faced with unprecedented social, economical, and political crises, we are today increasingly urged to treat any kind of otherness that challenges our fragile egos as an enemy … our basic hypothesis is that there can be no sincere appreciation of the other as another subject without acknowledging a more profound, albeit immanent, kind of Other: the linguistic/discursive nature of the animal that speaks and writes; its structural in-completeness and parallel desire for completeness.'

following features. They are guided by more than one question and inspire further considerations. 'Theory' and 'street' are intertwined practices, but how can we understand the 'street' as a practice or as an act of any importance at all? How were streets in the age of the festivals, and are they very different from those of our own towns?

4.3.1 Athens

It is most challenging that the numerous studies on the Athenian democracy are lacking an oversight or explicit mention of the 'streets' in Athens. The profile of pedestrians in that century recovers some meanings of 'theory' and underlines the importance of the fact that a specific *theoric fund* shaped the mind of the majority of pedestrians. Did the influence of this fund also have a determining function in view of the streets of Athens, or of their names? We know three important streets by name. They dominated the profile of the town and led ultimately to the Agora: the Piraean Street from the Piraean Gate and the Panathenaic Way from the Dipylon Gate led to the Agora, and the Street of the Tripods, on the east side of the Acropolis is also known by name. All were bordered by private houses, commercial or even governmental buildings, temples, toilets and baths – and all created a specific form of togetherness. A 'Main Street' is never mentioned in this context. Inscriptions related to a street are not only linked to dust, stones, rocks, bumpy roads and steep slopes of streets but also to water systems that were vital in urban layouts. No road was without water and water-delivery systems that support social behaviors. Research on Roman archeo-biology illustrates the relation between the street and what we nowadays call 'hygiene'.[19] Streets were in Greek city planning created by chance or habit and the desire to experience life in an urban environment that expressed and nurtured those ideals of its inhabitants. The streets were occasionally straight, broad, intersecting and retaining wide central areas for marketplaces and agoras. But they never met modern standards of cleanliness; Greek latrines always bordered streets (like the Romans' would later) and a public eye (most often from a Goddess: *Tyche* in Greek, *Fortuna* in later Roman days) was watching all details like a modern camera. Seats with stone slabs sticking out of the walls connected to water provisions gave the latrines public dimensions. Men were primary users, but women,

[19] Günter E. Thüry, *Müll und Marmorsäulen: Siedlungshygiene in der römischen Antike*, von Zabern, Mainz am Rhein, 2001.

slaves and freedmen (*metics*) as well as citizens rich and poor had equal access to the latrines.

The situation brought a rude confrontation with the unpleasant aspects of human life. Water was the sole means to soften it: Tyche's connection to water was as meaningful as water politics appeared to be an integral part of the 'street'-codes in Ancient Greek societies.[20] The power of water policy is not a privilege of the twenty-first century but seems as old as the Graeco-Roman culture itself. Public toilets or latrines bordering the street illustrate that the *street* must be understood as an *act* embedded in and sustained by a *theoria* as well as a *milieu* composed by city, State, individual personhood and togetherness. A Goddess was protecting the '*act named street*' like its modern counterparts today are protected by a Constitution – which means: founded in law what in earlier days was anchored in religion. If an Ancient Greek 'street'-concept had existed at all, then the concept would have embraced the act of inclusion and certainly not of any protected intimate other, which tends to exclude whatever form of otherness occurs on streets. The *street* thus embraces an altruism that shaped the social value of walking the street. Walking was in the first place experienced as well as understood in terms of togetherness and not of efficiency, as is dominantly the case in our days. The 'where am I now' dominated any 'where will I be as soon as possible'. It should be underlined that the expression 'talking about law on the street' *includes* and at the same time *creates* this togetherness. One of the differences between 'talking about law' and 'proclaiming for law' is created by the fact that the first is, and the second is not, built upon that notion of belonging.

A glance of Tyche was not only technically different from our camera observations but as a consequence of the spirit of that time also in mentality. Our cameras on street corners, in shopping centers, traffic lights and many other places are at a far distance from the notion that a human's individual fate and fortune are embedded in town and country and therefore socially engendered beyond his or her personal power. That feeling's function was as crucial as our feelings about law, order and safety of persons and their social frames. Tyche in the latrine, or better: in the bathroom, presents the Goddess and source of uncertainty that binds people in commonness at a most vulnerable moment of their

---

[20] On Tyche, toilets and the importance of water provisions, see Ann Olga Kokosi-Ostrov, 'Dura-Europos: Water, Baths, Latrines, and the Goddess Fortuna in a Desert City' in Lisa R. Brody and Gail. L. Hoffmann (eds), *Dura Europos: Crossroads of Antiquity*, McMullen Museum of Art, Boston College, 2011, p. 251ff.

physical existence. She is the Goddess of Otherness. If one cannot take one's fate and fortune in hand, one should at least perceive her image as if it were coins to pay for the acquired difference.[21]

Numbers of those who walked the street in the Ancient Greek fifth century that sustain our insights are available by approximation only. Contemporary authors studying Ancient Greek life and culture proposed such estimations regularly. They differ according to their references. One can refer to a legal-political criterion: the number of judges to vote in the Athenian Assembly.[22] The population in Athens just before the Peloponnesian War began, can be estimated at 172,000 citizens and 30,000 slaves, so that the total population in Athens during the fifth and fourth centuries BC was around 200,000 individuals. Referring to taxation of the Athenian population's wheat consumption, ownership of land and money, soldiers, slaves and children, the final number comes to 124,000 free persons, children included, and 20,000 slaves – a total of 144,000 individuals. Although '[t]he Athenians themselves would not have been able to answer ... with exactitude', Hansen brings the number of inhabitants of city and State to 150,000 Athenians.[23]

Many would not frequently walk the streets of the city. We do not possess a sociological investigation of any street population – not pertaining to Ancient times or the European Middle Ages or to our days. Pedestrians are seldom numbered, and the mentality, spirit or mind on the street and its social level, differs from any number of participants. It is,

---

[21] Jan M. Broekman, 'A Goddess for semiotics of law and legal discourse' in A. Palmisano (ed.), *DADA-Rivista di Antropologia post-globale*, Trieste, 2011, pp. 7–24; Jan M. Broekman, *supra note 1*, Ch. III.

[22] Sir Arthur Pickard-Cambridge, *The Dramatic Festivals of Athens,* Oxford University Press, Oxford/New York, 1991, p. 95 ff., studied elaborately the legal rules for selecting and acting for those citizens who were judges and voted during the performances which were organized as a contest. That issue must have inspired a massive 'talking about law' in public. It parallels the 'legal screening' of the entire number of visitors after the conclusion of the festival, because in those specific days children were born, people died or were murdered, thefts were to be correctly registered, and – ultimately – the entire organization of the festival had to be legally and financially checked before 'normal' life could go on.

[23] M. H. Hansen, *The Athenian Democracy in the Age of Demosthenes*, Blackwell, Oxford/Cambridge, MA, 1991, p. 86; Chester G. Starr, *The Birth of Athenian Democracy*, Oxford University Press, Oxford, 1990; H. W. Parke, *Festivals of the Athenians*, Cornell University Press, London/Ithaca, NY, 1977; M. M. Austin and P. Vidal-Naquet, *Economic and Social History of Ancient Greece*, California University Press, Berkeley, LA, 1977.

however, evident that men were in the majority on the streets, in the public toilets or the public spaces around these as well as the agoras or the theater scenes. Women and children were supposed to live in and around the houses, in particular in agrarian surroundings of the city centers. Registered aliens (*metics*) and slaves would also infrequently be seen on the street, although several of them were famously rich. Citizens as well as *metics* and slaves performed all sorts of agrarian work, which kept them mostly away from streets. An agrarian mentality dominates, as we can read in Plato's *Laws*, and that spirit is also not intensely street-directed. A relation between professional profile and street population, as we could discover today, is apparently already visible in Ancient Athens. The suggestion is that many were together on the streets, but that important streets were never overcrowded and that smaller and less important streets were more frequently used than the major streets because citizens and other individuals did not connect to anything comparable to our contemporary 'big town' mentality. These numbers are almost exclusively based on the estimation of numbers of registered citizens. For instance the *metics* were left out, because registered aliens did not possess any rights comparable to those of the citizens.

This does not, however, mean that citizens and metics on the street did not exchange opinions or have conversations. Some characteristics of the Athenian citizenship on the streets are imaginable for us. Legally acknowledged citizens were at a relatively low number compared to the totality of the population. Citizenship was not always easy to obtain, and this legal qualification was in certain periods very restricted, as for instance in the days of Pericles. The citizen's main privilege was political rights, and that embraced many consequences. Every adult male citizen had the right to attend the Assembly, to be a magistrate or a legislator or a juror, he owned further the right to financial and land property, to explore the minerals of the land and the rights to hold concessions. Men in possession of those rights were the prominent pedestrians – even while in low numbers and by no means always wealthy. So the streets showed a mixed population with a male dominance, without an important racial mixture but certainly with a mixture of those who were bearers of political rights and those who were not.

It is also clear that the *features of spatiality* were not based on distinctions we usually tend to explore. Differences between small and large, long and short, high-bordered or low-bordered streets are not found and thus did not cause a specific mentality. Streets were, not unlike words (no matter whether spoken or written), a component of a totality – houses, buildings, toilets, agoras and theater stages – but apparently not an issue in itself. Their Goddesses or Gods did not mark the image of the streets, despite some stone piles of Hermes in front of some houses bordering the street.

This has not drawn much attention to those who studied Ancient Greek cultures, but it illustrates a deeper layer of public life being anchored in religious motives. Streets were open spaces for debate, discussion and argument: speech was in those days *not* primarily for an exchange of information. The openness of the *polis* was demonstrated in the general sounds one could hear on the street, and not solely in the information that was exchanged: 'Greek culture took form by opening to an ever widening circle – and finally to the entire *demos* (community) – access to the spiritual world reserved initially for an aristocracy of priests and warriors', Vernant concludes.[24] Athenian streets were to a great extent filled with those who exercised their citizen rights, and that could only be done at the expense of slaves, women or aliens. The latter did not have rights and could not participate in the political life of the city. But: to enjoy your rights you need sufficient leisure.

Only a fraction of the total population had the possibility to take part in the directness or features of immediacy of the Athenian democracy: a 'have-not' may have been watched by the Gods but he received occasionally a small sum of money from one of the branches of the *theoric fund.* It paid citizens (and *metics*) to participate in the Liturgies, which often took place more than a hundred times a year and thus created for the streets each year more than a hundred liturgical and festive days. Those Liturgies profiled the street population in numbers and spirit accordingly; their organization was a duty for the wealthiest citizens nearly every two years but reached out to all ordinary citizens who could or wanted to participate. The preparation for a religious festival or a naval Liturgy took approximately a year. Numbers of citizens involved were high, and costs considerable – the latter were in the first place an issue for the well to do because their provision was forcefully understood as a 'public service for the State'.

The influence of the theoric fund *on public life was immense, and thus on life on the street.* The fund, like all funds in all ages, was a turning point in the flow from State wealth to private (dis)comfort. It impresses how strongly the festivals of Athens influenced a possible reverse of a psychological, philosophical or a financial situation. Many of the citizens, *metics*, and (perhaps sometimes) women participating, were

---

[24] J. -P. Vernant, *Les origines de la pensée grecque*, Paris, 1962 (English edition, *The Origins of Greek Thought*, Cornell University Press, Ithaca, NY, 1982), p. 51.

included with the individuals who were accepted as voters for the prizes which the authors of drama and tragedy received. Their majority was paid by the fund. The word *theorika* was on everybody's lips; it indicated a generally approved institution, in its most active and appreciated form during the years of Pericles. *Theoroi* were those who envisaged, had seen, experienced, attended and voted during the festivals for or against an author, in particular during the Athenian Greater Dionysia. 'Street' and 'theory' intertwine meanings; their togetherness is a key to understanding our citizens walking modern streets.

4.3.2 Paris

Whoever is invited to think of walking *Athenian* streets in the fifth century BC might think of Aeschylus, Euripides or any other winner of a Dionysian Festival or of dramatic, even comic texts from that period. Whoever thinks of *Parisian* streets at the end of the nineteenth Occidental century, thinks of Walter Benjamin and his Arcades Project. The indicative function of the title embraces much more than a title alone. Benjamin introduced the theme powerfully:

> They spoke of Paris as *la ville qui remue* – the city that never stops moving. But no less important than the life of this city's layout is here the unconquerable power in the names of streets, squares, and theaters, a power which persists in the face of all topographic displacement ... How many street names, even today, preserve the name of the landed proprietor who, centuries earlier, had his demesne on their ground.[25]

The two words that compose the title of his famous work (Arcades, and: Project) refer to his impressive English language publication issued almost half a century after the philosopher's death, as well as the formula Benjamin and his friends used for the totality of his work: books, essays, letters and other texts had the Arcades continuously in mind, and with that project *the issue of 'street'*.[26]

We mentioned already that a differentiation between interiority and exteriority seems untenable for Benjamin's project: facts and situations, events and circumstances, speech and context show always two faces of the same. A window mirror projects the outer world in the interior of the living room and the room is a room because it is filled with reflections of

---

[25] Walter Benjamin, *The Arcades Project* (edited by H. Eiland and K. McLaughlin), Harvard University Press, Cambridge, MA/London, 1999, p. 516.

[26] Walter Benjamin, *supra note 25*.

the exterior, Adorno once added.[27] A moment of the past thus becomes owner of the momentary and its future. The dissolution of spiritual and architectonic barriers between *internal* and *external* remains a powerful sign, no matter whether it is philosophically accepted or rejected. The 'street' always assigns the spirit of a new perception. The historical intrudes the actuality of the intimate continuously. Our perception is the product of such an intrusion.

Arcades illustrate variability – architectural conditions for the unfolding of a new life on the streets come with new actualities. While covering, indeed roofing the street, they form a veiled and concealed situation in which any dissimilarity of interior and exterior could be abolished. They constituted abstract communication lines between abstract individuals, and provided the necessary conditions for an equally abstract system of commodity exchange, as Popper foresaw and which is an almost global reality in today's life. Indeed: the imagery of a new economy and philosophy of State emerge in the citizen's mind as powerfully as possible. The pedestrian enters a scene that changes continuously and provides a sequence of associations like in an everlasting dream or phantasm. Architecture did what speech did in an equal rhythm, Hannah Arendt could have noticed; every step of the pedestrian concluded with 'amen' to embrace 'reality' and exchange commodities *ad libitum*.

It is not surprising that Benjamin focused on the *names* of streets in Paris in line with his earlier essays on a philosophy of language – their history, their changes, their sign character and their inner expressivity. He seemed guided by a specific observation, which reads:

> What was otherwise reserved for only a very few words, a privileged class of words, the city has made possible for all words, or at least a great many: to be elevated to the noble status of name. This revolution in language was carried out by what is most general: the street. – Through its street names, the city is a linguistic cosmos.[28]

Streets seem to contribute to the continuing variety of linguistic wealth by names (which are known and documented even two-and-a-half millennia ago) in the first place, and by conversations which are known

---

[27] Th. W. Adorno, *Kierkegaard: Konstruktion des Ästhetischen*, Tübingen, 1933 (English edition edited by R. Hullot-Kenter, *Kierkegaard: Construction of the Aesthetic*, Minnesota University Press, Minneapolis, MN, 1989).

[28] Walter Benjamin, *supra note 25*, p. 522

by topic and decision rather than by the words that were uttered on streets, plazas and avenues.

Names in that linguistic cosmos are in many regards a counter-example of the numbered streets, unless numbers are used as names, as is often the case in the US history of the street. Numbers express a greater distance to an historic mentality and seem to deliver more efficiency, so that the numbered streets were at risk of becoming an entity without identity. We do in general tend to forget, or at least to neglect, that the numbers of houses in streets – no matter whether those streets had a name or were simply numbered – were a component of the history of streets. Benjamin noted: 'the Quartier de l'Europe already existed as a project, incorporating the names of the European capitals, in 1820' and he furthermore mentioned:

> On February 4, 1805, houses were first numbered, by imperial decree. Previous attempts to do this – in January 1726 – had met with violent resistance. Owners of house declared themselves ready to number the side entrances, but not their carriage entrances. The Revolution had already introduced the numbering of houses according to districts; in some districts, there were 1,500–2,000 numbers.[29]

But it remains of great socio-psychological interest in correlation to Benjamin's view that we should notice in what historical settings the street numbers can also become a name: the New York Fifth Avenue is definitively *not/no longer* a numbered street. But the functions of streets in modern cities and their specific culture are no longer a component of the internal space of a town or village – they transited into spaces, fields of anonymity, plazas of phantasmagoria that were filled with anonymous communication, as the milliards of smart phones in those spaces indicate. Benjamin's observations in the Arcades Project seem to touch the borderlines of the above-unfolded theme introduced with the words 'street as communication'. He underlines that there are still 'little squares that are suddenly there, and to which no name attaches. They have not been the object of careful planning … and do not enjoy the patronage of world history; but owe their existence to houses that have slowly, sleepily, belatedly assembled in response to the summons of the century. In such squares, the trees hold sway; even the smallest afford thick shade.'[30] Street names, most of them originating in the eighteenth

[29] Walter Benjamin, *supra note 25*, p. 517.
[30] Walter Benjamin, *supra note 25*, p. 516.

century, are interesting for their implications of a philosophy of language and of Occidental culture.

A 'theory of street names' was quoted in the Arcades text, which formulated a pivotal insight and quoted Leo Spitzer's 1928 *Stilstudien* (*Style Studies*): 'Proper names, too, have an effect that is conceptually unburdened and purely acoustic ... proper names are "bare formulas" which Proust can fill up with feelings because they have not yet been rationalized by language.' Benjamin refers to numerous aspects of a street's name; he writes on 'the magic of street names' and contrasts a 'street' with the older expression 'way'. The fascination of the street name seems to exist since the French Revolution. The mirrors erected all around crossings of *arcades* at the end of the nineteenth century, the new light sources, their unknown quality affect the citizen's mind as well as the unexpected panoramas created by the new architecture. They build a bridge to the 'street'-concept of our days. The phantasmagoria of communication becomes more and more general in the 'street'-notion's political practice, and appears surprisingly intertwined with the Ancient Greek concept of *theoria.*

As if returning from contemplations on Athens in the fifth century BC, one reads Benjamin about our above-explored ideas about Athenian streets:

> 'Street', to be understood, must be profiled against the older term 'way'. With respect to their mythological natures, the two words are entirely distinct. The way brings with it the terrors of wandering, some reverberation of which must have struck the leaders of nomadic tribes. In the incalculable turning and resolutions of the way, there is even today, for the solitary wanderer a detectable trace of the power of ancient directives over wandering hordes. But the person who travels a street, it would seem, has no need of any waywise guiding hand. It is not in wandering that man takes the street, but rather in submitting to the monotonous, fascinating, constantly unrolling band of asphalt. The synthesis of these twin errors, however – monotonous wandering – is represented in the labyrinth.[31]

To *walk the 'street'* thus embraces a new meaning: while walking, the walker/pedestrian explores a wealth of possibilities of the Self, including the virtual dimensions of which a '*selfie'* is a sign. The latter is, at least, a sign pertaining to the fact that the 'street' cannot be understood without a notion of a multidimensional 'Self' and its constitutive powers. Greek streets are never studied in that light: the Self of the Ancient Greek

---

[31] Walter Benjamin, *supra note 25*, p. 519.

citizen walking the street appears in the first place a *politically determined* Self and not a psychologically understandable Self. The Greek notion emphasized a 'street-level power' with 'common' and 'communal' features – but these are no longer appropriate for the 'street' because the dimensions of the walking and talking citizen on the street are widened and touch today even the technical means of electronic communication, including the consideration of the effects of those techniques on the human mind. Hypostatic forces based on the social articulation of powers internal and external to the Self illustrate the need for a semiotic approach in view of law and society. Acceptance of the 'street' reinforces the *street credibility* of the Self beyond any type of State power. No one knows what Self will emerge once that credibility is established in a future 'street', and no one knows what social, philosophical or political changes will be relevant for the Self that electronically became a Sign Alone. The 'Self/Sign' and the 'Street' challenge us in Parisian streets where Benjamin was a '*flaneur*'. Indeed, streets, squares and avenues are not what they were before or what we think they will become. Their changes occur in relation to the ever-changing meaning of the pedestrian's *Self* – and, who knows, his *selfie*. How do we know about the streets of Athens? We study Ancient Greek literature, history and even archeology. How about Paris? We read the work of Benjamin. How about New York?

4.3.3 New York

Not by studying anything of its actuality but by studying its literature. That is indeed bewildering. What does it mean for the streets? A remarkable answer will be given: the streets of New York were not in the first place determined by their numbers and names, but by their role in a specific type of literature. Streets were read and presented in literature as signs of poverty, lack of education, poor opportunities, desire for new and expanding experiences and their contrast to other streets, lanes and avenues, which were assigned great wealth, affluence, or other Wall Street attitudes and behaviors. 'Talking on the street' was a matter of exchanging the signs one masters. The names of Broadway, Fifth Avenue or the multiple faces of New York City's Tenth Street were present in literary documents pertaining to the life at those locations, which all had their specific historic details and significant actuality. No New York street is without literature, from pieces of scrap paper to journals to novels or poems. Body and life, self and destiny, wealth and work – the street signifies. Bergmann mentions in his 1995 study on New York, writing while referring to Melville's Guidebooks from 1849 in which he describes the town's 1840 reality, that narration and panorama find their literary form almost everywhere:

> [The] 'literary panoramic paradigm in New York narrative pervades many genres – guidebooks, journalism, 'serious' journalism, charity-work reports, popular fiction, 'serious' fiction – but determining which genre a narrative belongs to is difficult. Works of fiction contain passages that seem much like journalism while the nonfiction often contains obviously fictional stories. Panoramic narrative is often a mixed form in which 'fact' and 'fiction' intermingle unstably.[32]

The power of signification by the street and its name remains a general New York feature, despite the public reduction of literature and its substitution by means of e-communication. Means have changed, as millions of *selfies* on Times Square illustrate, but attitudes evidently did not. However, it is clear that one has to go back to the literature of the last decades of the nineteenth and the beginnings of the twentieth century to obtain a deeper insight into the structure of this observation. That move brings us to the midst of the 1850s, to Herman Melville, Walt Whitman and others. And Hermes is in this context neither lost nor forgotten. 'Cities have their own god. Hermes himself came to town when trade was no longer a matter of guarding cattle and sheep', Bergmann remarks. 'New York narratives of the antebellum period took a Homeric pleasure in warning New Yorkers and visitors about the clever gods of commerce in New York.' He thus mentioned how they 'told and retold stories of encounters between representative people and a "genius" who was a tutelary god or attendant spirit attached to New York the way Hermes was attached to Athens. This is a genius with a readiness of speech and adroitness of action that still characterize the stereotypical New Yorker in American culture.'[33]

Street names also refer in a unique way to the *history* of town and culture. Read the Whitman poem in his 1891/92 *Leaves of Grass*:

> 'Mannahatta'
>
> I was asking for something specific and perfect for my city,
> Whereupon lo! upsprang the aboriginal name.
>
> Now I see what there is in a name, a word, liquid, sane,
> unruly, musical, self-sufficient,

---

32 Hans Bergmann, *God in the Street: New York Writing from the Penny Press to Melville,* Temple Press, Philadelphia, 1995, p. 49ff.

33 Hans Bergmann, *supra note 32*, 1995, p. 181.

I see that the word of my city is that word from of old,
Because I see that word nested in nests of water-bays,
  superb,
Rich, hemm'd thick all around with sailships and
  steamships, an island sixteen miles long, solid-founded,
Numberless crowded streets, high growths of iron, slender,
  strong, light, splendidly uprising toward clear skies ...

Streets in New York are further determined by another outstanding and unique component: the city's *skylines connected with the names*. The skylines fascinated any visitor in the midst of the nineteenth century: New York was pictured *in panorama* already since the years of the 1853 Crystal Palace Exhibition. Streets in panorama incorporated a change of dimension long before e-communication took over. Urban definitions appeared to become pillars of our understanding of a new culture, like 'The New Paris' without royal names or royalty support. Commodities in New York: they were at issue in newspapers on the street, and required a new explanatory dynamic of author and reader. The European-colored term '*flaneur*' was introduced and explored until our days.

Walt Whitman gave it his own specific American translation. Many of his texts strongly emphasize a general need to understand reality in terms of *wholeness*: street like body, city like life, commonness like equilibrium can be met in his poetry. This is not without interest for modernity. Whitman is in that regard a worthy survivor of his century's New York culture. The streets, panoramas and landscapes in his poetic mind are the city with that name, which unifies, bundles and signifies all street names of his life – no matter whether it is Broadway or Wall Street. The splendor of the city's life is reflected in names. Whitman's various articles on New York's quotidian life in *Life Illustrated* form a true catalogue of the town's locations to celebrate the virtues of its culture. But the flow of people in the street and the sights from towers, bridges or high buildings, the colloquial language at all those occasions, were not only recalled positively. Bergmann mentions words of Whitman in which a hidden New York was at stake: 'If some potent magician could lift the veil which shrouds, in alleys, dark street, garrets, and a thousand other habitations of want, the miseries that are every day going on among us – how would the spectacle distress and terrify the beholder!'[34] Were

[34] Hans Bergmann, *supra note 32*, 1995, p. 75.

Whitman's appeal to *wholeness* and his repeated suggestion to incorporate a mission for a mankind of the future based on his experiences of the city's streets? Is the appeal to reinterpreting *wholeness* not far beyond a poetic philosopher's intuition?

To see streets *in panorama* was in the middle of the nineteenth century an experience that bewilders. What has been perceived as undamaged in the horizontal and inspiring if not challenging, in the vertical, becomes disorder and confusion when the two are brought together. Where is unity, where are foundations, where is logic for life? Is *wholeness* not the sole solution? Whitman's poem in his 1891/92 *Leaves of Grass* entitled 'I Sing the Body Electric' could entirely be read as a poem of the city's streets all around:

> 'I Sing the Body Electric'
>
> I sing the body electric,
> The armies of those I love engirth me and I engirth them,
> They will not let me off till I go with them, respond to them,
> And discorrupt them, and charge them full with the charge of the soul …

The *body* is the most efficient metaphor for wholeness and perfection needed to live a life on the multiplicity of the city's streets. They include an equilibration of all the differences one encounters: in race, origin, language, habit, history, power or wealth. The poem speaks and writes around one particular sign: the unity of physical, corporal and social components of one's existence. A comparison with Hobbes' 1651 figure, which was already quoted in preceding pages, the *Magnus Homo*, is also of interest here. The body becomes an ultimate figuration of society, its interpretation has become uniform and simple: the interpretation of *one body*. Any 'talking about law' that once took place on the street, plaza, park or avenue is given solely *one place*: *in the body*. Commonness finally became a whole! A deep desire seems satisfied; singing the body transforms the poem into a song of the Self that is in peace and unity with itself – a theme from Hobbes to Whitman and New York's streets. The wholeness of the Self is found in its literature.

But, one should ask: why singing the body *electric*? At first, one experiences hardly any more how the word symbolized a new power and a newly invented source of energy that fortifies the required tendency of the poem: to sing the wholeness of the body. It is surprising to read the title in our days, in which New York streets are filled with individuals carrying and using their smart phones as an extension of their brain capacities. They have a substantial part of their brain in their hands and move it through the streets without experiencing any problem. 'Electric' became 'electronic', and the latter engendered new shapes of consciousness, which populate the city's streets. The street names are data for the phones; the phones are providing data as well as creating spaces to reflect instead of walk, to have conversations instead of bodily meetings, to know instead of hear the word. We sing the body electronic and are not aware that the city and its streets changed fundamentally: this time from bodily to data-driven awareness. The change is also literary: from Whitman to Eggers, from *Leaves of Grass* to *The Circle.* The novel does not sing anymore like the poem, but registers the outlines of our online culture that leaves us completely vulnerable to consume information as the determining force in our life. We do not *walk* the street anymore, we *orientate ourselves* according to the data of our smart phone and its many apps; we do not *talk* on the street anymore, but we *exchange data* on the preferred street-sections where WiFi is powerful or gratis. Our life experience on the street is the fiction from which we thought it was only-just-fiction.

Is the *wholeness* Whitman wanted to achieve, transformed into a *total loss* of identity – of the pedestrian on the street as well as the street (and its city) itself? That *wholeness* is described ironically in the first pages of Eggers' novel, *The Circle*. He introduces Ty to us, who had just devised a new e-communication system, the Unified Operating System. What was online was separate and sloppy: social media profiles, payment systems, passwords, mail accounts, user names, preferences and other personal specificities. 'You shouldn't have to have eighty-seven different cars' he was described as saying. And Ty had put all of it into one account, one identity per person: 'TruYou'.

This is – again – literature, and again literature about the streets of New York! Look around you while you walk Fifth Avenue, or the Avenue of the Americas, or just cross along Fourteenth Street and you will meet the walking smart phone that would like more than anything else *a new wholeness.*[35] Eggers' Ty designed that wholeness; there are no multiple identities anymore. Your devices knew who you were, and your one identity – the *TruYou*! The Eggers story unfolds. Ty had claimed that he did not have any idea of the commercial implications of his TruYou. The monetization 'came from two other Wise Men, who found ways to reap fund from all of *Ty*'s innovations, and it was they who grew the company into the force that subsumed Facebook, Twitter, Google, and finally

[35] *Wholeness* is a forthcoming issue of importance in legal theory. See Sarah Marusek (ed.), *Synesthetic Legalities: Sensory Dimensions of Law and Jurisprudence*, Routledge, London, 2016.

Alacrity, Zoopa, Jefe and Quan'.[36] Do not forget, even when you hear talking about law on the street that a desire for *wholeness* is a social and historical phenomenon in human culture. We keep that in mind when we walk on the streets of New York, Paris or Athens.

REFERENCES

Adorno, Th. W., *Kierkegaard: Konstruktion des Ästhetischen*, Tübingen, 1933 (English edition edited by R. Hullot-Kenter, *Kierkegaard: Construction of the Aesthetic*, Minnesota University Press, Minneapolis, MN, 1989).

Agamben, Giorgio, *La comunità che viene*, 1990 (English edition edited by M. Hardt, *The Coming Community*, Minnesota University Press, Minneapolis, MN, 1993).

Austin, M. M. and P. Vidal-Naquet, *Economic and Social History of Ancient Greece*, California University Press, Berkeley, LA, 1977.

Benjamin, Walter, *The Arcades Project* (edited by H. Eiland and K. McLaughlin), Harvard University Press, Cambridge, MA/London, 1999.

Bergmann, Hans, *God in the Street: New York Writing from the Penny Press to Melville.* Temple Press, Philadelphia, 1995.

Bergson, Henri, *Les deux sources de la moralité et de la religion*, Paris, 1932 (English edition, *Two Sources of Morality and Religion*, University of Notre Dame Press, Notre Dame, IN, 1935, 1977).

Broekman, Jan M., 'A Goddess for semiotics of law and legal discourse' in A. Palmisano (ed.), *DADA-Rivista di Antropologia post-globale*, Trieste, 2011, available at: www.dadarivista.com.

Broekman, Jan M., *Meaning, Narrativity, and the Real: The Semiotics of Law in Legal Education IV*, Springer, Switzerland, 2016.

Broekman, Jan M., 'Street as Theory' in Sarah Marusek and John Brigham (eds), *Street Level Sovereignty: A Reader*, Rowman and Littlefield, Lanham, MD, 2017.

Buchanan, James J., *Theorika: A Study of Monetary Distributions to the Athenian Citizenry during the Fifth and Fourth Centuries BC*, Augustin, New York, 1962.

Chiesa, Lorenzo and Raffaello Palumbo Mosca (eds), 'Figures of the o/Other: Brother, Neighbor, Stranger, Enemy', GSH Seminar Series at the Genoa School of Humanities, 2016.

D'Alisa, Giacomo, Federico Demaria and Kalis Giorgos, *Degrowth: A Vocabulary for a New Era,* Routledge, London, 2014.

De Haan, J. I., 'Essence and Task of Legal Significs', Amsterdam, 1916 (English translation in Jan M. Broekman and Larry Catà Backer (eds), *Signs in Law – A Source Book*, Springer, Heidelberg/New York/Dordrecht, 2013.

---

[36] Dave Eggers, *supra note 2*, p. 23.

Detienne, Marcel, 'L'espace de la Publicité: ses Opérateurs Intellectuels dans la Cité' *Cahiers de Philologie*, Vol. 14, Série Apparat Critique, Presses Universitaires de Lille, 1958.
Eggers, Dave, *The Circle, A Novel*, Vintage Books, New York, 2014.
Habermas, Jürgen, *The Crisis of the European Union*, Polity Press, Cambridge/ Malden, MA, 2012.
Hansen, M. H., *The Athenian Democracy in the Age of Demosthenes*, Blackwell, Oxford/Cambridge, MA, 1991.
Hertzog, C., A. F. Kramer, R. S. Wilson and U. Lindenberger, 'Enrichment Effects on Adult Cognitive Development: Can the Functional Capacity of Older Adults Be Preserved and Enhanced?' *Psychological Sciences Public Interest*, Oct. Vol. 9, No. 1, 2008, 1–65.
Hobbes, Th., *Leviathan*, 1651 (Latin edition edited by Hobbes, 1668; critical edition edited by N. Malcolm (ed.), Clarendon, Oxford University Press, 2012).
Kokosi-Ostrov, Ann Olga, 'Dura-Europos: Water, Baths, Latrines, and the Goddess Fortuna in a Desert City' in Lisa R. Brody and Gail. L. Hoffmann (eds), *Dura Europos: Crossroads of Antiquity*, McMullen Museum of Art, Boston College, 2011.
Koller, Hermann, 'Theoros und Theoria' in *Historia – Glotta; Zeitschrift für Alte Geschichte*, F. Steiner Verlag, Wiesbaden, 1958.
Marusek, Sarah (ed.), *Synesthetic Legalities: Sensory Dimensions of Law and Jurisprudence*, Routledge, London, 2016.
Parke, H. W., *Festivals of the Athenians*, Cornell University Press, London/ Ithaca, NY, 1977.
Pickard-Cambridge, Sir Arthur, *The Dramatic Festivals of Athens*, Oxford University Press, Oxford/New York, 1991.
Popper, Karl, *The Open Society and its Enemies*, 1945, 5th edn, Routledge, London, 1966.
Spitzer, Leo, *Stilstudien (Style Studies) (2 Vols)*, Max Hueber Verlag, München 1928, 1961.
Starr, Chester G., *The Birth of Athenian Democracy*, Oxford University Press, Oxford, 1990.
Taylor, Charles, 'Atomism' in Shl. Averini and A. De-Shalit (eds), *Communitarianism and Individualism*, Oxford University Press, Oxford, 1992.
The Invisible Committee (2014), *To Our Friends* (translated by R. Hurley) Semiotext(e), Pasadena, 2015.
Thüry, Günter E., *Müll und Marmorsäulen: Siedlungshygiene in der römischen Antike*, Mainz, Zabern, 2001.
Van der Walt, Johan and Jeffrey Ellsworth (eds), *Constitutional Sovereignty and Social Solidarity in Europe*, Nomos, Baden-Baden, 2015.
Vernant, J. -P., *Les origines de la pensée grecque*, Paris, 1962 (English edition, *The Origins of Greek Thought*, Cornell University Press, Ithaca, NY, 1982).
Wiley, Norbert, *Inner Speech and the Dialogical Self*, Temple University Press, Philadelphia/Rome/Tokyo, 2016.

Index